John Donaldson Ford

An American Cruiser in the East

Travels and Studies in the Far East; the Aleutian Islands, Behring's Sea; Eastern Siberia,

Japan, Korea, China, Formosa, Hong Kong, and the Philippine Islands

John Donaldson Ford

An American Cruiser in the East

Travels and Studies in the Far East; the Aleutian Islands, Behring's Sea; Eastern Siberia, Japan, Korea, China, Formosa, Hong Kong, and the Philippine Islands

ISBN/EAN: 9783743395374

Manufactured in Europe, USA, Canada, Australia, Japa

Cover: Foto ©Andreas Hilbeck / pixelio.de

Manufactured and distributed by brebook publishing software (www.brebook.com)

John Donaldson Ford

An American Cruiser in the East

An American Cruiser in the East

"Pass not unmarked the islands in that sea,
   Where nature claims the most celebrity,
   Half hidden, stretching in a lengthened line
   In front of China,   .   .   .
   Japan abounds in mines of silver fine,
   And shall enlighten'd be by holy faith divine."

CAMOENS, *The Lusiad*.

Yours truly
John D. Ford

AN
AMERICAN CRUISER IN THE EAST

Travels and Studies in the far East

The Aleutian Islands, Behring's Sea, Eastern Siberia,
Japan, Korea, China, Formosa, Hong Kong,
and the Philippine Islands

BY

JOHN D. FORD

*Fleet Engineer of the Pacific Station, United
States Navy*

WITH NUMEROUS ILLUSTRATIONS AND THREE MAPS

New York
A. S. Barnes and Company
1898

University Press:
JOHN WILSON AND SON, CAMBRIDGE, U.S.A.

CONTENTS

		PAGE
INTRODUCTION		1

CHAPTER
I.	THE START	5
II.	UNALASKA, ALEUTIAN ISLANDS	14
III.	CRUISING IN BEHRING SEA	24
IV.	PETROPAULSKI, KAMTCHATKA. EASTERN SIBERIA	38
V.	KAMTCHATKA, EASTERN SIBERIA	44
VI.	YOKOHAMA, JAPAN	51
VII.	TOKIO, THE CAPITAL	76
VIII.	KOBE, JAPAN	124
IX.	OSAKA, JAPAN	153
X.	CONSTITUTION AND GOVERNMENT OF JAPAN	185
XI.	POPULATION AND INDUSTRY OF JAPAN	190
XII.	A TRIP TO THE NORTHWESTWARD	227
XIII.	A TRIP TO KOREA	237
XIV.	SEOUL, THE CAPITAL OF KOREA	251
XV.	PING-YANG, KOREA	259
XVI.	KOREA	278
XVII.	SHANGHAI, CHINA	293
XVIII.	NINGPO, CHINA	305
XIX.	FORMOSA	320
XX.	AMOY, CHINA	331

Contents

CHAPTER		PAGE
XXI.	CANTON, CHINA	343
XXII.	THE GOVERNMENT AND PEOPLE OF CHINA	376
XXIII.	HONG-KONG, CHINA	399
XXIV.	MACAO, CHINA	411
XXV.	MANILA, PHILIPPINE ISLANDS	417
XXVI.	THE PHILIPPINES	432

APPENDIX 443

LIST OF ILLUSTRATIONS

John D. Ford	*Frontispiece*
	PAGE
The Point of Tomioka, Japan	48
A Japanese Torii and Lanterns	49
Fujiyama	51
The 101 Steps at the Bluff, Yokohama, Japan, with the Celebrated Zenaba Tea-House on the Left . . .	52
Yokohama, Japan	53
The Grand Hotel, Yokohama, Japan	56
Yokohama Bluffs, Japan	57
Jinrikisha in Japan	59
The Imperial Japanese Government Buildings, Yokohama, Japan	61
A Japanese Sampan	63
Japanese Green-Grocer's Shop	65
A Japanese Actor	66
Dai Butsu, the "Great Buddha," near Kamakma, Japan .	67
Enoshema, Japan	70
Japanese Junks	72
Harvesting the Rice in Japan	73
A Street Scene, Tokio, Japan	77
Making Rice Flour, Japan	79
Wistaria	80
A Garden, Tokio, Japan	81
Entrance to Kwanin Temple, near Tokio, Japan	85
Vegetables in Japan	87
Japanese Acrobats	88
Sweets and Toys	89
Japanese Jugglers	90

List of Illustrations

	PAGE
ENTRANCE TO THE MORTUARY TEMPLES OF THE SHOGUNS AT SHEBA, NEAR TOKIO, JAPAN	91
JAPANESE TROUBADOURS	93
TEMPLE OF THE SHOGUNS, SHEBA, NEAR TOKIO, JAPAN	95
THE TEMPLE FONT AT THE SHOGUN TEMPLES, SHEBA, NEAR TOKIO, JAPAN	97
ANCIENT JAPANESE ARMOR	98
TEMPLE OF THE SHOGUNS, SHEBA, NEAR TOKIO, JAPAN	99
TEMPLES OF THE SHOGUNS AT SHEBA, NEAR TOKIO, JAPAN	101
TOMB OF "ROKU DAI," THE SIXTH TOKUGAWA SHOGUN, SHEBA, NEAR TOKIO, JAPAN	102
TEMPLE OF THE SHOGUNS, SHEBA, NEAR TOKIO, JAPAN	103
A JAPANESE SCHOOL	106
JAPANESE WRESTLERS	107
JAPANESE WRESTLERS	109
A LOTUS FIELD	110
IN A JAPANESE RICE-FIELD	113
THE MIKADO'S PALACE AT TOKIO, JAPAN	115
BAMBOO GROVE AT FUKIAGU, TOKIO, JAPAN	118
CHRYSANTHEMUMS	120
A SEDAN CHAIR IN JAPAN	121
SHIMONOSEKI, THE ENTRANCE TO THE INLAND SEA OF JAPAN	124
"THE FALLS" AT KOBE, JAPAN	125
JAPANESE WOOD-PEDLER	126
KOBE AND THE INLAND SEA OF JAPAN	127
JAPANESE FRUIT SHOP	129
DRY GOODS SHOP, KOBE, JAPAN	130
JAPANESE DANCING-GIRLS, — THE "GEISHA"	131
JAPANESE BABIES	132
A TRIP INTO THE COUNTRY, — THE "KAGA"	133
JAPANESE CARPENTERS	135
A JAPANESE BARBER SHOP	136
NUNABIKI WATERFALL AT KOBE, JAPAN	137
ONE METHOD OF IRRIGATING THE LAND IN JAPAN	140
A JAPANESE CLOG-MAKER	142
A JAPANESE HOME DINNER	143
JAPANESE DOCTOR AND PATIENT	144
HOW THEY SLEEP IN JAPAN	145
THE FAMILY BATH, JAPAN	146

List of Illustrations

	PAGE
MAKING THE TOILET, JAPAN	147
THE HAIR-DRESSER IN JAPAN	148
THE SICK BABE, JAPAN	149
A TATTOOED JAPANESE	150
JAPANESE COOPER	151
PICKING TEA LEAVES IN JAPAN	153
JAPANESE CABINET-MAKER AT OSAKA	154
JAPANESE POTTERY AT OSAKA, JAPAN	155
ENTRANCE TO NAGASAKI HARBOR. PAPINBERG IN THE DISTANT CENTRE	157
JAPANESE SAMPAN FERRY	159
UP THE MOUNTAIN STREAM, NAGASAKI, JAPAN	160
THE HILLSIDE GRAVES	161
AN OLD STONE BRIDGE, NAGASAKI, JAPAN	163
JAPANESE TOY PEDLER	165
FISH AND FRESH PROVISION SHOP, JAPAN	166
NAGASAKI HARBOR AT NOON ON A FOURTH OF JULY	167
ARTISTS DECORATING LANTERNS	169
A FUNERAL PROCESSION IN JAPAN	171
COFFIN AND FUNERAL ORNAMENTS, JAPAN	172
A JAPANESE COUNTRY HOUSE NEAR NAGASAKI, JAPAN	173
IN THE RICE-FIELD	174
THE DRY DOCK AT NAGASAKI, JAPAN	175
JAPANESE BULL CART	179
"THE OLD MILL" AT NAGASAKI, JAPAN	180
MOJI, JAPAN	182
HILLSIDE GRAVES OF THE MARTYRS, MOJI, JAPAN	183
ANCIENT JAPANESE WARRIOR	187
JAPANESE FIREMEN ON PARADE	193
SHINTO PRIEST, JAPAN	196
BUDDHIST PRIEST, JAPAN	199
JAPANESE WOOD-CARVING	200
JAPANESE HOMES	202
JAPANESE TRAMPS	204
A COOLIE	207
MAKING UMBRELLAS IN JAPAN	209
JAPANESE WOOD-CARVER	211
JAPANESE LACQUER WARE	213
AN INSTRUMENTAL CONCERT, JAPAN	217

xii List of Illustrations

	PAGE
JAPANESE ARTISTS DECORATING PORCELAIN	221
A CHINESE CART	227
CHEMULPO, KOREA	237
A DELEGATION OF KOREANS VISIT THE "ALERT"	245
KOREAN MOURNING COSTUME	247
SEOUL, THE CAPITAL OF KOREA	251
GATEWAY TO SEOUL	253
GATEWAY TO THE KING'S PALACE, SEOUL, KOREA	255
THE KOREAN ARMY	257
PING-YANG, KOREA	259
FORTIFICATIONS AND GOVERNOR'S HOUSE, PING-YANG INLET	263
A KOREAN YOUNG WOMAN	265
A KOREAN HOUSE, PING-YANG INLET	266
FORTIFICATIONS	267
KOREAN BUDDHIST PRIESTS	270
BROUGHTON BAY AND GEN-SAN	272
HIS MAJESTY LI-FIN, KING OF KOREA, AND HIS ROYAL HIGHNESS THE CROWN PRINCE	280
THE PRIME MINISTER OF KOREA	282
THE "CHOSON," THE ONLY VESSEL IN THE KOREAN NAVY	284
A KOREAN FAMILY	286
SACRED WHITE HORSE OF JUNGU TEMPLE	288
THE KOREAN ARMY,—SKIRMISH DRILL	289
CHINESE JUNK	293
A ROAD IN SHANGHAI, CHINA	303
WATER-FRONT, NINGPO, CHINA	305
A CORNER OF THE CITY WALL, NINGPO, CHINA	307
THE PONTOON BRIDGE, NINGPO, CHINA	309
A NINGPO CHINESE FAMILY	311
NINGPO CHINAMAN	316
CHART OF THE WORLD	321
OLD BANYAN-TREES	327
THE DEIFIED ROCKS AT AMOY, CHINA	332
FOREIGN RESIDENCES AT KORLANGSOO, AMOY, CHINA	335
LAMPOTOH TEMPLE, AMOY, CHINA	337
WOMAN OF SWATOW, CHINA	340
MAP OF OLD CANTON	349
THE BARE PAGODA, CANTON, CHINA	357
CHINESE PUNISHMENT,—IN THE CAUGUE	359

List of Illustrations xiii

	PAGE
A Knotty Case in Old Canton	361
A Cantonese Family	363
Execution of Chinese Rebels	366
Temple of the Ocean Banners, Honan, Canton	369
The Water-Front of Old Canton	373
Camel Caravan Bound for Peking, China	391
Hong-Kong	399
The Queen's Road, Hong-Kong	401
The Water-Front, Hong-Kong in a Fog	403
The Parsee Cemetery in the Happy Valley, Hong-Kong	404
Residence of the Tartar General, New Chwang, China	411
Woman of Northern China	415
Manila, Philippine Islands	419
An Indian Warrior of the Philippine Islands	422
Natives of Manila, Philippine Islands	423
A Native of Manila, Philippine Islands	427
A Native of Manila, Philippine Islands	429
A Cock-Pit at Manila, Philippine Islands	431
The Untamed Indians of the Philippine Islands	433
Natives of Manila, Philippine Islands	436
Native Bull Sled, Manila, Philippine Islands	438
Native Woman of Manila, Philippine Islands	439
Japanese Mounted Infantry. By a Japanese Artist	446
Imperial Chinese Troops	459
Japanese Artillery. By a Japanese Artist	464

Introduction

AFTER a term of duty at the Baltimore Manual Training School, having watched its growth from nothing to five hundred students; having seen four classes of one hundred and twenty young men graduated, settled in good employments, and well started in their chosen lifework; having witnessed the material increase from two bare floors in the old schoolhouse on Courtland Street to the acquisition and equipment of the entire building, together with the lease and equipment of the annex, on the opposite side of the street, and the erection and furnishing of the five-story building adjoining and connecting with the old schoolhouse, — I opened my mail, on the 2d of July, and found an order which required me to report for duty in San Francisco on the 13th of the month.

The work had been laborious. There were some data for other circumstances, but none to suit our conditions. We were doing pioneer work. Every lesson and every course of study, both in the laboratories and the draughting-rooms, had to be studied out and devised, in order to obtain such as would furnish the largest amount of hand and eye work, so that it could be made to supplement the purely literary work, blending together and producing the desired result, thus solving the problem, How to adjust Manual Training to the Public-School System? The results show how well or how ill the work has been done.

Although my official relations with the school had been severed by the receipt of the order, I devoted the remaining days to getting things in shape for my unknown successor, and had never realized until then how it had endeared itself to me. But the last day came, as last days always will come!

His Honor the Mayor, and the Officers and Members of the School Board tendered me a farewell dinner at the Rennert. After sitting through the feast, from the oysters to the black coffee and cigars, where all had kind words and pleasant wishes, we all stood and sang "Auld Lang Syne." Then came the hardest part of all, the "good-bye" and the "God bless you."

A little later, I bade farewell to dear old Baltimore, and took my seat in a Pullman sleeper of the "Overland Flyer," on the hottest night that has been known in this section for many years. As the train was rushing through the tunnel and beyond, I remembered how kind and helpful all had been to the work I was leaving behind. Our Senators and Representatives had interested themselves in it from its inception. The newspapers had sent their representatives, investigated, and commended. The Mayor, the Councils, and the School Board had been generous in their appropriations. The Chairman and Committee had always been a unit for the school. The Faculty was devoted and zealous, and the great majority of the students appreciated their opportunities.

The next night Chicago was reached and left behind us, and we were still rushing through the great flat, treeless plains towards the Rocky Mountains. Council Bluffs, Omaha, Grand Island, Cheyenne, Laramie, Green River, Granger, Ogden, Winnemucca, Reno, Trucker, and Summit, seven thousand feet above the sea-level, and scores of other cities and towns, were passed by as we sped from prairie to desert and over hills and mountains. From Summit the road ran down the Pacific slope, through Sacramento to Oakland, where we crossed the bay in the big steamer to San Francisco, having left Baltimore late on Tuesday night and arrived in San Francisco on the following Sunday morning. The car services, sleeping and dining, left nothing to be desired.

Having completed my duty in San Francisco by the end of September, I repaired to the Mare Island Navy Yard, and joined the U. S. S. "Alert" for a cruise in Behring Sea and the far East. The cruise was very interesting, and the experiences were valuable. Behring Sea and Korea were revelations to me. During a large portion of the cruise we visited Japan, China, Hong-kong, and the Philippines, which gave me the opportunity to compare, modify, or confirm the impressions of years ago; and my desire is, to show those countries and their people as I saw them.

An American Cruiser in the East

CHAPTER I

THE START

ON the morning of the 18th of June we cast off the lines that bound us to the water-front of the Mare Island Navy Yard, and steamed down the river towards San Francisco. After reaching the bay, we changed our course to keep clear of the great steamer which plies between that city and Oakland; and passing by the city, we rounded to, and stood through the Golden Gate, running against a stiff breeze and a heavy chopped sea. As soon as we were well outside of the land, upon the bosom of the broad Pacific, bearings were taken, and the vessel was headed for Unalaska, Aleutian Islands, about twenty-two hundred miles away. The clouds lowered and became almost black, and the once chopped sea gradually increased until we had a heavy head sea, causing the old ship to roll and pitch in a most uncomfortable manner.

The little ship, that was to be our home for the next two years and a half, was an iron steamer, 175 feet long, 35 feet beam, 15 feet 6 inches deep, and of 1,020 tons' displacement. It was full bark-rigged, and had an old-fashioned bow. Her armament consisted of one eleven-inch smooth-bore pivot gun, two nine-inch smooth-bore broadside guns, one sixty-pounder breech-loading rifle, and several machine guns and brass pieces.

We had a lot of almost worthless Japanese for servants, — poor fellows, who had left their island home to seek their fortunes in America. They had met with poor success, and were discouraged and homesick. To get away from their uncongenial surroundings, and with the hope of ultimately reaching Japan, they shipped as servants for our cruise. They made poor seamen; for as the gale increased, boy after boy disappeared, — sick, down with *mal de mer*, — and before the close of the day we had but one servant in condition for service. One boy to look after a dozen of us!

Our head wind and sea stuck to us, and continued to increase, as though winds and seas never came from any other direction. After experimenting for four days, it was determined to abandon the direct course to Unalaska, and to make a leading wind of the present freshness, running into Victoria, British Columbia, to refill our bunkers and to make a new start.

The bad weather we were experiencing gave us the opportunity of testing the seamanship and endurance of our men, as a great deal of sail-drilling was necessary; and before the end of it we realized that we had about as fine a crew as ever went to sea. Many of them were not only good seamen, but possessed qualities that promote the happiness of a ship's company. There were some jewels in the engine department, — men who worked well, and in the early watches of the night excelled in song and dance; they could " spout " quotations from an " improved " Shakespeare or the dime " Ready Speaker," with a fervor and gesture that would cause an actor to blush. These interested and amused the forecastle and the fire-room, and made Jack's time pass pleasantly during the loneliest hours of the nights, from tea-water to hammocks. We had men who were formerly elegant " barn-stormers," but had been financially wrecked in their showy ventures; also an ex-negro minstrel from down the coast, and an athlete who had seen

Sullivan; but the cream of the crew was the dude barber, whose carroty frizzes were always parted in the middle. He wore the finest embroidered trousers and shirts, and the ship's name, in solid silver, on his cap ribbon; his clocked silk hose and elegant pumps were the envy of all the youngsters, from the forecastle to the maintop. He could trip the light fantastic toe, in hornpipe or jig, make good music from almost any instrument, " splice the main-brace," or jump aloft as nimbly as any. Of course, such a paragon soon became the favorite of the crew, and, to his credit, he held this good opinion throughout the cruise. As I have stated, we had artists and poets amongst the crew, and many of their stories of imagination, told to a gaping auditory in the dark midnight watches, might "cause each particular hair to stand on end," or provoke mirth that would disturb the slumbers of the watch below; and we had some old fellows who were so salt that they would secure all the sea water they could stow away, to use for bathing purposes when the vessel was in fresh-water rivers.

Early on the 24th, we sighted the Olympics and headed for Cape Flattery, the most northerly point of land projecting from the State of Washington, and just opposite Vancouver Island. We entered the Strait of Juan de Fuca, between the cape and the island, and headed for Victoria, British Columbia. On one side of the strait, the great black mountains are covered with dense forests until the snow-line is reached; beyond which the darkness is transformed into an eternal whiteness, rending the heavens and piercing the clouds, thousands of feet above us. Several Indian villages are scattered along the foot of the mountains. Braves, and squaws with their pappooses, stroll along the beach and admire the great white war-canoe that is forging its way through the waters. Others paddle their canoes upon the quiet waters, or haul seine or line in pursuit of unwary members of the finny tribe.

A cool breeze and calm sea bring our late, not sea-sick, but sick of the sea, messmates from their rooms, with appetites as big as the ship. Crackers, cheese, and beer are in demand; and the stentorian voice of our most excellent caterer is heard in vain protests against this dangerous raid upon the sea stores. As the day passes into night, the Olympics, with a nearly full moon shining upon them, appear like masses of blackness capped with dancing gold; and the old ship speeds on through placid waters, carrying a mass of silvery waves at her bow, which make faint dashes, and are lost upon the beach, where the tiny lights and fires of the Indians dance like "will-o'-the-wisps" amidst the blackness. About ten o'clock we anchored near the inner harbor of Victoria, and were soon surrounded by a little fleet of pleasure-boats, whose happy occupants gave us some fine music, instrumental as well as vocal; and we found that these good people were as curious to see a Yankee man-of-war as the Indians of the strait had been.

Victoria, British Columbia

Victoria is situated on the southern end of Vancouver Island, in the Strait of Juan de Fuca, and has grown from old Fort William, a trading post, which is nearly as old as the fur-trade on the North Pacific coast. It is still a seat of the Hudson Bay Company, which has fine storehouses in the city, where almost anything can be purchased or traded.

The fur-trader was close behind the hunter, and they were soon followed by the prospector and the miner, as vast quantities of gold were supposed to be hidden in the hills. The finds were not equal to the expectations, and the rush soon cleared out what was there; but the coal mines that were discovered have proven themselves vastly more important to this portion of the world than the precious metal could possibly have been. The mines at Nainaimo and vicinity supply the whole upper Pacific coast, including San Francisco as well as the railroads and shipping, and make life, manufactures, and commerce possible. Timber is abundant, but the government cares for it, and its cutting, on a large scale, is discouraged.

The business portion of the city is built around an inner harbor which is protected by a point of land that juts out into the strait. Many improvements are being made in this part of the city: roads and streets are being changed and graded; hollows and low places are being filled in, and hills removed, giving the place a "fussy" appearance. There are many handsome buildings that would be ornaments in any city. Through the streets several lines of cars are run, driven by electric motors. They make good speed, are easily handled, and have many advantages over the cable cars run in San Francisco. The poor car-horse is on the eve of emancipation, and there seems to be no excuse for his further employment in that capacity. The streets — roads, they are called — are lighted with electric lights.

The curious old custom is preserved in Victoria of firing a warning gun at nine in the evening; and at nine thirty a second gun is fired, when all the public lights are extinguished and the streets and roads are in darkness.

Everything moves slowly here. Business is done in a very quiet way, and the shopkeeper's life seems an easy one. There is no push or drive, and no advertising, as we see it in our home cities. No attempt is made to push goods in the shops: they are shown, on inquiry the price is named, and you buy or not, as you please; and yet a vast business is done in this quiet, easy way, and handsome profits are realized. Business does not begin until after nine in the morning, and ends at four in the afternoon.

The hotels are excellent, and are conducted on the English plan.

The residents' portion of the city extends over hills and valleys, and far up the strait, where, surrounded by neat little gardens filled with beautiful flowers or carefully kept lawns, stand villas and cottages, — the homes of the people. The roads are hard, smooth, and admirably cared for. They are bordered with trim hedges, and brightly painted gates open from them into little gardens. In the quiet summer evenings, the air is laden with sweet perfumes from these dainty gardens of roses.

The houses are picturesque and varied, and of a composite order of architecture that is convenient and attractive. Many of the houses are built of bricks with handsome stone trimmings, while a larger number are of wood, painted in pleasing tints; and all have an air of quiet refinement and elegance. The climate is invigorating and healthy. The summers are delightful, and the winters are comparatively mild, for the latitude. The city contains about twenty thousand inhabitants, its population having doubled in the last three years.

We drove to "Beacon Hill" to see the magnificent sunset, and sat through the long twilight, which lasts about two hours. The route led over a fine, hard road, surrounded by handsomely hedged gardens, whose delicious perfumes filled the air; and the elegant houses lent their beauty to the ever-changing panorama, as we wended our way up among the hills. Beacon Hill is a bare knoll of greensward, with a flagstaff from which the British jack is thrown to the breezes. From this spot a most magnificent view is obtained.

In the valley below us nestles a village with its cluster of gardens and bright little cottages. We see the coast-line, with its restless, ever-lashing sea; and beyond, an arm of the sea studded with islands, while here and there little boats and steamers are feeling their way through the winding channels. Yonder, the forest-covered Olympics, and in the far-off distance the snow-capped mountains of the Pacific hold up their heads in solemn grandeur.

As the "day-god" sank into the bosom of "Balboa's ocean," the tints changed from blue to silver, to gold, to fiery vermilion, the outlines of the mountains were tipped with old rose, and finally all melted into one streak of rosy red, when the heavens and the earth seemed to meet each other, and we realized that it was night, and the stars were on guard.

The guns having been fired, the lights were extinguished, and our ride back to the hotel was dismal. The lonely watchman threw the rays of his dark lantern upon us, peered at us through the darkness, and cried out: "Ten — o' — clock, — a — clear — bright — night!" Then all was dark and still.

At Sea

On the 30th, we said good-bye to our new-made friends and made another start for Behring Sea. When we had cleared the land, and the vessel's course was set, we found ourselves confronted by head winds and seas that caused the ship to pitch and roll to such a degree as to make life miserable. On the night of the 3d, the wind and sea died out, and the 4th opened with almost a calm, with a smooth sea and as bright a sun as ever shone. The boys had not sufficiently recovered from their second attack of sea-sickness to make any attempt at celebrating the day, and the "glorious Fourth" came and went with only the "storm flag" flying.

During the night of the 4th, the fair weather left us, and by daylight we had strong head winds and seas, with cold, gloomy weather. The 6th brought us some remarkable weather, — a cold Scotch mist with drizzly rain.

Through this the sun would shine brightly for about twenty minutes; then the mist would shut the sun out for about the same length of time, — and so it went on, repeating the order for the whole day. The next day brought us a heavy sea with a dense fog. The ship, having been lightened up considerably by the use of stores, rolled very deep, and the creaking bulkheads and blowing steam whistle were not soothing music for nerves already strained in endeavors to penetrate the fog and discover the rocky shore ahead.

Owing to the flatness of the earth in these latitudes, there are chances for grave errors in estimating distances; and the fact that these waters have never been carefully surveyed and charted, makes navigation extremely hazardous. After leaving Victoria, our only visible neighbors were several schools of whales and numerous stray seals.

Early on the morning of the 9th, the fog having cleared away, the peculiar haze, which the seaman knows to be land, was discovered ahead of us. Keeping on our course, we were soon between snowy mountains, whose chilly winds sent cold shivers through our frames. The grandeur of the scenery was fascinating, and held us almost spellbound, in spite of the cold, as we felt our way through the Onalga pass, which leads into Behring Sea. On one side of us were rugged, snow-capped mountains, upon whose rocky sides not a vestige of verdure could be seen, with here and there mad torrents of melted snow plunging into the sea almost at our feet; or mountain sides of emerald and black, up to the snow-line, from whence began their covering of white. On the port hand was Mount "Makooshin," 5,500 feet above the sea, sending forth ashes and smoke; on the starboard, mighty cone-shaped "Shisaldin," towering 8,500 feet towards the heavens, with its everlasting mantle of snow, the mad waters of ocean and sea dashing themselves against its rocky base. All about us were islands and great snow-capped peaks, which we passed and left in the distance. "Priest Rock" stood out of the sea, tall and slender, in cowl and gown, and "Egg Island" and "Old Man" were passed as we felt our way into Behring Sea. An interesting native village about six miles away, and Beaver Bay, where Captain Cook refitted his little fleet in 1778, were visible; and by five in the afternoon we moored the ship in the outer harbor of Iliuliuk, Unalaska.

CHAPTER II

UNALASKA, ALEUTIAN ISLANDS

Ice-built, ice-bound, and ice-bounded,
  Such cold seas of silence! such room!
Such snow-light! such sea-light confounded
  With thunders that smite like a doom!
  Such grandeur! such glory, such gloom!
  Hear that boom! hear that deep, distant boom
    Of an avalanche hurled
    Down this unfinished world!

Ice seas and ice summits! ice spaces,
  In splendor of white, as God's throne!
Ice worlds to the pole! and ice places,
  Untracked and unnamed and unknown!
  Hear that boom! Hear the grinding, the groan
  Of the ice gods in pain! Hear the moan
    Of yon ice mountain hurled
    Down this unfinished world!

JOAQUIN MILLER.

ILIULIUK is a beautiful harbor, surrounded by snow-capped mountains and green valleys. Unalaska, the settlement, has been built upon a natural crescent of low hills and plains on the southern side of the harbor, and consists of a Russian church, six large residences, sixty one-story wooden shanties, a few sod-houses, two storehouses, and a lot of sheds. These are the property of the Alaska Commercial Company, whose agent, called "Prince Paul" by the natives, manages the place, under the observation of some of our own officials.

Unalaska, Aleutian Islands

An inner harbor is formed by a point of land jutting out from the shore, opposite the middle of the settlement. Near by is a third harbor, opening into the main one, known as Dutchman's Bay, around whose shores a rival company is erecting storehouses and shanties for use of its people in future operations. At the foot of the mountains, behind the settlement, there is a large fresh-water lake, which is formed by the melted snow from the mountain's side.

"Prince Paul" came on board to pay his respects, and to invite us to a ball which was to be given in the palace that evening in honor of our arrival. But as the notice was short, and as we had not been sufficiently long beyond the pale of civilization to indulge, we were compelled to decline the honor. We lunched the "Prince;" and when he had said good-bye, he insisted upon returning to the shore in his own barge, which, by the way, was managed by only one man. Soon after he left the vessel, a local breeze and heavy rain came howling through the little valley ahead of us. The whitecaps soon sprang up from the smooth surface of the bay, and the "Prince's" man Friday could not pull against the wind and sea. Their barge was blown upon the beach on the opposite side of the bay, where, in a drenched condition, they were compelled to abandon the boat and wade through swamp and mud to the head of the spit; here they secured another boat and were landed near the palace.

The principal part of the settlement of Unalaska faces a roadway, which extends along the beach for about two miles from the inner harbor to the little cemetery on the hillock towards the sea. In this little cemetery there are twoscore or more quaint graves marked with the double cross, and heavily fenced in to protect the inmates from the raids of hungry wild beasts.

The islands are of volcanic origin. Immense rocks have been thrown up from the bottom of the sea in some past age, and a thin layer of soil has been deposited upon them. The tops of the hills and mountains are covered with snow, and there is nearly always an icy breeze blowing from the mountains, a drizzly rain, or a fog. Efforts have been made to cultivate the soil. In well-sheltered places the experiments have been partially successful, but not very encouraging. There is not a tree or a bush in the neighborhood. A tall, rank grass grows in sheltered places, where a few cattle are pastured until killing time.

A great variety of small wild flowers, including violets and heliotrope, grow about the sheltered valleys. I found more than one hundred specimens, which I pressed and sent to the President of the Woman's College of Baltimore. A fine scarlet berry, which the natives call the "salmon berry," as large as a cultivated blackberry, and of delicious flavor, grows abundantly in sunshiny places, where it has protection from the cold winds.

Unalaska is the huntsman's paradise, whether with rod or gun. There is no end to the sport. It is just beyond civilization, or rather just on its border. There are no hotels and no boarding-places, and one must rough it all the time. The "globe-trotter" and the tourist have not penetrated its boundaries, climbed its hills, nor drank its sparkling waters; neither has the hotel clerk's headlight flashed along its beach. There are many fine sites for hotels, huts, or tents, and the hills are filled with brown and green stones, that are almost prepared for buildings.

It is delightful to live the summer through in such freedom. So close to nature! All is so peacefully quiet, and the musical, silvery chimes from the old church belfry are only disturbed by the dashing of the surf upon the rocks, or the howling winds that come tearing like mad from the mountain-tops.

Wolves, deer, and foxes abound on the islands. Ptarmigan are plenty, and ducks and geese frequent the waters from September to May. The waters fairly teem with whales, sea-lions, seals, cod, salmon, halibut, flounders, and herring. Gamy trout give sport in the streams, while fine oysters and clams are abundant.

The principal occupation of the inhabitants is hunting and fishing. They build small canoes ("kiaks") of the raw hide of sea animals, which they sew over a light framework of wood. These they deck over, leaving an opening large enough to get their legs through. Their hunting and fishing garments are made of the entrails of sea-lions or other large animals; consequently, they are waterproof. These garments are called "kamlika." After taking his seat in the "kiak," the native securely fastens the skirt of his "kamlika" to the rim of the deck opening, or hatch-combing, and with the hood of the "kamlika" secured about his head, he is prepared to encounter any sea, as, with the exception of face and hands, he never becomes wet. The paddles used in these "kiaks" are double-ended, with broad blades, and are made of such wood as can be procured from whaling vessels of the Trading Company.

The melted snow from the mountains behind the settlement is collected in a little reservoir, which has been terraced into the mountain, from whence it trickles down the hillside into a fresh-water basin.

Down upon the beach, among the rocks, pebbles, and shells, a noisy family party, assisted by neighbors, were preparing hundreds of fine salmon for the winter's food supply. A right merry crowd of merry-makers they were, and the occasion might be called an Aleute harvest. The older members of the party cut the great fish down the back, removed the entrails, and passed them on to the youngsters, — little "tackers," whose ages, perhaps, ranged from four to ten years. They chopped off the heads and carried the bodies of the fish to the rear of the "home," where they were thrown upon the ground in a heap until some old women strung them over great ridgepoles to dry. The fish were placed high enough to be out of reach of any wild animals that might be forced into the settlement in search of food. They were neither washed, salted, nor covered. There was no other preparation than I have noted. Many of these fine salmon would weigh twenty or thirty pounds apiece, and the cod, in these waters, are just as heavy.

During the long winter season, the men devote their time to repairing boats and seines, making lines and spears, and lounging. Many of them, when they can obtain molasses or sugar, distil it into " hoocheno," a fiery rum, which they frequently use to excess. To prevent this, the agents are particular to sell these articles in very limited quantities; but it is surprising to see the devices of the natives to obtain the fiery beverage.

Their women devote the long hours of winter to making baskets, mats, and many other curious ornaments from finely split grasses, with which they weave gay-colored wools and silks. They also make odd trinkets from dried skins, and ornament them with fancy colors. The summer nights are nearly as light as the day. I could read a newspaper on deck until eleven at night, afterwards a deeper twilight lasted until about two in the morning, when again the paper could be read without the assistance of artificial light.

The Aleutian·Islands number about one hundred and fifty, and belong to the United States, being a part of Alaska. They form a chain which extends from the west coast of America to a point within eight hundred miles of Asia. They lie in about 55 degrees of north latitude, and separate Behring Sea from the Pacific Ocean. They are naturally divided into five groups, are of volcanic formation, and show evidences of earthquakes on every hand.

The smoke of several volcanoes can be seen at great distances on clear days.

The whole number of inhabitants on all the islands is about fifteen hundred, who, from their circumstances and surroundings, are compelled to live in a shiftless condition, and lead miserable lives. They are poor stunted Indians, who gather salmon and cod in the summer for the winter's supply of food. They live in caves and holes in the ground, or in huts made by piling rows of sods upon each other, over which they thatch a roof, and fasten the skin of some animal to a lintel to serve as a door, unless they are so fortunate as to obtain some old boards for the purpose. They dress in skins of animals, or in " store-clothes," which they receive in trade for the skins they have captured. They live on in this way until they are put into another hole in the ground, where they will remain until the last trumpet shall sound.

In the settlements, the Aleute has undergone a great change since he made his first bow to the Russian in the seventeenth century. His condition is not much improved, although he has changed his language, religion, and dress. His main reliance is still upon his fish, which he captures at the old place, and in the same old way. He has learned the use of civilized goods, and rather enjoys them. Canned goods and rum are two of his chief delights. He still lives in his cave, or hut, which he would gladly exchange for a comfortable Japanese cottage, with its charcoal fire and kerosene light, and he would have no prejudice against changing his garb for " store-clothes." He is the true son of his ancestors, and inherits many of their qualities. He is a member of the Russian Church, and can read and write the Russian language, which he has been taught by the priests. He is dependent upon the Trading Company for his living, being paid for the skins he captures, and for the work he does about the warehouses.

It was curious to see a coal vessel unloaded by women and girls, who carried great baskets filled with coal from the vessel to the coal sheds.

In the centre of the settlement there is a neat little Russian church, which is noted for its beautiful silvery chimes, and its fine pictures. Several of these are truly works of art, and it is surprising that they are in this out-of-the-way place. A painting of the " Last Supper," which hangs behind the altar, is particularly fine, both in its grouping and colors. A picture of the " Madonna and Infant," on the left of the altar, is also fine, and there are several in miniature that are excellent. The solid silver altar service is artistic and massive.

On the right of the entrance to the church there is a solitary grave marked " Nestor, a Bishop of these Islands." The monument states that at one time " Nestor had been a Lieutenant in the Imperial Russian Navy, and in civil life a Baron;" the monument fails to narrate the romance which caused the change in the man's career, and brought him from the gay scenes of St. Petersburg to these bleak rocks beyond Siberia; but here he sleeps under the shadow of his little church, where the silence is only broken by the chimes of the silvery bells.

A stroll along the beach from the boat-landing to the cemetery, about four in the afternoon, is very interesting. The fashionables of Unalaska are out for an airing; to see and to be seen. The ladies of the station are dressed in fur or velvet cloaks, gay-colored skirts, and headgear that rivals the rainbow's colors; together with their escorts, in neatest outfits of the San Francisco tailor. The reverend priest, in black gown, with bared head and stooping form, has a cheering smile and a kindly greeting for all. He strokes the heads of the little ones, and imprints a kiss of love and peace upon the rosy cheek of the babe. All reverence the good father, and bow low to him in passing.

The ladies of the "Aleute Colony" are on the promenade in gowns of quiet colors, with wraps as bright as their own sunny smile, their hair parted in the middle and carefully made into "Psyche" knots.

The half-breeds, like the creoles in southern climes, have forms and features of surpassing loveliness and great, flashing black eyes. They dress in the blackest products of the loom, and have cloaks of the sea-otter for handy use in the chilly breezes. They daintily pick their way over the pebbly walk that ends in the little valley beyond the cemetery, where the beautiful wild flowers may be had for the gathering. The population of the settlement is about four hundred, of whom one hundred are whites, and three hundred are Aleutes and half-breeds.

Every day, after our arrival, we enjoyed fine cod and salmon, some weighing as much as twenty-five pounds. The trout, ptarmigan, oysters, and clams were very fine and of delicious flavor. Cod or salmon, boiled and seasoned with drawn butter, a dash of salt, pepper and Worcestershire, with a steamed potato, as *entrée*, and a half-pint of Sauterne, is very appetizing after a climb over the hills or a stroll along the beach.

Prospectors are continually rapping, sounding, and "divining" about these islands and hills on the mainland. We could not go anywhere without meeting their eager, anxious, speculative faces. Why not leave these islands as spots in which to hunt and angle, haul the seine, or tong the oyster and clam that wait to be lifted out of the water?

Every two or three days, and sometimes every afternoon, a gale is loosened in the icy mountain-tops among the snow, and sweeps down upon us in all its fury. The cables become taut, an ugly chopped sea is raised, and cold chills are sent through our frames, the only relief being found within our little rooms near the heaters. Sometimes the days are beautiful, when the sun shines brightly and there is just a " baby-breeze," when greatcoats and storm-caps are comfortable.

Such we have found the Aleutian Islands, their people and climate, after spending many " summer days " in the full enjoyment of the good things nature has so bountifully supplied. But it must be remembered that the Aleutian Islands are only a small portion of our territory in this great northwest. Alaska, of which they are a portion, is an immense territory, about one fourth the size of the entire United States. From it twenty States, each as large as any of the older States of our Union, could be formed. The distance from Eastport, Maine, to Attau, the most western island of the Aleutian group, spans about one third around the globe. Alaska is very rich in minerals and coal, and its fishing interests are immense. Its grass lands could supply cattle for the world, and it is believed that the hardier cereals, fruits, and vegetables would flourish, if cultivated in its sheltered places.

On the afternoon of the 30th of July one of our quartermasters — Thompson — was killed in going from the coal bark to the shore. He had been visiting a party of friends on the vessel, which, nearly emptied of its coal, was high out of water, and the gang-plank was very steep. When Thompson reached the rail, he missed his footing and fell, striking his head against a large beam of wood placed in the water to keep the vessel from the wharf. When the man was picked up by the horror-stricken people about the wharf, life was extinct. The body was taken on board our ship and prepared for burial. All night long his messmates guarded the remains, and on the afternoon of the next day a funeral party from our vessel and other ships in port went on shore to bury the dead.

The music, his messmates, and then the body, in a neat box covered by the " Union Jack," were followed by the Marine Guard and Blue Jackets, men from our other vessels and many from the British war-vessels which were there to assist us in patrolling the sea. The "Third Watch" acted as chaplain as well as commander of the funeral party. After these came the British and our own officers, in reverse order of their rank. Slowly the cortége moved along the beach to the tump, tump, tump, of the muffled drums, or the mournful strains of the funeral march. Nearly all the inhabitants of the settlement stood uncovered in the drizzling rain as the procession moved by, and then accompanied it to the cemetery. Having arrived at the grave, all uncovered, and the "Third Watch" read the solemn service for the dead, when all that was mortal of our late shipmate was tenderly lowered into his last resting-place, that had been prepared by his messmates on the edge of the little cemetery.

As Thompson had not been a Catholic, the priest could not officiate, neither could his remains be buried in consecrated ground; but who can say that no drop of water or ray of sunshine from the heavens has consecrated the ground

> "Where, wrapped in his tarpaulin jacket,
> A poor sailor lies low"?

Thompson had served long and faithfully. He was a good man and an excellent sailor.

CHAPTER III

CRUISING IN BEHRING SEA

WE cruised about Behring Sea for thirty days, guarding the passes, hunting for illegal sealers, and going into port only to replenish our coal. We found the work very disagreeable, both on account of the reduced temperature and the weather. Fogs, with Scotch mists or drizzly rains, were not conducive to happiness; and if we were so fortunate as to have an exceptionally sunshiny day, the fog had a disagreeable way of working in between us and "Old Sol," making it very annoying for those who were responsible for the navigation of the vessel. The steam-whistle could not be used, as it would betray our position, so we kept the lead going to ascertain the depth of water, and kept sharp lookout about us, slowing the engines.

On the 15th, we overhauled a schooner which proved to be all right. On the 16th, the weather being thick, we sighted a schooner which "took to her heels." Her people crowded on all sail in the effort to get away from us. Every few minutes the weather cleared a little, then the fog settled down thick, so that we were unable to see as far as the length of our own vessel. We were gaining on the schooner, but slowly, and the chase was becoming exciting. In one of the thick spells, the schooner's course was altered, in the hope that we would keep on our course and run by her, while she would be making "to the good" on the new course, and thus elude us. Our "Skipper" anticipated the move or "chanced it," and the schooner's people were very much astonished, when the fog lifted again, to find us almost running over her. She proved to be engaged in the contraband work, and her master was warned to take her out of the sea.

Our vessels cruise at a great disadvantage in these waters. The sealers and whalers are accustomed to keep a sharp lookout, day and night, at their vessels' mastheads for seals, whales, and other game; and as their profits mainly depend upon it, they become very expert at the work. While they are watching for game they also keep a lookout for the tall masts, smoke-pipes, and the long line of black smoke which betrays our position. At the same time, their shorter masts and smaller hulls are a protection to them; so it is only by chance that we are able to see them through the fog and mist.

Later we anchored for about an hour, and gave all hands an opportunity to catch some fish. Some magnificent cod were hauled in, about a yard long, and weighing from thirty to thirty-five pounds apiece, while scores were taken that averaged more than twenty-five pounds. Some lines had two and three of these struggling beauties when they neared the surface, and assistance was necessary to land them safely.

On the 16th, we sighted the island of St. George, on its eastern side, and ran close in to see if any unauthorized vessels were loitering in the neighborhood. This side presents to the sea a bold, rocky bluff, about three hundred feet high, and almost perpendicular. Millions of birds were flying from its top towards the mainland, and the sickly sunshine was darkened to twilight by their passing between sky and sea. Hundreds of "killer" whales were sporting in the sea, rolling and blowing; but they are not attractive to the hunter, and seem to have been created for the sole purpose of thinning out the smaller fish which abound in these waters. We headed about and stood to the northward, going at a very slow rate of speed, but with everything in readiness to "crowd on" in case of necessity.

After a week's cruising in dense fog, chasing schooners, with scarcely a ray of sunshine to gladden our hearts, or to assist us in determining our position, we felt our way in under the lee of St. Paul Island, and anchored on the night of July 21. The stillness was broken by the rolling and dashing of the surf and the almost human cries of the seals. All night long these nervous, restless creatures kept up a chatter and din that made the night hideous. The next morning, Sunday, we steamed around to the village, where we found the "Mohican" and the "Thetis," the "Bear" and the "Corwin," H. B. M. S. "Nymphe" and "Pheasant," and the mail steamer "Farallon."

After devoting the remaining portion of the forenoon to official calls and the functions incident to the day, and having partaken of a "sea luncheon," a party of us started in the gig for the shore to see the island, particularly the seal rookeries, and the hauling and killing grounds. As we approached the shore, we found many hidden dangers from rocks close under the surface of the sea, over which our boat bumped and grated, much to the discomfort of all hands; but by poling here, pushing there, and an occasional pull on the oars, we succeeded in getting the boat safely through the surf, and landed on the rocks at the foot of the village road. After "pulling ourselves together" and making a hasty survey of the surrounding country, we dismissed our boat to the ship, and started for the north beach, or rookeries, from which the sounds that we had enjoyed (?) the night before had proceeded. Leaving the village for future inspection, we started over the hills, which are covered with soft, fibrous turf, from which a rank grass has grown, amid which there is neither path nor road. In a rain that had lasted perhaps since the last winter, we trudged along over the uncertain, slippery ground. So uncertain was the footing that at almost every step great exertion was required to hold the position we had gained, or to make any progress toward our destination; but this, like all other things, must have an end, and after a couple of miles of such travel, with much puffing and blowing, and some very poor attempts at pleasantry, we finally reached the rookeries, and beheld the celebrated amphibious animal in all its glory.

The beach, or rookery, which we visited extends for about a mile and a half along the seashore, and gradually slopes up from the sea for about sixty feet to a point where the rocks are covered with soil, whither the seals never go. The beach is formed of hard rock, worn smooth by the rise and fall of the sea, and by the friction of the seals moving about upon it. Rising from this smooth surface, at intervals more or less great, are shelving rocks, or seal's pillows, — natural formations, which vary in size and shape, some of them being only a few inches in height and area, while others are several feet high.

The male seal measures about six feet in length, and weighs about five hundred pounds. Its head is very small in comparison with the size of its body, and its eyes are bluish, changing to hazel. It has a long yellowish-gray mustache, and sits very nearly erect. The female seal is about four feet in length, much more shapely than the male, and has a handsome head, eye, and body, and an expression of much intelligence. The young seals, or "pups," are awkward, ungainly little animals, of a black color, with large heads and small eyes, and of not much intelligence. They huddle together in groups, and spend the first weeks of life apparently in wondering why they were born, and if life is worth living.

The hunting season is in the months of June and July. There is nothing novel or exciting about it, it being rather a piece of cold-blooded butchery. The seals are singled out and driven like domestic animals.

The Pribyloff Islands (St. Paul and St. George) and the Commander Islands (Behring and Copper), having clean, shelving, rocky beaches, free from mud and sand, are peculiarly adapted to the habits and comfort of the seals during the breeding season. Here they live from May to October in perfect peace and security.

The business of hunting the seals, curing the skins, and trading with the islands has, for the past twenty-five years, been a monopoly of the Alaska Commercial Company of San Francisco, which has made a point of protecting the seals required for breeding purposes, but has not enjoyed its franchises undisputed. Many vessels have been fitted out each year, both in our own country and in Canada, to prey upon the seals when they leave the rookeries. It is claimed that these poachers have wantonly frightened and destroyed the seals in great numbers by the use of fire-arms; and it is also said that the crews of such vessels have raided the rookeries, and have even gone so far as to raid the salt-houses and carry off the skins, under cover of darkness and fog.

After gathering some specimens of beautiful wild flowers and coarse grasses, we retraced our steps to the village landing, where we found a motley crowd of young natives who were curious to see the strangers. We were soon in our boat again, and after having experiences similar to those on our way to the shore, we reached the vessel, thoroughly tired out and wet, but well repaid, we thought, for the trouble it had cost us to see the seals and rookeries.

The next morning we sailed from St. Paul, heading towards St. George and Unalaska, going very slowly and keeping a bright lookout for our friends, the poachers. We arrived at St. George Island on the morning of July 23, and were soon headed for the rookeries to see our other dear friends, the seals. St. George lies to the southward of St. Paul, and has less than half its area. The approaches and the landing are in better condition than those at St. Paul. The extent of the rookeries is about one sixth as great as those at the main island. There are about one hundred inhabitants on the island, — Americans, Russians, Aleutes, and half-breeds, — whose occupations are all connected with the seals or the government of the islands.

We were greatly interested in the efforts that a gentleman was making here to instruct some of the native boys in the art of working the bones and teeth of the seal into ornaments and other articles of commercial value. Both this island and St. Paul are strewn with bones and teeth of whales and seals, and they appear to be useless. They are, however, susceptible of manipulation, and may be given a fine polish. I have seen beautiful articles manufactured from them, such as buttons, card-cases, paper-cutters, etc. Such training and employment will be of great benefit to the natives, as it will broaden their contracted range of winter employments.

At the landing we saw about twenty young Aleutes and half-breeds lounging about to see the arrivals. They ranged from twelve to twenty years of age, and were resplendent in store-clothes, most of which were too large for the wearers, and were "baggy" upon them. Each one of the natives had a heavy watch-chain across the front of his waistcoat, loud neckgear, pins, and finger-rings, which they took a great deal of trouble to display. They were veritable know-nothings, for we could not get an intelligent answer to any of our questions, though we afterwards learned that the under-employés of the Company are not permitted to answer the questions of strangers.

The seals were chattering to themselves, and the little settlement was before us; so we concluded to do our own piloting, and struck out on our own account. The formation and soil of this island is about the same as at St. Paul, except on the eastern side, where a great elevated plateau, about three hundred feet high and almost perpendicular on the eastern sea-front, gradually slopes inland, and is lost in what may be called the general level of the island on all other sides. The settlement contains a little Russian church, with musical chimes and a beautiful white Virgin and Infant, and a schoolhouse, where the children are taught the catechism, the creed, and the elements of a secular education. Its fifty houses are built of wood, with no attempt at ornamentation, but all had an air of comfort, and some were elegant in their furnishings.

Leaving the village behind us, we started off for the beach and rookeries, guided by the well-known chatter of the seals. After a hard tramp we approached the rookeries, where all before us, as far as the eye could reach, spread a dark-coated, restless, chattering mass, — like a crouching army, ready to dash upon an enemy's lines. The beaches on all sides, except the east, are similar to those at St. Paul, and are well suited to the habits of the seals.

Hundreds of little groups of these interesting creatures were huddled together. These were the "harems," or families, and near by the "pups" were cared for by the rough old males, or "bulls." Over yonder, thousands of unmated "bachelor" seals were assembled in large parties bemoaning their fate, while thousands more were disporting among the breakers in the surf. Among all these thousands of restless, nervous seals, the rights of each seemed to be respected. Occasionally, a dissatisfied female would start off with the intention of deserting her lord, but a few roaring howls, and a savage bite on the neck, would cause her ladyship to return to her allegiance in short order.

The "bachelors" spend their time in lamenting their fate, and they are the first victims of the conscientious hunter's blow and knife. The seals begin to leave the rookeries about the middle of July, and these are entirely deserted by the middle of September, when the young have learned to take care of themselves.

The study of the movements and sports of these interesting creatures was both instructive and entertaining. From what we have seen, there can be little doubt that the man who originally reported a mermaid had seen a female seal sporting in the sea. Their heads and bodies are shapely (almost human in form), and their arms are handsome to the elbows, from whence the forearms become great black rubber-like flippers; while from the hips down the body tapers into a double tail, instead of legs.

As we took a farewell look at the rookeries, what a din and chatter there was! There were old seals and young seals, males, females, and "pups," — sportive, meditative, and quarrelsome. The males were guarding their "harems" while the females were lying about in enjoyment of their leisure and ease. Seals are very shy, and all about us were evidently disturbed by our presence. Whenever any of us approached too near, within ten or twelve feet, the males assumed an angry, threatening attitude, and they expressed their anxiety with trembling form, shaking of heads, flashing eyes, gestures, and loud roars of voice.

We saw the sun, a great ball of dull red, sink into the far-off west, and in the twilight we retraced our steps to the landing, and took places in our boat to return to the ship.

After the poor forlorn bachelor has become a regular Jeremiah by spending the season in lamentations, he is driven to the hauling grounds with his fellows, knocked in the head, stabbed to the heart, and skinned. The skin is salted, pickled, and cured, after which it is plucked and dyed. Every here and there over the seal's body a coarse white hair grows out from the fur, and these hairs must be plucked out so carefully that the fur is not injured, otherwise the skin will be depreciated in value.

A little while ago a countryman of ours invented a machine for removing these hairs. An enthusiastic furrier witnessed some experiments with the machine, and was so well pleased with the rapidity of the work that he invested in hundreds of unplucked skins and set the inventor to work. When the work was finished it was discovered that a small tuft of fur had been plucked out with each hair, and the skins had all been ruined. The plucking is all done by hand now. After the plucking, the skins are dyed; for it must be remembered that until the dyer has satisfactorily performed his operations upon it, the seal's skin is of a dark silver-gray, or mouse-color, — not the beautiful brown with which we are familiar.

After leaving St. George Island, we cruised about, inside of the Aleutian Islands, as far west as Pass No. 72. The scenery was beautiful beyond description. Nearly every high hill was covered with snow, and below the snow-line were great frowning rocks, palisades, and valleys, while here and there mad, tumbling, rushing torrents flowed from the gorged streams of melted snow. Yonder, a handsome greensward, a lawn of nature's own making, containing whole acres as smooth as our decks. A fine buck with ten-foot antlers was grazing near the beach, but was gone before a rifle could be reached. Just the faintest stain of smoke, within the beautiful blue vault of heaven, indicated a volcano, that some night may be in full eruption, and send forth fire, ashes, and smoke in great volume, while changing the physical geography of the neighborhood.

After heading to the northward for a day, we saw a sail and made chase. On overhauling "the find," it proved to be a whaler whose master told a gloomy story of losing a boat's crew of five men, while trying to secure a whale. The men had stuck their harpoons into the whale, which, as usual, started off, pulling the boat with it. Suddenly diving, the whale dragged the boat, with all hands, under, the men being drowned and the boat lost. Besides this, he had a small mutiny to subdue. Some of his men were sick, and the others thought the old vessel was too short-handed to continue on the hunt, so wished to go into port for additional help. They refused to work, but the old skipper meted out the punishments of low diet and double duty. This, together with the presence of several men-of-war in the sea, caused the men to change their minds and go to work. The burly old skipper hummed psalm-tunes as he stowed his papers away, and cast a long, threatening look towards his forecastle. Our surgeon went on board and did what was necessary for the comfort of the sick.

Three days afterwards, while a fine breeze was blowing, we sighted a sail and gave chase. After running nearly all day, and burning more coal than would supply several houses for a winter, we came up with the sail, which proved to be our old friend, the whaler. Well! we were not giving anything away, so we spoke him, returned his "dip," and kept right on the course as though we were going somewhere in a hurry. We could not afford to let that crowd have the laugh on us.

On the next day, we sighted a schooner, which kept just beyond our range while her people were "doing" all the seamanship they knew, evidently with the hope of getting away, whether as a joke or for more substantial reasons, we could only conjecture. It was one of those intermitting, sunshiny, and foggy days so common in those latitudes. After having been led in the chase until it began to look as if the schooner would escape us, a charge of powder and a shell were put into the sixty-pounder, and in a moment of sunshine it was "let go." It was a fair line shot; and in less time than I can write it, our friend was almost drowned in a shower of water. The rapidity with which he let all his "sails fly" was a sight that would have delighted a yachtsman. Our vessel was soon alongside of the schooner, — a poacher, of course, — whose master was ordered to take her out of the sea.

After more of such cruising and the enjoyment of the fine scenery about the islands, we worked our way into the harbor of Iliuliuk, and made preparations for the trip to Japan, *via* Kamtchatka.

UNALASKA TO KAMTCHATKA, SIBERIA

Early on the morning of September 10, we said goodbye to Unalaska, and started for Petropaulski, Kamtchatka. We ran along in full sight of the Aleutian Islands, once more enjoying the grandeur and beauty of the magnificent scenery. Late in the afternoon, we reached the latest addition to United States soil, the changeable island of Bogaslov. Bogaslov is very much like a child's " Johnny-jump-up," only Bogaslov jumps up out of the sea and then sinks into it again, to rise again in a new place. Now we see it as a great volcano sending forth dense clouds of steam and vapor, not only from its crater, but from crater and fissures in its sides, giving it the appearance of a whole mountain on fire. This steam and vapor are formed by water of the sea running into the fissures of the island where it comes in contact with internal heat and is sent forth seething and boiling.

The old volcano Bogaslov, known to the Russians for more than a hundred years, is near by. In 1882, it burst forth, after having remained quiet for more than half a century, and a new volcano was thrown up from the sea and added to our possessions. This great mass of matter issued from a submarine volcano. The particles, it is believed, worked up and around the outside of the crater until they reached the sea-level, where they formed the foundation of our new Bogaslov. So far as known, no human being witnessed the birth of this island, for it was never reported. Ships sailed by the spot without observing it, and, later, ships sailed by, and it was there. It was first seen in 1883, being then in about the condition we saw it, with the addition of a strip of land and a series of immense rocks, known as " sail-rocks," — from their resemblance to a full-rigged ship, — which connected the old and the new Bogaslov. These connections have sunk into the sea, and vessels of large draught of water can sail over the place where they once were. Extremes meet in this Behring Sea! The internal fires in both old and new Bogaslov never cease, and yonder are great mountains from whose peaks the snow never melts.

Our path lay across the 180th meridian, and crossing this meridian for the first time is an event in a Pacific cruise almost equal to crossing the equator. The greenhorns are made to pay their footing and are warned to look out for the line; to watch and see that the ship is not tripped up by it, and there is always a jolly time. This meridian marks the division of time between the eastern and western hemispheres, and is exactly opposite Greenwich. In going westward, when we cross the 180th meridian, we drop a day from the calendar; for instance, one retires on Friday night and awakens on Sunday morning.

There is a tradition, in our service, of an old salt who would not drop the day, and when his vessel fell in with the fleet he was still running his own time. As the days rolled on, he held his Sunday service on Saturday, so when the fleet was having Sunday routine, our friend started off with "general quarters," and there was a great deal of noise and racket on board of his vessel. The senior officer signalled him to change his time and go on with the Sunday routine; so our friend dropped the day, and ever afterwards insisted that he had kept two consecutive Sundays.

The weather continued fine until the morning of the 12th, when our head wind and sea had increased to such strength that we could not steam against them. The vessel was "hove to" under steam and sail until the evening of the 14th, when the weather moderated, and we were enabled to increase our speed.

The next day and night were beautiful, but it was so cold there was no pleasure in being on deck. On the night of the 17th, we picked up a gale that blew right in our teeth for two days and a half, and the ship was worked in under the lee of Behring and Copper islands, where we remained until the 20th. There we experienced some of the effects of the kurisowo, or Japanese warm current, which sweeps up the coast of Asia, and is divided somewhere to the southward of Attau. One portion flows up into Behring Sea; the other, being diverted by the Aleutian Islands, extends along the northern Pacific, moderates the temperature, and renders the islands habitable, but increases the dangers of navigation by the fogs and currents it produces.

As the gale subsided, we worked the vessel closer in to Behring Island, and we saw the place where Behring's little vessel was wrecked, and further on the spot where he is buried. The memories that cling about this island are sad. Near this spot, shipwrecked and broken in health, the intrepid Behring was stricken with scurvy. In the hope of checking its ravages, he was buried in the sand, but in a few days he died of the disease. A cruel fate! a horrible death!

After taking a look at Cooper Island, we headed for the entrance to Petropaulski, Kamtchatka. We sighted the coast at about two on the morning of the 22d and pushed on into the outer harbor of Petropaulski. As we ran down the coast, the lightning flashed, the thunder roared, and it rained in torrents; but as the land is bold and the coast well charted, we kept on our course and anchored in the bay.

The bay of Avatcha measures about ten miles across in every direction, and is surrounded by mountains from seven to ten thousand feet high, whose sides are covered with dense forests of birch, which extend almost to their peaks; while in the distant background are mountains holding their heads seventeen thousand feet high, and perpetually covered with snow.

It had been snowing here for two weeks, and it was a glorious sight to see the sunshine. Along the outlines of some of the mountains, the sun's rays playing upon the snow-banks gave all the prismatic colors of the rainbow. At this season of the year, the weather changes very rapidly. One night the elements will be warring and the rain coming down as though the very flood-gates had burst, while the next night will be calm, bright, and beautiful, and all the world seemingly at peace, until we discover by the howling, the yells, and the barking that we are anchored near kennels of native dogs. These creatures make the most horrible noises that can be heard outside of Cairo in Egypt. The noises made by the seals at St. Paul Island were painful, because human-like, but they were music in comparison with these dogs.

CHAPTER IV

PETROPAULSKI, KAMTCHATKA. EASTERN SIBERIA

THE Russian settlement of Petropaulski stands at the head of the harbor of Avatcha, Kamtchatka, in an amphitheatre, on the slope of two hills, which form a valley that is covered with reeds and grasses. The settlement is composed of about two hundred small log-houses, surrounded by handsome little courts and gardens, which are neatly fenced with palings and interwoven twigs. Peter the Great took a great interest in the place, and more than two hundred years ago it was a flourishing port, but now it contains less than one thousand inhabitants. Behring was able to build his ships here, and from this place he started on the voyages of discovery that immortalized his name and added so much territory to the Russian Empire. Petropaulski has long been abandoned by the Russians as a military station. It is an interesting, dilapidated old place, whose history has been honorable, and it is likely again to play an important part in the affairs of the world.

At the lower part of the settlement, in the valley, stands the old church, remarkable for its fantastic architecture. It is fast falling into ruins, and is not now used. A high railing has been built around the grounds for protection, and the church is looked upon as an almost sacred thing, as it stands, a monument to the marriages, the baptisms, the funerals, and all the solemn and grand religious outbursts of this hardy people. Before Behring and his followers were blessed there, bishops, priests and people had sung masses and chanted the Miserere within its little white walls. A new church has been erected on the hill, adjoining the governor's palace. On one side of the church, a monument has been erected to Behring; on the other side is a monument to Clerke, the successor of the famous Captain Cook. There is also a monument to the navigator La Pérouse.

On a point of land which separates the inner from the outer harbor, there is a handsome granite monument which commemorates the victory gained by the Russians over a combined British and French naval force in 1854. During the Crimean war, the British and French attacked the place in force, having six vessels and three thousand men. The Russians had several land batteries, and a frigate in the harbor. After having been twice repulsed, the commanders of the allied forces determined to make an assault. A large force of sailors and marines was landed, and an attempt was made to take the place in the rear. The Russian sharpshooters picked off the assailants with deadly aim. Later a rush was made by the Russians, and in the panic the enemy was driven over the steep, sloping cliff, two hundred feet high, into the plain below. It is said that more than two thousand of the enemy were slain, and five hundred Russians. The British admiral committed suicide early in the attack. In two immense trenches, side by side, sleep the Russians and the enemy who fell that day, and a handsome chapel has been erected on the plain.

The houses of Petropaulski are built of heavy logs, one piled upon the other, the ends being halved out to receive the ends of the cross logs. The joints are calked like the seams of a wooden ship, and the interiors are lined with boards and painted or covered with paper. No attempt is made to ornament the exteriors. A few of the houses are elegant, many are comfortable, but the great majority are in keeping with the people, who are miserably poor and shiftless. Religious pictures and engravings are seen upon the walls, and a shrine, containing a representation of the patron saint, is placed in the principal room of every house, and in the shops. When entering a shop it is customary to remove the hat in honor of the saint.

The men of the lower class are great drunkards, their favorite beverage being "swadka," a raw brandy full of fire, which they do not hesitate to pour down their "copper-lined" throats by the tumblerful. The evenings, which usually close with a supper, are generally spent in card-playing, drinking, smoking, and tea-drinking.

The tea used by these people is of a superior quality, and is made in a very careful way. The "samovar," or tea-urn, is seen in every Russian house, and is found from Behring Sea to the Baltic. It is a portable furnace, — a brass urn through which passes from bottom to top a cylinder, a couple of inches in diameter. The cylinder is filled with ignited charcoal, and the water is heated by it, remaining hot as long as the fire continues. A porcelain or earthenware tea-pot is warmed with hot water before the dry leaves are placed in it, then boiling water is poured upon the leaves, and when the pot is about full it is placed on top of the samovar. It is kept hot, but does not boil, and after several minutes the tea is ready. The Russians drink their tea from tumblers. It is sweetened with loaf sugar, and a thin slice of lemon floating upon its surface gives flavor to the delicious beverage.

Just before dinner, a luncheon is served on a side table, in the dining-room, and consists of cordial, wines, bitters with herring, caviar, dried meats, and fish. The dinner follows in a few minutes, and is served in this order: fish, soup, roast beef and vegetables, chops and cake, cream and jellies, the whole interspersed with wines and spirits. The fish is always served before the soup.

The houses are heated by large brick stoves, which are from four to six feet high, and so arranged as to extend into the corners of two or three rooms. The furnaces are remarkably small.

The women have attractive features, but their dress is old-fashioned and plain. The children are a merry, noisy, bright-looking lot of youngsters, full of fun and frolic, except when the governor appears; then the fun ceases, and they act as if a "boogy man" were about. They have schools, where they are instructed in the Russian language, writing, and arithmetic. They are not encouraged to learn enough to make them dissatisfied with their lot in life.

There are several good shops where almost anything can be purchased, from sugar to a full dress-suit. The fashion of the latter may be a little ancient, but the goods will be all right.

The governor of Kamtchatka is a colonel in the Russian army, and he is assisted in the administration by a captain and fifty Cossacks. They wear a butternut-brown uniform, long gray overcoats, and flat-top brown caps, being armed with rifles of superior make. These troops are stationed about the settlement, and little wooden shanties protect them from the rain and snow. The people hold the governor in great awe. Wherever he goes, hats are removed and hands fall to the seams of the trousers, until his pleasure is known, or he leaves the place.

Coal is brought from the Shaghalen Islands, and is expensive. There is plenty of wood, the hills being covered with forests of young birch, which is used for all constructions as well as, in part, for fuel. The forests are cared for by the government, and only such trees as it permits can be cut. Timber is cut by hand or imported from California, as there are no saw-mills in the country.

The melted snow flows down the mountain's side, and is diverted into ditches which have been made on one side of every street. From these little artificial brooks the people get their supply of water for household purposes.

Years ago the cultivation of wheat, rye, and barley was introduced with considerable success, but for some reason their culture has not been continued. The people depend upon the government supplies of rye-flour, which is brought here and sold at cost price. Potatoes, turnips, cabbages, and lettuce are grown in the little gardens, but neither the cabbages nor lettuce will head. The hills are covered with beautiful wild flowers and tall rank grass. Some few of the hardy flowers are raised indoors and under glass, but they do not succeed in the open air. A large supply of cattle is kept on hand, and the beeves are killed to order.

There are some delightful walks and climbs about Petropaulski. A little "clearing" on the point between the harbors is delightfully situated for magnificent views of the snow-clad mountains, the hills, the bays, and the plains beyond. In the autumn, the days and nights are fine, clear, cold, and bracing; the leaves have taken on their yellows, browns, and reds, and are about to die.

The weather is fine until the middle of October; after that it is cold and wet, and the snow falls, which does not disappear until June. During the winter, violent storms occur, the cold is intense, snow falls in such quantities as to lie even with the house-tops, and the people cannot get about. In their imprisonment, with storehouses full, they sleep and idle the time away until the thaw. The roadstead outside is rarely frozen over.

The summers are short and hot. Vegetation is of remarkably rapid growth; as soon as the snow disappears, the trees send forth their buds and blossoms, and the hills and valleys take on their beautiful verdure. In the same week the snow and ice may melt, and the trees begin to bloom. The temperature ranges from sixty to seventy-five degrees, Fah.

Fish form the basis of the native's food, and the salmon

is his choice. The fishing season lasts for nearly two months, when the salmon ascend the streams. They are taken in seines, and immense numbers are caught each year. Salmon intended for the winter's supply are split and dried in the sun. The odor from one of these drying establishments is abominable and sickening. The natives in the interior catch the salmon in nets and with spears, while the dogs, wolves, and bears catch them with their mouths.

Kamtchatka dogs are famous, and those of Petropaulski are second to none for the noises they can make. There are about two thousand of them owned in the town. They can bark, but they seem to prefer to howl. They begin about sunset, and keep up the most dismal howling until morning, making sleep and rest almost impossible, and life miserable.

Kamtchatka has no industrial interests except its trade in skins and furs, and that is very limited. Trade is conducted on the barter plan, and the poor native finds his furs are cheap and the store goods are high priced. Sable is the principal fur trapped by the natives, and all their ingenuity is expended in its capture.

The poll tax of the natives is paid in sable skins at the rate of one skin for every four persons, and the governor makes an annual visit to all the villages, to collect the tax. Foxes, sea-otter, silver foxes, and bears are also caught in small numbers, and traded to the merchants. Bears are plentiful, but their skins are not desired for export. Bear-hunting is one of the sports of the community.

There are about one thousand inhabitants in the settlement, consisting of Russians, Cossacks, Kamtchadales, and half-breeds. The port is free, so far as import and export duties are concerned. The local government is supported by the fines and dues of various kinds.

Exiles have not been sent to Kamtchatka since 1830.

CHAPTER V

KAMTCHATKA, EASTERN SIBERIA

THE Russians say: "Even the distant shores of the cold and fog-covered Sea of Okhotsk are not, however, quite the *ultima Thule* of that dreariest of regions, Siberia; Kamtchatka lies beyond."

The peninsula of Kamtchatka extends out from the northeastern extremity of Asia, and lies between the Sea of Okhotsk and the Pacific Ocean. It is about eight hundred miles long and two hundred and fifty miles at its broadest part. The entire peninsula is a vast range of volcanic mountains, many of which are in a state of activity, and earthquakes are of frequent occurrence. Two of these volcanoes have thrown ashes and stones for more than a hundred miles, and Avatcha, just behind Petropaulski, has sent out showers of stones and water. Kamtchatka is included in the province of Eastern Siberia, and Petropaulski is its capital.

The Kamtchatka is the only navigable river, and empties into the ocean on the eastern side of the peninsula. There are many smaller streams, which contain great quantities of fish and water-fowl. Whales, walruses, seals, cod, and herring abound in the seas, and many salmon are found in the rivers. Game is plentiful near the coast, and on the streams ducks, teal, divers, quail, and woodcock are abundant; while tracks of larger game are found all over the country.

Avatcha Bay is a very extensive basin, nearly circular in shape, and is about ten miles across. It is formed at the foot of a larger outer bay of the same name, near the southeastern end of the peninsula, and would afford secure shelter for all the fleets of the world. The harbor of Petropaulski, on the eastern side of Avatcha inner bay, is small, deep, and well sheltered, and is a very convenient place in which vessels may refit, although there is no dock.

Three aboriginal tribes still inhabit the peninsula. The Kouricks and Ohlutors divide the north, while the Kamtchadales roam over the south. They are a dirty, repulsive set, of short stature and filthy habits, and they subsist by means of fishing and hunting. They have no settled home, but wander from place to place, leading their most precious treasure, the " mean yellow dogs." The whole population of Kamtchatka is less than five thousand.

The dog is a native of the country, and is as ugly as his master. He has many of the instincts of the mastiff and the wolf, both of which he resembles, having the body of the former and the head of the latter. He is of a dirty yellow or silver color, his senses are keener in the night than in the daylight, and his bark and howl are peculiar. He is alert and nervous, but obedient under the lash. He has no feelings of attachment, and he should always be driven by the hand and the voice that have trained him. It is very necessary to keep him in good temper with his neighbors, and it is not safe to let him loose at any time. The half of a dried salmon is his day's ration when idle; and this is materially reduced when he is at work, as it is believed that he will work better when on the verge of starvation. The young dogs are considered the most dangerous.

Kamtchatka being situated between the ocean and the sea, and influenced by the Japanese warm current, it has a somewhat milder climate than is found in the same latitudes on the Asiatic continent, but it is a cheerless, dreary place.

AT SEA. — ON PASSAGE TO JAPAN

The midnight of the 25th ushered in a beautiful day, and in the early morning we left our anchorage and shaped our course for Japan. On the way through the waters of Avatcha we took a farewell look at the land. Just north of the settlement, Mount Korianski stands 1,100 feet high in its mantle of newly fallen, glistening snow, resplendent in the glorious sunshine, while all about it lesser mountains and hills crowd upon the vision; and behind all, great black clouds work down from the northward. Further on down the bay, the whole coast is one mass of jagged mountains, hills, and deep ravines. Wiluckneski, 7,250 feet high, and Flat Mount, both snow-clad, sparkle like great masses of diamonds amid the forest of black hills.

After leaving Avatcha Bay, we had our usual rain and mists, with head winds and seas. The winds and seas increased until Thursday morning, when we found ourselves in a lively gale. From about five o'clock we had a succession of rain squalls, for two hours after which the old ship wallowed in a very heavy, confused sea with no wind. The stifling, oppressive influence that always accompanies the typhoon was present. The barometer registered about 28, and the vessel rolled from side to side with a deep lurch that was slow of recovery; but in her own good time she changed the motion, came up, and started off on the other roll. The hatches were battened down, and spars and masts were sent from aloft and secured. At every dip, green seas rolled over the rail, and for a time it seemed as if the ship must swamp. The bulkheads set up a melancholy squeaking that added to the unpleasantness. To keep the vessel under control, the engines were turning ahead slowly, the men at the wheel met the seas and tried to hold her up to them. Thick oil was dripped from a canvas bag at her bow, while the boiling seas chased each other over her sides from every direction.

Later in the day, the seas took on more form, and as a great roller was approached, the engines were speeded to their utmost. The sea, like an angry child, was making havoc with our luggage below, article after article, singly, in pairs, and in crowds, being dashed from their places into the filthy water that was swashing over the floors of our rooms. Bibles were chased around by boots and shoes, nautical and musical instruments followed; packs of cards, books, and articles of clothing were tossed about like wreckage upon a beach when the tide is low.

At sundown, a faint breeze was discovered, which increased during the night. As it freshened, sail was set, the vessel's speed was increased, and by daylight we had a fine breeze, and were bounding along, under steam and sail, with nothing to mar our happiness except the recollection of the wreckage in our little rooms.

On the morning of the 4th, we sighted the Japanese coast, and ran along near the islands. In the afternoon, we passed close enough to see a large native city with its thousands of houses and huts, some of its temples, and much of its bustle and life, while off its harbor more than three hundred junks were riding at anchor or engaged in fishing.

As we worked to the southward, we picked up fair weather, and enjoyed smooth seas and pleasant skies. Old Neptune became so extremely polite and so careful of us that our late unpleasant shaking up was almost forgotten. The life lines and extra lashings were removed, exercises and drills were resumed, the lately sea-sick crawled out from their little rooms, and the vessel once more became tidy and trim. The great sodden cloud-shapes in the mysterious, ever-changing vault were replaced by glorious skies. Our sun sank behind that great purple-black streak, the Empire of Japan, and the fantastic shapes and colors presented to our view would make an artist famous if he could but reproduce their beautiful effects upon his canvas.

Our half-ill servants were soon on deck, to take a look at the outlines of the country which was their home, and while they did not indulge in the old songs of "Home, Sweet Home," or "Home Again," we could easily see that they felt all the sentiments of those songs, and more. Their mobile, jaundice-like faces lighted up with almost

THE POINT OF TOMIOKA, JAPAN.

sickly smiles as they bowed low towards their country, and to each other, and congratulated themselves upon their good fortune, or joined in animated conversation about their past disappointments and their new-found hopes.

We soon rounded Nasima light, on Cape King, and stood up Yeddo Bay towards Yokohama. From the dreary waters of old ocean, with their gloomy background, to the westward, we now turned towards a beautiful panorama. Terraced hills, of beautiful green, crowned and combed with bamboo, lined the broad bay on each side.

Here and there were towns, villages, and hamlets of native houses, and huts surrounded by neat little farms, gardens, or groves. Scarlet or unpainted wooden torii marked the temple path, which ends in a grove of fine old trees. The great towering chimney of modern bricks sent its curling black smoke like clouds over the little hamlet, while the hum of machines announced the fabrication of beautiful silks and satins. Great steamers ploughed through the waters, and little ones rushed up or down like mad, as

A JAPANESE TORII AND LANTERNS.

they sent a deafening whoop from their tiny steam-whistles. Unpainted junks, with bright-bronze fastenings, and square white sails streaked half-way down with black, stood across the swift running waters; and all about little fishing-boats, with picturesque people managing sails or oars, caused us to slow, to port, to starboard our helm, or speed the ship to avoid collision. As we approached the city, the scene became still more animated. The houses were more pretentious and closer together. The hum and din of machinery was heard, and the great red ribs of a leviathan steamer were seen upon the ways as we passed near the shipyards. The people in the little native boats were noisy and boisterous. Steamers were swinging at buoys, in the outer reach, while taking cargoes of coal, or silk, or tea from great lighters, and the breech-clothed coolies sang merrily as they passed up bags, or bales, or boxes. These coolies were stalwart, handsome fellows, with splendid muscles standing out as they bent and pulled and lifted the heavy weights. Along the beach, crowds of men, women, and children were bathing in the surf, while some of the more venturesome were swimming in our wake, and others beyond it were heading for the opposite shore.

FUJIYAMA.

CHAPTER VI

YOKOHAMA, JAPAN

IN the afternoon we moored the vessel inside of the breakwater at Yokohama, and before the first anchor was on the bottom, we were besieged by a long line of "sampans," or native boats, made of pine boards, propelled by two long stern oars, worked by the little brown boatmen. These boats contained representatives of nearly all the business houses in the town, and their occupants ranged from washermen to the business managers of great commercial houses. Americans, Britons, Germans, Japanese, Parsees, Chinese, and natives of India and Africa helped to swell the cosmopolitan mob, for mob it was, until our master-at-arms took charge of the ship's gangway, and arranged for the people to come on board in an orderly manner. Some of these people were old acquaintances. Many, soliciting trade, presented their cards and recommendations, whilst others brought samples and specimens of their wares. In most cases, the wares were beautiful, the offers tempting, and the merchants and their assistants courteous and graceful.

Loath to leave this bazaar-like scene upon our decks, we turn from these interesting merchants to look over and

THE 101 STEPS AT THE BLUFF, YOKOHAMA, JAPAN, WITH THE
CELEBRATED ZENABA TEA-HOUSE ON THE LEFT.

beyond the rail, to see the bay well filled with merchant steamers, sailing-vessels, native craft, our old " Monocacy," and several Japanese war-vessels, whose gay ensigns flutter in the breezes.

On low, undulating ground, between two ranges of low hills, lies the town, studded with neat little Japanese houses and gay shops. The hills, called "the Bluffs," are about one hundred and fifty feet high, semi-circular in trend, and stretch inland for a mile or more. Far away, and over

Yokohama, Japan.

the town, snow-mantled Fujiyama looms up 15,000 feet towards the heavens, while a great white cloud cuts its beautiful cone between snow-line and base. Fujiyama, as Fujisan, has been almost deified. It is the object of many pilgrimages, and has always held the first place in the affections of the Japanese people. It is the first thing looked for and greeted in the morning; and when the gloaming is darkening into night, and Fujisan is disappearing from view, millions of people bid it goodnight.

The harbor is naturally exposed to strong winds and seas, and a semi-circular breakwater, twelve thousand feet long, is in process of construction for its protection. This breakwater extends from the entrance to the canal, under the bluffs, to the northern extremity of the settlement, and has an opening six hundred and fifty feet wide at its middle part, through which we entered the harbor. There are fixed red and green lights on the sides of the entrance, and buoys of corresponding colors are placed well inside and outside of the works as ranges for the navigator, and as marks of the channel. This breakwater is a great undertaking, and a magnificent piece of engineering. Its massive granite walls would reflect credit upon the working-men of any country. A great iron pier, two thousand feet long, at which vessels may discharge and take in cargo, is being built out into the bay, at the northern end of the town.

Yokohama is situated on the western side of Yeddo Bay, and is about eighteen miles from the capital, with which it is connected by a fine double-track railway, or by water, for vessels of very light draught. The foreign residences are situated in handsome gardens on "the Bluffs," — a special concession made to foreigners when the present town of Yokohama was an insignificant fishing-village. "The Bluffs" are reached by a system of winding roads, or by one hundred and one granite steps. The views from the top of these hills are fine, and the location is the healthiest in this section of country. The tea-house at the top of the steps is one of the most celebrated in Japan. There is a fine Public Garden at "the Bluffs," and the race-course, which has a good track and is well enclosed, is situated about a mile beyond. The semi-annual meets are well patronized, and attract crowds of people from the open ports. Chinese and Japanese ponies are usually run, and

THE GRAND HOTEL, YOKOHAMA, JAPAN.

the sport is thoroughly enjoyed. A public hall, combining theatre and assembly-room, is also located on "the Bluffs."

The Bund is a fine hard roadway, extending along the entire water-front of Yokohama, and upon this many of the principal houses and hotels front. There are churches, mission-houses, and schools of many Christian denominations in the settlement, and near the centre is a very dilapidated recreation-ground. The public water-supply is excellent in quality and quantity. The hotels of Yoko-

YOKOHAMA BLUFFS, JAPAN.

hama afford excellent accommodations. The Grand Hotel, for example, situated at the southern end of the settlement, and facing Bund and bay, is one of the finest in the East. It has all the modern conveniences and appliances, and, under the management of " Fussy little Louis," who haunts the markets for delicacies, its menu is second to none in the world.

Several daily and weekly newspapers, in the English language, are published here, and the latest news from all parts of the world is obtained.

JINRIKISHA IN JAPAN.

At Yokohama, the visitor from the United States has the first glimpse of beautiful Japan, and of its wonderful people. Whether you land at the canal or at the " Hataba," you are met by a crowd of jolly, laughing jinrikisha men, each offering his vehicle, and soliciting your patronage. If you except the customs officials, the jinrikisha men are about the first acquaintances one makes in Japan. Each of these worthies is clad in a close-fitting white-knit shirt, dark-blue, skin-tight pantaloons, or his bare, brown legs display the splendid muscles that rival those of an athlete. The sun's rays are warded off by a large flat helmet, and he is shod with sandals of plaited straw. If he is at all " dudish," he wears a close-fitting, dark-blue coat, having scarlet edges and a great white monogram, or character, emblazoned upon the middle of the back. These poor fellows are intelligent, faithful, and honest. As soon as you engage one you can trust him, and your property is perfectly safe in his care. The fare for these jinrikishas is ridiculously low, fifteen cents paying for an hour's ride, ten cents for any short distance, and seventy-five cents for a whole day's service.

Two men should always be employed with a jinrikisha, one to pull and one to push. The overheating and sudden cooling, incident to the work, is very injurious to health, and produces throat and lung troubles, which are frequently followed by consumption and death. An excellent authority places the duration of life of a " rickshaw " man at less than five years. After my attention had been called to these facts, I never permitted myself to be pulled about by one man.

The government buildings in Yokohama, — built of stone in the foreign style of architecture, — and the Consulates, are grouped near the centre of the native settlement. The Consulates are surrounded by handsome, well-kept grounds, situated on wide streets. The town has grown[1] so rapidly

[1] Yokohama has grown rapidly since 1859, when it was thrown open to foreign trade. It is the port of entry for Tokio, a considerable coast, and the surrounding country. The population is about one hundred and fifty thousand. The number of foreign residents is about six thousand, of whom four thousand are Chinese. The imports consist chiefly of cotton and woollen goods. The value of the imports is $30,679,508. The total value of the exports is $50,450,489. Silk is the most valuable of the exports, being valued at $40,570,286.

THE IMPERIAL JAPANESE GOVERNMENT BUILDINGS, YOKOHAMA, JAPAN.

that the native houses, as a rule, are not equal to those in other towns. The roads are unmended, and in the rainy season almost impassable.

On the Bund, one sees all sorts and conditions of natives. The man yonder, in the gray suit, like our letter-carriers, is in the Imperial Customs service; the little fellow in blue-cloth sack suit, with the great goggles on his nose, and sword by his side, is a policeman, and the little box on the corner is the place in which he takes his rest and finds shel-

A JAPANESE SAMPAN.

ter from sun and rain. The man who is coming down the middle of the road, at a dog-trot, is a mail runner; the tiny parcel, suspended from the bamboo rod over his shoulder, is the mail. These men, by relays, go all over the Empire, conveying packages over mountains and through valleys to the most remote places, and they are said to make remarkably quick time.

We meet representatives of every nationality in cosmopolitan Yokohama: the sight-seeing American, who landed from the last steamer from 'Frisco, or who is loitering to see more of the country; the Englishman, who is making the "grand tour;" the Frenchman, who is interested in beautiful curiosities; the German, in quest of raw silk and mattings; the Russian, whose interest centres in furs; the Parsee, in search of desirable stocks; the Aleute, stranded from a Japanese sealing-schooner; the Indian, who mysteriously brings from the folds of his garments the most wonderful necklaces, brooches, rings, and unmounted stones of dazzling brilliancy, all sworn to be "first water" and "perfect," but at prices so astonishingly low as to excite suspicions of their genuineness; the Chinaman, bent on legitimate trade, who keeps a furnishing or a grocery shop, and adds to his gains by the sale of Manila lottery tickets; and the native of South Africa, who offers a few Cape Colony "diamonds" of exceptional brilliancy, which he has "smuggled" into the country from Africa, or perhaps imported from Birmingham.

We pass on, beyond the Government buildings and Consulates, make a couple of turns in the road, and enter the Benton Dori, a road which extends westward, and contains many native shops. It is a veritable "Japanese old curiosity bazaar" on an extensive scale: old armor, swords, bows and arrows, pikes, spears, battle-axes, and all the war-gear for man and horse. Their fashion and workmanship are beautiful. Many of them are marked and inlaid with gold and silver, while many others are mounted with rich bronze, which was considered more precious than gold or silver. These arms, which cost hundreds, and in some cases thousands, of dollars to manufacture, can now be obtained for a few dollars apiece. They are graphic relics of Japan, her noble families, her arms, and her military glory, from the early ages of her history to the present time, and they should not be scattered all over the world, but should be gathered together and deposited in a great museum at

Tokio, where they could remain on exhibition for all time.

The Benton Dori is not all made up of arms and armor. Brocades, silks, porcelains, masks, and portraits, and beautiful embroideries, old bronzes, ivory, and wood carvings, — much of it marvellously fine, — is to be seen in almost every shop. The very fronts have been removed from the little shops, and the whole interiors are exposed to view. How artistic is the arrangement of the beautiful and odd

JAPANESE GREEN-GROCER'S SHOP.

wares! What temptation there is to empty one's pockets, and say, "Give me anything; all is so charming!" Thus it is, shop after shop, on both sides of the road, for the mile or more of its length, crowds of bright little men, women, and children thronging its thoroughfare, and peals of merry laughter ringing out in unison with the sounds of the clogs upon its walk. One is always dissatisfied in this great bazaar, where the more that is seen, the greater is the desire to see more and to examine closer. Hours are instructively and entertainingly spent in roaming from shop to shop, inspecting the beautiful wares, while chatting about their manufacture and history with the bright little shop-keepers or manufacturers.

A JAPANESE ACTOR.

Retracing our steps to the end of the road, where we entered, we make a sharp turn to the right, and find ourselves on the gay Isszakicho; and a little further on we are among the theatres, museums, booths, tea-shops, and bazaars which line its road. Here all is noise and gayety. Banners and streamers float on the breezes, bright lanterns add to the

Dai Buisu, the "Great Buddha," near Kamakma, Japan.

brilliant scene; and beating drums, the samesan, the high-pitched voices of the actors, the criticisms and applause of the audience, — all increase the noise and confusion of the place.

We entered the best-looking theatre on the road, and sat through some pantomime acting, which was novel to us. The stage was bare of scenery. The actors and actresses were painted and made up with faces like those of the Chinese, although their costumes were ancient Japanese court dresses. The play was founded on a Japanese love-story, in which a maiden was carried off by her lover and his friends, after all the members of her family had been murdered, and their house burned. The story had no moral, for in the last act the "sweet girl" and her new-made lord were enjoying great happiness, after the Japanese fashion, notwithstanding the murder of her people.

We visited a museum of wax-works, a series of tableaux from the life of a Japanese saint, or hermit. These we found very interesting, both as works of the imagination, and in artistic treatment, and some of them were startlingly life-like.

The booths and bazaars, which line the road, were filled with the hundreds of trinkets peculiar to the native's use; while in the little tea-shops we could obtain tiny draughts of the delicious beverage, and sweetened rice-cake, which is so toothsome to the natives.

Taking jinrikishas early in the morning, with sufficient help to travel comfortably, we set out for Enoshema, to see the colossal bronze statue of Buddha, the "Dai Butsu," near the temple of Hachiman. After a delightful ride over a portion of the "Trocado," the old damio road to the capital, over hills and through valleys, stopping at the little tea-houses on the way, for refreshments and to rest our men, we finally arrived at the temple, which is situated in large grounds where priests are continually in attendance. The temple has great altars and shrines, and contains many specimens of beautiful armor, swords, spears, and banners, ancient trappings of war, and many trophies which have been committed to the custody of the god; for this is the temple of Hachiman, the war god. Hachiman was not born until after his mother, Jingu, had subdued the Koreans, and placed her arrow over the palace gate at Seoul. After examining the beauties of the temple and the old swords and armor, we rode on another mile, which brought us into

ENOSHEMA, JAPAN.

the grove of old trees, through which, in the distance, we could see the great image.

Buddha sits alone upon his granite base, surrounded and shaded by old forest trees. Tradition says: "He was the altar-piece of a great temple which flourished centuries ago, and fell into decay; and these great old trees now shade the form of the ' Dai Butsu.' "

The statue is fifty feet high, and is made of bright bronze which is now greened with age. It was made in sections and riveted together. The expression of the face is mild and benevolent, well fitted for Buddha. The sacred snail is coiled upon his head to ward off rays of the sun. He holds the sacred lotus in each hand, and massive lanterns and vases are placed before him. The interior of the image contains a shrine, and the priest in attendance never tires of narrating the traditions of Buddha and the temple.

A further ride of about five miles, through a beautiful rolling country, brings us to Enoshema, and after a short walk through a dark grove of old trees we are at the celebrated temple of the goddess " Benten." After inspecting the temple and grounds, and enjoying the magnificent views both inland and seaward, we repair to the little tea-house, where we enjoy an appetizing luncheon of delicious fish, while watching the everlasting surf splashing upon the opposite beach of Katase. The journey back to Yokohama was very enjoyable. The evening was refreshingly cool, and the light of the moon, breaking through the trees, which line both sides of the " Trocado," showed us the way.

YOKASUKA

From Yokohama, in one of the little steamers to Yokasuka, the Japanese Naval Arsenal, was a very interesting trip, and revealed many facts about these wonderful people. The dry dock and slips for building vessels are large and well planned. Here we see great vessels, their engines, boilers, and auxiliaries in all stages of construction and repair; and a visit to this place would awaken in any one great respect for these people, as constructing engineers and mechanics. To see the begrimed little fellows at their work of bending, framing, riveting, or plating, attending the shaping machine, or drill press; at the moulding trough, sweeping up, or pouring the metal, — all was a revelation, so cleverly did they work. Battle-ships, cruisers, and torpedo vessels, such as any nation would be proud to fly its ensign upon, were in process of construction or undergoing repairs.

On leaving the dockyards, we strolled over to the hill where poor Will Adams lies buried. Adams was an Englishman who came here in 1607 on a Dutch trader. The natives soon discovered that he was able to instruct them in the art of shipbuilding, and they detained him in the country. Spiritless and broken-hearted, without hope,

JAPANESE JUNKS.

with a consuming longing for his far-off island home and loved ones, he went about his task as best he could, until finally he drooped and died of a broken heart, and was buried in this lovely spot.

THE RIDE TO TOKIO

The railroad travel from Yokohama to Tokio, the capital, partly along the bay shore, is through a country of varying scenery, and is full of interest. The roadway is

Harvesting the Rice in Japan.

about eighteen miles long, well made and ballasted. The cars are luxurious, and are divided into compartments for passengers of different classes. On leaving Yokohama, the train passes under the shadow of a large temple, on the suburb, then along the fishing village of Kanagawa, which was the first designated place of residence for foreigners in Japan. We pass through the noted tobacco-fields, and through Tsumi, where the planters congregate and exchange experiences over their cup of saki. As we go by Kawasaki, we see its fleets of busy sampans, and later the bare plains of Owair, whose porcelains have never been surpassed. Through Kamada, at full speed, we pass to Ikegawa, whose greatest treasure is the temple of the " Wealth God," old " Dai Koku," whose pictures of the god, sitting on bags of rice which rats are gnawing, remind us of the famous Gambrinus sitting upon his kegs of beer. In passing through Shinegawa, we have reached the head of the bay, and are at the home of those noted fish with the wonderful popping eyes, ill-shapen bodies, and fan-tails. Soon we round through the suburb of Tokio, passing Mita and Shambashi on the way, and have arrived at the station in Japan's capital

CHAPTER VII

TOKIO, THE CAPITAL

TOKIO is situated at the head of Yeddo Bay, and is about ten miles square, containing about one million and a half of inhabitants. It is the seat of the Imperial Government and the residence of the Mikado. The Shiro, or palace, occupies a commanding position, and is the most notable building in the capital. It is one of the finest specimens of the old feudal castle to be found in Japan, and its many stories, huge ramparts, wide moats, and grove of old trees make it very attractive.

Tokio is a busy, pushing city, with the hum and noises of a great metropolis. The streets are bustling streams of life and animation, and are full of novelties. As the people are changing their garb and customs for those of the European, the streets show many extremes and contradictions. The officials and many private citizens wear garments made in the western fashion, while thousands adhere to the ancient dress. The grave, picturesque, quaint, and grotesque meet, crowd, and pass on. The jinrikisha races by, the street car moves along the rails, and the sedan-chairman dodges under the horses' heads. A crowd of human beings tug and pull as they move great loads on wheels, while the stately coachman drives by in livery. The pulsations of the steam-engine mingle with the sighs of the poor coolie as he tries to rival it in pounding rice into flour. The dingy kerosene lamp is beside the arc-light. A little fellow with bushy head, in ancient dress and clogs, passes by the side of one in the latest tailor-made garments. The

A STREET SCENE, TOKIO, JAPAN.

musūme, in bright kimono and handsome coiffure, trips merrily by the side of her sister who is gowned in American fashion. Men with bared heads, in dark-blue coats and tight pantaloons, and little women in demure kimonos; men in full-dress, wearing high silk hats, greeting others whose only covering is a coarse shirt; little soldiers in black uniforms and burnished helmets; the business-like policeman with sword by his side; the hurrying postman and the clatter of the clogs upon the walks; the shuffling of the

MAKING RICE FLOUR, JAPAN.

throng, and the prattle and laughter of the merry children, who are playing along the streets; the quaint little shops, with their dark-blue awnings and patient attendants; the little white-and-black houses in almost endless lines, like rows of fireproof safes; the thousands of odd, ugly, and pretty things that we see in shops or streets; the chatting, smiling people; the lowly bows and happy, flowery salutations and greetings amongst the people; and the nobleman's carriage at his poor friend's door, — all help to make up the bustle and noises, and the contradictions and extremes of this great city of the Mikado.

The Japanese have great appreciation and admiration of the beautiful in nature. They wander about the country in little bands, visiting some mountain, waterfall, or other beautiful scenery. They are great lovers of flowers, from the blossoms of the early spring and the roses to the imperial chrysanthemum. In the season, groups and

WISTARIA.

crowds of old, middle-aged, and young can be seen strolling through the gardens, or on the roads, admiring the blossoms of the wistaria or the chrysanthemum.

Even the poor coolie decorates his person, or his surroundings, with blossoms, buds, or flowers. From plants growing in a handful of soil, in pot or box, to those of the garden, all are cared for and nurtured. The Japanese will devote years to training vines and growing flowers, shrubs, and trees. The patience displayed is wonderful, and the results of their efforts and skill are the crosses and new

A Garden, Tokio, Japan.

species in flowers and shrubs, and the dwarfed and twisted trees which they so well know how to produce, or the enormous, overgrown productions that would astonish the judges at one of our county fairs. They can carry a hundred-year-old tree in a flower-pot, or grow chestnuts that weigh half a pound, or potatoes that could not be put into an ordinary keg.

The dwarfing is obtained with great patience and care by pinching off the rootlets week by week, and rubbing off and trimming the ends of the branches until the tree is stunted and will not measure over a few inches in height; the other condition is obtained by patient cultivation and forcing. These dwarfed trees are planted on little hills in the gardens, amongst rocks, miniature rivers, and waterfalls, and the effects are not unlike the little artificial gardens we used to make around our Christmas trees.

A ride through the beautiful, picturesque capital brings us to the suburb of Asakusa, where we visit the celebrated temple of Kwanin, whose golden image of the goddess was found by a fisherman's net at the bottom of the river. It was a fitting find, for Kwanin is the goddess of the sea, and her temple is the favorite of fishermen and seafaring people, who pay their devotions to her, to supplicate for fair weather and prosperous voyages, or to return thanks for past mercies and blessings.

At all temples, the worshippers perform ablution by washing their hands and mouths before entering the temple, for which purpose large fonts or basins of water are placed in the grounds near the entrance. Each person using the water is expected to deposit a small coin in a box placed conveniently for the purpose. On each side of the entrance to the temple is a great red cage with heavy iron gratings, containing colossal guardian gods, hideous and fierce fellows, whose terrible countenances and attitudes seem to belie their peaceful mission of receiving repentant sinners and looking after the welfare of children.

Having purified himself, the worshipper devoutly enters the temple and selects the particular deity he thinks will suit his needs. This temple contains four shrines and gods, besides the goddess Kwanin: one makes fair weather at sea, another gives a prosperous fishing season or voyage, a third cures the stomach-ache, and the fourth is the patron of women and girls. The votary pulls a bell-rope to attract the attention of the deity with whom he wishes to commune, drops a coin into a grated box, places his hands together, and whispers his supplication; after which, he claps his hands to let the god know he has finished, and retires.

The entrance-grounds to the temple contain many handsomely sculptured stone lanterns, several grim-grinning foxes, and some fine specimens of the Japanese lion. Flocks of tame pigeons and doves swarm and coo about the temple's eaves and grounds, and as they are believed to contain the spirits of the departed, they are held sacred. Old women sell rice and peas, which the pious purchase and feed to the birds.

Kwanin, like all temple-grounds, is used for pleasure as well as for pious purposes. The place is crowded with theatres, shows, archery-galleries, tea-booths, and exhibitors of wax-works, some of whom rival the famous Mrs. Jarley. A large model of the sacred mountain, Fujiyama, is visited by hundreds of people who view the city and surrounding country from its crater. The pagoda, which is also near the temple, is approached by a stone walk, lined on both sides by gay little booths for the sale of toys, ornaments, and refreshments, where the women and children love to loiter and wonder over the gaudy trifles.

All the children of Tokio seem to be here to-day; the din, chatter, and noise of these happy youngsters can only be excelled by one of our Fourth of July celebrations at home. Tin horns, fire-crackers, toy balloons, waving

Entrance to Kwanin Temple, near Tokio, Japan.

flags, and grotesque kites add to the merriment and enjoyment of the young Japanese and his mother.

All Japan is a paradise for the aged and the children. Gray hairs are eminently respectable, and great deference is paid to age. Old age and a clean, honorable life are honored by all. Old people are saluted in the most respectful language; a mother's heart rejoices if an aged person speaks kindly to her babe, and the words are treas-

VEGETABLES IN JAPAN.

ured as good omens for the child. Children with shaven heads, bright black eyes, rosy brown cheeks, clad in gowns which almost reach to their feet, play and frolic where they will, in the highways or quiet places, with ball or kite or at catches. They are never interfered with or molested. There are no displays of ill-temper, or bad words, — all is hearty fun and frolic. Even the poor coolie, with his heavy burden, will go a long way round rather than disturb the children's play.

Little companies of juvenile acrobats travel about and give exhibitions of their skill, wherever they meet children at play. The little acrobats are clad in dark-blue tights, with great red turbans, and just enough bright tint to relieve the monotony of the blue. They tumble, cross, pile, and roll, and perform a number of very clever feats to the sound of a gourd-like drum. At the climax of each feat they call out " Hic ! " — " See ! " — as they extend their tiny arms in graceful acknowledgment of the applause; and when

JAPANESE ACROBATS.

they have finished their programme, a small contribution is gratifying, and they move on in quest of other audiences.

With all their love for the young, and their beautiful wares, the Japanese are far behind the rest of the world in the use of common toys amongst their own children. Within the exception of some very poor specimens of monstrous cats, fishes, flowers, and rattles, I have not seen anything that was worthy of the name of toy for children's use.

The "wandering" candy manufacturer is a genius, an artist in sweets, and he always succeeds in gathering in a large number of small coins. He moves from street to street with his little stand, upon which is displayed his

SWEETS AND TOYS.

stock of birds, fishes, flowers, sticks, and drops. One end of his stand is fitted with a tiny charcoal furnace, above which a large basin of molten sugar is kept ready for use. From this, he forms into shape and colors such articles as may be desired. Some beautiful forms are fashioned from the sweet, and it is a pleasure to watch the clever fingers in their manipulations, and the wide-eyed youngsters gazing in astonishment as the work progresses. The candies made of pure sugar, while beautiful in form and color, are not flavored to our taste. Other candies are made of highly sweetened rice-flour, which is also moulded into beautiful shapes and highly colored.

The juggler amuses, and may be called a friend of the children in this beautiful land. A poorly clad and ofttimes wretched-looking man steps in among a crowd of merry

JAPANESE JUGGLERS.

children at their play, when, much to the amusement of all, he will open an umbrella, perhaps, and begin to twirl it on his wrist. Suddenly a great ball is seen travelling rapidly over its surface in the opposite direction. He places a small roll of paper in his mouth, and proceeds to draw therefrom marvellous yards of gay-colored ribbons; next, he may draw a sword from his girdle, give a history of the bloody weapon, and with great flourishes proceed to swallow its blade. He will plant a

Entrance to the Mortuary Temples of the Shoguns at Sheba, near Tokio, Japan.

Tokio, the Capital

couple of seeds in the ground, cover the spot, mumble some words, and make some mimic passes over it, and then remove the covering, revealing a beautiful plant in flower; or he will place a child in a basket, thrust a great two-handed sword through and through it, up and down, right and left, while the screams and finally the groans from the child are heard. Then all is quiet, the basket is uncovered and found to be empty. Thus he gives trick after trick, in rapid succession, until his stock is exhausted, when he solicits contributions and moves on.

A man will be seen feeling his way along in the middle of the road, blowing an occasional blast on his little reed pipe. Every one gives way to him, for he is blind, and his occupation is to give massage treatment to any who need his services. He will pull and pound, knead and rub you, until every joint and muscle of your body aches, and your skin rivals the

JAPANESE TROUBADOURS.

color of a boiled lobster; but the reaction soon comes, and you feel like a new person. This treatment is thought to be good for rheumatism and some other ills that Japanese believe themselves afflicted with, and the poor man has a very lucrative occupation, notwithstanding his apparent helplessness.

The Troubadours are usually from the country districts, and are dressed in quaint apparel. They bear a shrine of some celebrated saint or hermit about the city; and wherever they can find an audience, they proceed to recite, in a monotonous, sing-song fashion, the deeds of the good man.

SHEBA AND UYENO PARKS

A ride through gay Tokio, with its beautiful life and novel sights, and into the country beyond, where the old trees meet across the broad roadway and shut out the sunshine, almost the daylight; through an open country where hundreds of picturesque natives are at work in their little gardens; over a stretch of broad avenue, hedged with handsome stone fences, enclosing green terraces, with fine old trees, and a stream of silvery water rippling beside the granite roadway, — brings us through the suburb and into famous Sheba.

Through the dense shade, we behold the high, moss-covered white walls, with their quaint scarlet lacquer trimmings, sparkling in the subdued sunshine, and the great granite torii, with its bronze crests, standing in the open space before them; while just beyond is the gold and scarlet black-roofed gate that gives entrance to these temple-grounds of the Tokugawa Shoguns.

Having reached the gateway and exchanged our shoes for straw slippers, we were ready to enter the sacred place. The priest, our guide, conducted us into a porch from which we beheld a scene of bewildering splendor, — courtyards and groves, filled with beautiful temples, tombs, sculptures, and bronzes, all magnificent examples of artistic handiwork. The ancient Japanese hut and the Tartar tents are enlarged and beautified in these wonderful structures, which glisten and sparkle wherever a ray of sunshine strays through the dense foliage and falls upon them. It is a strange order of architecture, pleasing, bright, and warm,

TEMPLE OF THE SHOGUNS, SHEBA, NEAR TOKIO, JAPAN.

even in the subdued sunlight, the almost gloaming. The assemblage, grouping, and colors are wonderful, and one stands at the very threshold of all this beauty amazed at the magnificence.

The court of each temple is enclosed with massive stone railings. Great rows of sculptured stone and bronze lanterns, figures in bronze and iron, belfries, sacred wells, and handsome gateways, are seen in bewildering profusion, and

THE TEMPLE FONT AT THE SHOGUN TEMPLES, SHEBA, NEAR TOKIO, JAPAN.

the whole is surrounded by dense groves of old fir-trees which add nature's covering to the beautiful scene. The massive temples are warm and bright with gold, scarlet, green, and black lacquers and carvings; Tartar-fashioned eaves, tipped, ringed, and edged with weather-greened bronze, are placed under highly sculptured and massive black roofs which form their covering, splendid and confusing; and, through and over all, the triple asarum leaf is everywhere to be seen.

A beautiful greenish-black building is decorated with carved panels in scarlet, white, green, gold, and blue, which form the frieze around its sides. A space of black wood, spotted with bright bronze, extends up to the cornice under the eaves, which is beautifully carved and painted, and the great dark-bronze and gilt roof is dotted over with the Shogun's crest. A flight of broad stone steps leads to a massive platform, upon which eight white columns, embellished with delicate tracery, support a great lintel which is wrought in monstrous dragons, and banded with greenish-brass, the whole giving support to the bronze, tiled roof. Two fierce warriors, in ancient armor and armed with bows and arrows, occupy niches in walls of handsomely carved flowers, while guarding the temples.

ANCIENT JAPANESE ARMOR.

Projecting capitals are formed by half-bodies of fierce monsters with outstretched paws and open mouths, under a cornice of black and gold, from which project other gilded monsters, with contracted brows and hideous mien, who give support to a beautifully carved balcony. The balcony, a series of little panels of children romping among vines and flowers, has columns extending to the roof and

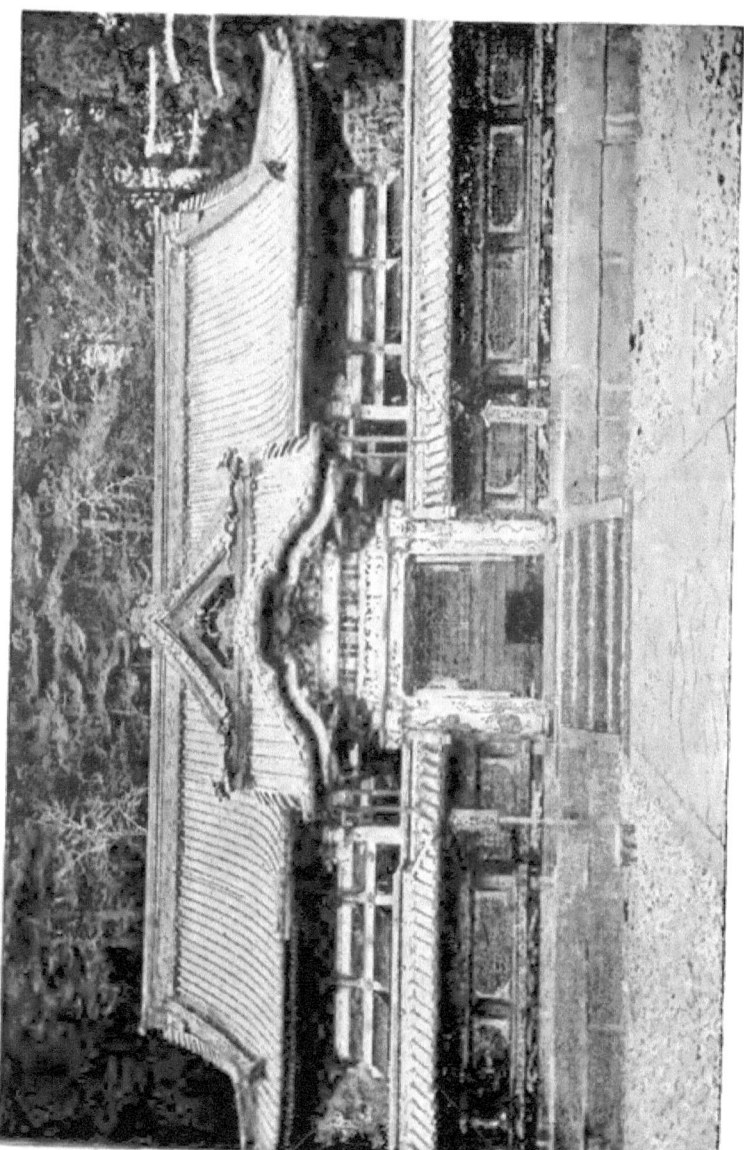

Temple of the Shoguns, Sheba, near Tokio, Japan.

Tokio, the Capital

crowned with monstrous dragon-horses. In the centre, a great white-and-gold dragon is supported between two massive columns; and all around the cornice, and up among the rafters, are hundreds of fierce dragons in threatening attitudes.

A great terrace, within a covered court, is enclosed by rich gilt walls; its polished black floors are covered with snowy matting of finest texture; its altar and shrine are rich in gilt and scarlet and black lacquers; the ceiling is

TEMPLES OF THE SHOGUNS AT SHEBA, NEAR TOKIO, JAPAN.

wonderfully carved and colored, while the nave and chancel are decorated with exquisite carvings and gold.

Another broad flight of massive stone steps brings us to a base of immense granite slabs, surrounded by a handsome wall of highly ornamented stones, from which great black-and-gold brackets reach up and support projecting gilt rafters that carry the massive roof; and between them is a band of frieze of rich-colored carvings in birds and leaves and flowers. Black and white and gold carvings are used in profusion; while the walls are covered with delicate tracery and lattice-work, wrought in exquisite patterns of flowers and leaves, in whites and lilacs, lavenders, rose, and gold.

Ascending a bronze stairway to a beautiful lacquered platform of the shrine, which is supported by four great white columns, we see monster dragons crawling about over the doorways, golden monsters frowning from the roof, and monkeys and birds carved on the frieze and band of the temple's face. The interior recesses and panels are

Tomb of "Roku Dai," the Sixth Tokugawa Shogun, Shieba, near Tokio, Japan.

filled with beautiful carving in bewildering profusion; strips of white sacramental paper, and a sacred metal-mirror are suspended from the main lintel; snow-white mats cover the dark, polished floor. Gilt columns separate the central walls, and help support the massive roof, whose ceiling is emblazoned with conventionalized carvings of birds and flowers, and the crest of the Shoguns.

It was nearly sunset as we turned from this magnificence and left the temples. Ascending a broad stone stairway,

TEMPLE OF THE SHOGUNS, SHEBA, NEAR TOKIO, JAPAN.

we passed between two hideous stone lions, and entered the famous bronze gateway, turned short to the right, and were soon before the tomb of Roku Dai, the sixth Shogun of the Tokugawa family. On a stone table before the tomb, are bright-bronze storks, lotus-flowers, and vases, — ornaments of the Buddhist faith.

The tomb is beautiful in its conception and its simplicity, — an artistic combination of geometric lines and shapes which form the Japanese covered bell. A base of five massive, octagonal, bronze steps gives support to a domed cylinder that is covered by a pyramid, from the top of which a forked flame shoots up and serves as finial. The tomb is of bright-bronze which is now becoming green. The triple asarum leaf is repeated ten times upon the beautiful bronze doors of the tomb which contains the ashes of Roku Dai.

Retracing our steps a short distance, and ascending a slimy, moss-covered old stairway, we pass along the great stone galleries until we reach the tombs of all the old kings of Japan, before which stand rows of bronze incense-burners and gigantic storks; but these tombs are insignificant when compared with the tombs of the Shoguns.

On our way out of the grounds we looked through the lattice of the dancing temple. A great black shadow fell across the floor, but the lithe form of the "woman in white" had vanished in the darkness.

Some of these temples are Shinto, and some are Buddhist. The Shinto, "way of the gods," is the ancient religion of Japan, and is now the official religion of the country. It is founded on relationship and duties, ancestral worship and nature. Its service is spiritual and ceremonious, no sound being heard in the temple, where there is neither decoration nor color, the white sacramental paper and the sacred metal mirror being the only ornaments. The temples are reproductions of the ancient Japanese hut of unpainted woods with thatched roof,—the homes of the spirits of ancestors. The Buddhist temples are rich in decoration and colors, shrines and drums and bells; and rows of low stools, containing scrolls of the law, are placed for the convenience of the devout.

We devoted three days to the Museum and the Zoological and Botanical gardens, which are filled with most interesting specimens, and are cared for by gentlemen who are highly cultured in science and art. The pleasure and profit

A JAPANESE SCHOOL.

of our visits were greatly enhanced by conversations and discussions with these enthusiastic scientists.

The imposing buildings of the Imperial University are grouped near the Botanical Garden, where professors and students have the benefit of museum and garden, for study and recreation.

Japan has made wonderful strides in educational lines as well as in other directions. Her system of free schools range from the Primary Department, through all grades, to the University. Separate schools are maintained for the

Tokio, the Capital

nobility, and all male students are required to wear a white linen cap with the Emperor's crest upon it.

The people of Japan are good-natured, flowery, and respectful in their address. When speaking of themselves, they are depreciatory and humble.

The Club and hotels of Tokio are conveniently located and are managed in the European style. Any one can be as comfortably housed and as well cared for there as anywhere in the world.

JAPANESE WRESTLERS.

We visited a colony of wrestlers near the Ragoku Bashi. Gay banners, standards and flags were floating in the chilly breezes. The sounds of clapping hands and the " Hic! Hic!" voices from the interior of the tent attracted our attention and excited our curiosity. After settling for the admission, we entered the tent. The tent is held in place by a framework of bamboo, and is large enough to shelter several thousand people. The ring in the centre of the tent is about twelve feet in diameter, is filled with black earth, and is formed by bags of rice arranged in a square about twenty feet on each side.

There is a red pole at each corner of the pavilion, before which a judge, in black kimono, is seated. The umpire, decked in ancient costume, asserts his importance by shrill screeches, while the spectators, smoking their tiny pipes, sit upon the ground or on the platforms, which are arranged around the ring much after the fashion of the seats at our circuses.

The wrestlers squat around the pavilion, outside of the ring. They are entirely naked, with the exception of a band of silk about four inches wide, which is fastened around the waist, passing between the legs, and tied at the back, leaving a fringe to hang over the thighs.

Two of them enter the ring and are received with great applause. What giants they are! They gulp down great swallows of water from buckets conveniently placed in the pavilion. They squirt the water into the air, and it falls back upon their naked bodies in a spray. They wipe themselves down with sheets of paper, and then begin to strut and pound upon their chests with their great fists. They slap their thighs, strike out with their legs, and bring their feet down with an energy that shakes the ground.

One old Chinaman, who should have been preparing for a better world, was busy taking all the bets that offered, and he was well patronized.

After this display, they take places on opposite sides of the ring, bow to the umpire, judges, and audience, then sit on their heels and stare each at his opponent. They then approach the centre of the ring, bend over, place their great fists on the ground, and glare defiance at each other. The wrestlers next rub themselves down with dirt from the ring, where they squat and glare at each other again. When the signal is given to close, they crouch like beasts, and spring together. Each tries to grasp the belt of his antagonist. They clutch each other. The great bunches of fat are crowded into great hills of muscle.

Mammoth, overfed, shapeless, nude human-brutes, clinging, pushing, pulling, and crowding, each endeavoring to overcome the other by mere weight! Their arms and legs become like great chunks of iron. They quiver, and one has grasped the waistband of the other, lifts the great beast as if he were a child, and throws him over the ring. There he drops with a dull thud, as if an elephant had fallen. What a pandemonium! How the crowd yells! The umpire frantically beats his fan upon his hand and screams out the name of the victor. The defeated walks off with ashamed face. The victor squats in the centre of the ring, while the umpire proclaims him successful and awards the silk apron embroidered in gold.

JAPANESE WRESTLERS.

The victor and his followers march off in triumph. Then another couple appear, and a similar struggle ensues. Some of these matches are settled in about a minute, while others are so well contested that they last for half an hour.

These games are about as dangerous as football with us. It is a common occurrence for these people to have ribs, arms, and legs broken, and sometimes a skull is cracked. There is no hitting or striking; the work is done by pushing, pulling, clutching, and throwing.

The training and methods of these wrestlers are entirely different from those of our athletes. They eat and drink large quantities of meat and beer, — anything and everything that will increase their weight. Many of them weigh from two to three hundred pounds, and their muscles are hard and firm, although their bodies are so large. Wrestling matches have been favorite games in Japan from the earliest times, and wrestlers did great service for the feudal lords in ancient days.

A LOTUS FIELD.

Muscle still tells in this land, where the work of beasts of burden is done by men, and athletes still have their place as workers, but they are no longer useful as military bullies. Rapid-fire guns and rifles have settled all that, and their occupation is gone.

The next day a pleasant drive brought us to the Botanical Gardens, where we were curious to learn about the flora of these islands. The oak, elm, beech, birch, laurel,

Tokio, the Capital

mulberry, walnut, chestnut, bamboo, pine and palm in many varieties, the wild plum, cherry, cycods, hydrangeas, azaleas, camellia, camphor, poppy, tea-bush, shepherd's purse, monkshood, dandelion, violet, lotus, mistletoe, rose, wistaria, chrysanthemum, celandine, chickweed, mallow, plantago, golden-rod, thistle, dock, burdock, burweed, loquat, cotton, yam, vegetable wax, varnish plant, rice, sesame, and tobacco are all well known.

The well-known birds are the pheasant, snipe, woodcock, wild-duck, wild-goose, stork, tit, crow, shirkie, wagtail, jay, owl, finch, earget. Our investigations were cut short by a low, rumbling noise. The building seemed to heave with the undulating motions of a ship at sea, then all was quiet again. The phenomenon was of only a very few seconds' duration, but it was quite long enough to convince us that we had experienced the shock of an earthquake. It was a small affair, however, and there was no material damage done.

Japan is a land of earthquakes. It experiences about five hundred shocks every year, and on many occasions some parts of the country have been severely shaken up. At times, great cities are shaken and rocked like rafts upon the ocean. There is a great strain, as if the internal pressure had overcome the imprisoning earth, and the surrounding country is made to oscillate violently. Slighter shakings on the surface, with crumblings and underground noises, follow, until finally this dies away, though perfect quiet and relief may not be obtained for months. In such years, an additional five hundred or more shakings are added to the average five hundred.

When earthquakes are not felt, the country is threatened with volcanoes, and a terrible eruption may take place at any time, and without warning. On the 15th July, 1888, an eruption took place on the grass-covered Bandaisan, and in less than fifteen minutes more than a hundred and fifty square miles of country were buried beneath a hundred feet depth of earth. The labor of years was wiped out. Villages and farms were buried, and about six hundred people lost their lives.

There are three well-known lines through which the subterranean forces act. The first of these comes from Kamtchatka, through the Kural Islands, Yesso, and Nippon, where it is met by a second line, almost at right angles, which runs through the Bonin Islands to the Ladrones in the Pacific Ocean. The third line comes from the Philippines, through Formosa to the centre of Kinshin, where it terminates in the volcano Assan, whose crater is ten miles in diameter.

Severe earthquakes are as frequent in the middle of Japan, where there are no volcanoes, as in other parts of the country. They are more frequent along the eastern coast, and do not come from volcanoes, neither do they seem to have any relationship with volcanic action as displayed at craters. The latest supposition concerning the cause of these mighty upheavals attributes them to the vapor of water.

Water is supposed to soak downwards to the heated regions, and the resulting steam is the motive-force of the volcano and the earthquake. The fact that many earthquakes occur in volcanic countries near the ocean, where both moisture and heat are present, seems to support the theory, — notably, the frequent changes and eruptions at Bogaslov in the Aleutian group. There appears to be a complexity of causes which may enter into the production of earthquakes, and the proper investigation of them may lead to foretelling the advent of these terrible phenomena.

One of the latest great disturbances in Japan was on the 28th October, 1891, about six o'clock in the morning, in the prefectures of Aichi and Gifu. In an area of over four thousand two hundred square miles the destruction of buildings and great engineering works was complete; and stone and brick buildings were affected over an area exceeding twenty-four thousand square miles, while the shocks were distinctly felt from Sundai to Nagasaki, an area exceeding ninety-two thousand square miles. There are neither volcanoes nor volcanic rocks about Gifu, the plain being a bed of alluvium lying in a basin of paleozoic hills. It was

IN A JAPANESE RICE-FIELD.

in these hills that the disturbance had its origin, and earthquakes have been frequent in this place.

The surgical report upon the effects of this earthquake states that: "One thousand one hundred and fifty cases were treated, mostly simple and compound fractures, especially of the spine and pelvis. A great number of wounds in consequence of neglect were dirty and suppurating; some were covered with maggots. Numbers of the patients were feverish and suffering from tetanus and erysipelas, but by strong antiseptic treatment and care, good results were obtained, and only four out of the 1150 died. These patients were treated and cared for by members of the Red Cross Society, medical officers from the Hospital of the Imperial University, and doctors from the Imperial Household, the Naval and Military Departments, and from the missions."

The hospital in which these unfortunates were treated was constructed from, and upon, the ruins of fallen houses, and the report further says : " The result of nervous excitement showed itself in the form of tetanus, spinal, and other troubles rather than in any general mental paralysis. . . . The fact that Japanese are less nervous and excitable than Europeans may be partly accounted for, perhaps, by the fact that the former nation has been cradled amongst earthquakes and volcanoes, the manifestations of which rank amongst the greatest of nature's terrors."

I received an invitation for the 10th, to attend a gathering in the gardens of the Emperor's Palace at Asakusa, in Tokio, to view the imperial chrysanthemums. Our party left Yokohama in the morning, and arrived at the capital in time to drive to the hotel, take a hasty luncheon, don our uniforms, and reach the palace.

After driving through the city at a rapid pace, we reached an open, rolling country, through which winds the Imperial roadway. This road was kept clear of traffic for a mile or more from the palace entrance. At short distances, a soldier, clad in blue uniform with scarlet trimmings, stood statue-like at " attention," and only relaxed from this position to salute the occupants of each carriage, as it passed, bearing the guests of his master. The road is broad, finely made, and hard, bordered on both sides by great old trees, whose branches meet overhead and shut out both the sunshine and the rain.

As we wound onward and upward, the scene became gayer and more animated. Lines of handsome equipages,

THE MIKADO'S PALACE AT TOKIO, JAPAN.

whose prancing steeds dashed fire from their heels upon the hardened road, bore grave ministers of state, ambassadors, and representatives from all the civilized nations of the earth, clad in handsome uniforms, and escorting fair women, to the Emperor's reception. After a hard ride of nearly an hour, we reached the entrance and left our carriages under cover of an exquisite little Japanese house, whose architecture, finish, and decorations are marvellous even in this land of beautiful things.

After presenting our cards, we were ushered into the presence of the Minister of the Imperial Household (representing the Emperor), who was surrounded by gentlemen-in-waiting, and, near by, a host of servants. We were each presented to the Minister, who said some kind things about our country and the President, and expressed the hope that our visit to Japan would be pleasant and profitable.

The Minister and gentlemen wore black frock-coats, light-colored trousers, and each wore the button of his order of nobility. The servants were bright in blue cutaway coats, with bright yellow facings, black knee-breeches, white hose, and shiny leather shoes with great silver buckles; a chapeau under the left arm.

We loitered awhile, with some British naval friends, to admire the beauty and exquisite taste displayed in this little entrance-house, where everything was charming.

The walls were covered with a rich rose-drab, difficult to describe, more difficult to imitate, and so effective as to linger in one's memory like a pleasant dream. The floor was inlaid with hard woods, in simple but elegant designs and colors, and the walk over it was laid with a broad rich velvet carpet in bright colors.

As we strolled along towards the chrysanthemums, through park and garden, we saw much to admire and to astonish us: a cluster of trees so grouped that their commingling colors of greens and reds and browns appear like a huge bouquet in the autumn light; a pond, a quaint little lake of sparkling water, with its sportive gold and silver fishes, with great popping eyes and fan-tails; yonder a lawn, so smooth and so green it would tempt a tennis-player to brave the anger of the guards to play upon it; a great waterfall, crashing and roaring as its mad waters dash into the pool below; and beautiful old trees and shrubs and bushes everywhere. At every corner of the walk and bend in the road stood a member of the house-

BAMBOO GROVE AT FUKIAGU, TOKIO, JAPAN.

hold guards, clad in black uniform and polished steel helmet, at "attention." These soldiers neither bend nor salute, but stand like black statues to ornament the grounds.

When we reached the pavilion, the bands were discoursing sweet music,— a selection from the opera of the "Bohemian Girl." Brave men and fair women were promenading, admiring the chrysanthemums or expectantly awaiting the coming of the Emperor. Two gayly decorated pavilions had been erected on a commanding eminence in the garden, — one for the use of the Emperor, and the other for the exhibition of the chrysanthemums.

While we exchanged greetings with friends and enjoyed the magnificent sights about us, the bands finished their selection and commenced playing the Japanese National Air. Couriers were approaching in great state, bowing low as they cleared the way. After them came the gentlemen-in-waiting, and soon the Emperor.

The Emperor was clad in the undress uniform of a general, and walked with a firm, stately tread, indicative of good health and power, and looked every inch the ruler. The Empress, dressed in a magnificent yellow satin gown of western fashion, came next after the Emperor, and she was followed by the Princesses and ladies of the court, each magnificently gowned in satins of western fashion. After the ladies came the notables of the Empire, ministers of State, judges of the Supreme Court, generals, admirals, and other dignitaries in order of their rank.

As the Emperor approached, we all gathered on the roadside and remained uncovered, until the party had passed by, when we joined it. The Emperor is a great lover of flowers, and led the way to the pavilion containing the chrysanthemums. This particular flower is his family crest, and, as may be imagined, the display was exceptionally fine and beautiful for the Imperial inspection. The chrysanthemums were in great variety of form, size, and color, from the smallest imaginable to a gigantic size, plain, curly, and feathery; ranging through all the colors of the rainbow, from the " rival of snow " to golds and reds and blues and pinks, with many intermediate shades and blendings.

When the flowers had been sufficiently admired, the Emperor led the way to a large pavilion on the opposite side of the roadway, where an elegant luncheon was served. The Emperor and the Empress were seated at a table at the head of the pavilion, and the Princesses sat facing them. Below this point a long table extended to the extreme end of the pavilion, and there were numerous small tables on the green, just outside of the enclosure.

Our places were at the long table, quite near the Emperor, who was evidently gratified, and enjoyed the beautiful scene fully as much as any of his guests. Sitting here in such presence and with such surroundings, I could but think of the wonderful changes this great man has wrought

CHRYSANTHEMUMS.

in this fair land and its people. Within the years that I have lived, the person of this man, whose guests we are, was considered too sacred for mortal eyes to gaze upon. No foreigner and very few natives could have access to him, — to look upon him was punishable by death. He lived in seclusion, surrounded by his court, the source of all honor and power, without actual knowledge of his people or their needs. Another, even mightier than he, by inherited usurpation, administered the active duties of the

A Sedan Chair in Japan.

Empire. But this great Emperor, when only a boy in years, tore away the traditions that had hedged about his family for the two thousand years or more that they have ruled Japan. When the Tartars conquered China, his family was an old reigning one in this country. He has wiped out feudalism, changed the entire social system, given his people a constitutional government; made the practice of religion free; established a free public-school system, where rich and poor can receive a liberal education; encouraged and extended railroads, workshops, and electric plants; opened up mines; extended industries and enlarged commerce until the flag of Japan is seen in every eastern port. He has made his army and his navy the most powerful in the far East, and watches over all with jealous care, seeking always for the best in personnel and material; and should the time ever come for Japan to defend herself, it will be a woful day for her enemy, come from whatever quarter he may. Such is the work of this great Emperor, who sits with us, in his scarlet blouse and blue trousers, sipping a cup of tea.

Perhaps I should not have intruded my thoughts here, as my intention was to describe the garden party, but the greatness of this man fills me with enthusiasm, and overshadows the simple story. I cannot help contrasting the history of Japan as I have read it, and the country and the people as I knew them twenty years ago, with the Japan of to-day as this great Emperor is shaping it.

The rain that had been threatening all day commenced to fall in gentle patter upon the pavilion roof, and about the same time the Imperial party arose from their seats, which of course was the signal for all to follow, and we were soon outside of the gardens, racing through the rain towards our hotel. Later in the evening we took the train for Yokohama, very tired but greatly pleased with the day's experiences.

SHIMONOSEKI, THE ENTRANCE TO THE INLAND SEA OF JAPAN.

CHAPTER VIII

KOBE, JAPAN

ON the next afternoon we sailed for Kobe, where we arrived on the second day. We kept as close to the shore as possible, and had the full benefit of the beautiful scenery. Terraced hills, valleys, and picturesque villages that are scattered along the land varied the scene and delighted the eye. All about us, the little fishing-boats were sailed, sculled, or worked about in such manner as to compel us to pick our way, while the mischievous boatmen seemed to enjoy getting under our bows, and forcing us to change our course. The little shock-haired, browned fishermen would dip their colors and cheer us on every hand. The trip was more like an ovation than the dignified passage of a man-of-war, and I have no doubt that these good people remembered the old ship and were glad to see her again, expressing their pleasure in this boisterous manner.

Kobe and Hyogo adjoin each other, and are situated on the Idzuminada, at the entrance to the beautiful Inland Sea. Both cities face the land-locked bay, stretch along its shores for about three miles, extend inland for about a mile to a range of lofty hills, where they struggle up for a little distance, then lose themselves under the almost perpendicular heights, whose tops form the beautiful plains of Arima.

'THE FALLS" AT KOBE, JAPAN.

The foreign settlement, at Kobe, is governed by a Governor and a Council, composed of all the foreign Consuls, and three members elected by the property-holders. The settlement is well laid out with wide, clean roads, and is lighted with gas and electricity. The water-front is protected by a massive stone wall, which extends the whole length of Kobe, and behind this is a handsome road and driveway called the Bund. The landing is at the foot of massive stone steps, situated nearly in front of the middle of the settlement. The foreign houses are large and airy, being built of bricks covered with mortar, tinted in some pleasing shade, and they are surrounded by handsome grounds. Many of these houses face the Bund and waterfront, and add to the beauty of the scene.

HYOGO-KOBE, JAPAN

The old native town of Hyogo is separated from Kobe by the river Minato, a narrow mountain stream spanned by a substantial stone bridge. Hyogo was not opened to foreign trade until 1892, when it was declared to be a part of Kobe.

JAPANESE WOOD-PEDLER.

Hyogo is a very interesting town, where we see a busy, thriving native population, who are not much influenced by foreigners. Walks through its streets and glimpses of its gay, open shops and little manufactories are entertaining and instructive. Everything is so novel and so different from what we have seen in the other cities and towns. The wares, the shapes, and the colors have been made to suit the native taste and use. Quaint and strange-shaped bowls and dishes, plaques, and tiny cups, in odd pieces and in sets of two, confront us in the shops, — Liliputian saki-bottles, in blue and white, or ugly browns and greens; wide-mouthed vases, with chrysanthemum-like top broader than the base, and scalloped around the edges like the teeth of a saw; wrought-iron tea-kettles, beauti-

Kobe and the Inland Sea of Japan.

fully inlaid with silver filigree work, representing vines, monsters, or gods; brass kettles, that have been pounded into shape, then chased and graven; hair-pins, and the scores of knick-knacks that women use in their hair; bows of blue, or pink, or red, to give brightness to the kimono; mirrors in metal and in glass; hundreds of cheap prints, novels, and fairy tales; queer-looking and queer-tasting cakes and jellies, and great chunks of sweets, and nameless toys; cats and dogs, that might scare the crows

JAPANESE FRUIT SHOP.

from a field, and cocks that are just true enough to nature to have a place in a collection; radishes that are two feet long; tomatoes, potatoes, and chestnuts that would easily take the prizes at our country fairs; old oak-trees that you could put into your coat-pocket, and hundreds of queer and odd things made for the every-day use of the natives.

Beyond, and away from these streets of shops and trade, we come to other streets and roads just as full of people, who are moving to and from the temples. The temple of Shinkoji has a very large bronze Buddha, which is placed in front of the building, where he smiles upon all who pass up or down the road, and no toll-keeper collects more willing contributions than does this silent pile of bronze. Poor indeed is the man, woman, or child who can pass by that face and not drop a cash or more. There is a curious old monumental stone in the courtyard, which

DRY GOODS SHOP, KOBE, JAPAN.

declares in Japanese, Chinese, and English that "Buddhism was first introduced here, from China, more than a thousand years ago."

Several hundred young girls were performing a religious dance in this temple, while its courtyard and the roads were filled with people participating in the festivities. When the dancing was ended, gifts of money and food were thrown from the tops of high bamboo towers to the poor people, who filled the temple-grounds.

There is an interesting old cemetery near the temples,

which is filled with quaint, moss-covered stones and monuments; and near by, in a grove of old trees, stands a monument that was erected in 1268 to the memory of the Japanese hero Kujormori. Thus does Japan honor the brave.

Near the end of the town is an interesting little temple noted for its plainness and poverty. Materials have been most sparingly used in its construction. Its exterior is unpainted, weather-stained, and moss-grown; but the in-

JAPANESE DANCING-GIRLS, — THE "GEISHA."

terior is full of beauty, so fresh and bright that no one would dream it had weathered the storms of three hundred years and more. Its shrine contains a great brown Buddha, which at the time of our visit was almost buried in flowers, while crowds of gayly dressed musümes were coming in, their arms filled with blossoms and flowers for its further adornment.

Close by stands the old circular stone fort which has been there since before the days of the Dutch. It was burned out, and is not susceptible of enlargement or strengthening, but stands with its cracked walls and closed ports, a wreck upon the land.

As we retrace our steps, we see great streamers, flags, banners, and lanterns, which are displayed from the housetops, giving the town a holiday appearance, and most astonishing signs hung out to advertise wares. Bareheaded men, gayly dressed women, with wide-eyed babies upon their backs, or following along in the crowd, make discordant music upon the hard walk with their little clogs. The scene, the bustle, and the great surging, polite, good-natured throng is thoroughly Japanese, " kimono and obi " prevail, while the people trip along, and bargain and shop from place to place.

We crossed the great stone bridge, which spans the Minato and connects the two towns. It is almost like the aerial bridges of China, except that it is wider and heavier. We were forcibly impressed by its unnecessarily high ascent; so great it is that jinrikisha men are compelled to go from one side to the other in making the ascent, and to repeat the operation in descending on the other side. The temple dedicated to Kusumski Masashegi stands near, on the Kobe side. This great warrior is famous in Japanese story for his loyalty and valor. He fell on the spot in 1336, during the unsuccessful war for the Restoration of the Mikado's power.

The railroads in Japan are as fine as any in the world.

JAPANESE BABIES.

Kobe, Japan 133

Kobe is connected with Osaka, twenty miles distant by a double-track road. This line has been extended to Kyoto (the old capital), a distance of twenty-seven miles from Osaka, to Nagoya and to Yokohama and Tokio. The whole system is called the Ko-kaido Railway, and its entire length is nearly four hundred miles.

Another road, the Sanyo railway, is being rapidly pushed

A Trip into the Country,—the "Kaga."

on to Shimonoseki at the Yellow Sea entrance of the Inland Sea.

At this place the Japanese government has extensive dockyards which contain a patent slip capable of accommodating a vessel of two thousand tons, where the government builds, and fits out, a large tonnage in cruisers, gun-ships, and torpedo vessels for its navy. It is nine hundred feet long, three hundred feet long above the water, thirty-eight feet broad with a declivity of one in twenty, and is worked by hydraulic power.

The Imperial arsenal is situated in the eastern end of Kobe, where we saw a cruiser, with ram bow, and six torpedo vessels, together with their boilers, engines, and auxiliaries in process of construction. The entire work was done by native superintendents and mechanics, and the intelligence, care, and workmanship displayed were surprising. The arrangement and equipment of the dock, arsenal, and shops are admirable, and as complete as could be desired.

We had been curious to discover what opportunities the boys had for acquiring a knowledge of a trade, and learned that the boy is apprenticed by his father to a working-man whom he is expected to serve " faithfully and well." The man obligates himself to impart all the information he can, and to explain, to the boy, the various operations and methods of his work. The boy commences his apprenticeship when about twelve years of age, and remains until his majority. Whenever, from any cause, the working-man changes his place, the boy goes with him, as the shop-owner has no control over him, except in the matter of deportment; and as Japanese boys are well behaved, there is seldom any trouble. These youngsters frequently become draughtsmen and superintendents, as the door is always wide open to the deserving young man in this progressive Japan.

Shipbuilding is a very important industry of Hyogo-Kobe, and a number of iron, steel, and wooden vessels are built here annually.

We strolled up the hillside to the temple of Hachiman, " the war-god," which is situated in a beautiful grove, and is surrounded by shrines and treasure-houses, that are filled with ancient armor, swords, spears, pennants, and trophies from Korea. Near by is the cage of the sacred white horse and the huts of the priests. The temple is approached by a broad roadway of masonry,— a noble

Kobe, Japan

avenue, — which extends through the city for several blocks, and is crossed, at intervals, by great stone torii and lanterns.

To the beautiful grove of old trees crowds of people resort, after their devotions, to admire the trophies, eat rice and dainties, smoke tobacco, and sip tea, while exchanging gossip or telling stories. The younger members of the party wander off to feed beans to the poor imprisoned

JAPANESE CARPENTERS.

horse, with his projecting ribs and pink eyes, clap their hands in merriment at the antics of the acrobats, climb over a blear-eyed god, and laugh and chatter over the fun and frolic.

The raised river-bed of the Minatogawa, lined on each side with magnificent old pines, as straight as masts, many of them a hundred feet high, is a pleasure-ground for the inhabitants of both cities. Under the old trees, little summer booths line the greensward banks, and tempt natives and foreigners to sip the saki, or lemonade, while enjoying the gentle breezes, the music of the soft samisan, and the song of the musüme; old men fly kites, and boys toss the shuttlecock with the heels of their clogs.

A JAPANESE BARBER SHOP.

Near by a merry family-party stops to rest; the old man takes three whiffs from his infinitesimal bronze and bamboo pipe; the little women and men gambol on mats and greensward; the demure musümes chatter in undertone as they cast fugitive glances at the promenaders;

NUNABIKI WATERFALL AT KOBE, JAPAN.

while the mother of the party chats with a neighbor over the fence.

All seem happy and joyous in Japan. No sad faces are seen, and if sadness fills any heart the clouds do not appear upon the countenance.

The Montomachi, main street, running from the centre of Kobe through Hyogo, and losing itself in the country beyond, is a revelation and a delight. It is lined on both sides with tempting little shops, where beautiful wares are displayed. The fronts are all open, and the interiors can be seen from the street, which is only about twenty feet wide.

Works of art, ancient armor and arms, bamboo furniture and ornaments, porcelains, fans, lanterns, jewelry, curios, old and new bronzes, wares of gold and colored lacquer; carvings in ivory and woods; embroideries, silks, and the hundreds of nameless things that make up the native woman's finery; fish, garden-produce, fruits and sweets, — are all temptingly arranged by the cunning, artistic shopkeepers, who are patiently squatting upon their little square mats, gazing into vacancy, apparently indifferent to the world and its surroundings, but well knowing that their beautiful wares are sure to draw you into their nets.

Further down the street are establishments where some of the most precious articles of the ancient order can be seen, — articles that in the days of the Shoguns were sacred heirlooms in families that have been deposed. Many of these beautiful works of art are in gold, silver, bronze, steel, ivory, lacquer, porcelain, and silk; armor that has resisted the spear's thrust, the arrow, and the battle-axe at the very gates of Seoul; swords that have hewn down countrymen and strangers, or perhaps have performed the hari-kari and saved a noble family from disgrace; old ivories, bronzes, and porcelains, that decorated castles for hundreds of years, — all have found their ways here. As the setting sun seems to gather the last rays of light and cast them like uncertain, scattering tints toward the eastern sky, so here we find the last trophies of the dying clans, gathered within the walls of these museums of art, where you and I may have our choice for the merest trifle.

The dark hills behind Kobe, reaching to a height of twenty-five hundred feet, make a beautiful background for the settlement and its approaches. In the morning sunlight the hills are brightest green and purple, shading into

ONE METHOD OF IRRIGATING THE LAND IN JAPAN.

the color of night, while in the evening their blackness is dotted over with little red lights, which shine from the native huts that are scattered on their sides.

The Nunabiki gathers its waters about the tops of these lofty hills, meanders for awhile, until, suddenly reaching a shelving place, it leaps over and dashes full a hundred feet into a basin that is surrounded by perpetual green, around which, as well as up the hillsides, the nature-loving natives have placed charming little summer-houses and tea-houses, where they enjoy the beautiful scenery and the waters.

The waters, like sportive maidens, frolic and play in the basin, and then make another leap of a hundred feet, and go laughingly on to the sea. The scenery is just as it came from the hands of the Creator, wild and weird, a place of beauty, quiet, and rest; and little bands of pilgrims come from every part of the country to wonder at, admire, and enjoy its beauties.

The plains of Arima are situated behind these lofty hills, and as far as vision extends, — until lost on the horizon, where the fields seem to meet the sky, — nothing is seen but a vast greensward plain, smooth and level, like our own prairies of the West.

MIDDLE-CLASS HOMES AND HOSPITALITY

We were frequently entertained by native friends; and as the native houses of Kobe are similar to millions of others all over this fair land, I will describe one where we visited.

The house stands about three feet above the ground on a foundation of bricks. It is two stories in height, built of wood, with an all-around projecting hip-roof of tiles. The sides and rear are enclosed by wooden walls with small openings for windows, while on the front both stories have sliding doors of thin wooden frames, covered with white paper. At night, and in stormy weather, heavy wooden shutters are set up in front of these papered frames, and secured on the inside. An oiled and polished wooden porch, about thirty inches wide, extends across the front.

Vines are trained upon the enclosed sides of the house for beauty and for their cooling effect in keeping off the sun's rays in summer. A litttle vestibule, or reception-room, is just outside of the front door, where visitors are received, and are expected to exchange their clogs or shoes for slippers before entering the house. It would be a gross insult to go in upon the beautiful white matting with soiled clogs or shoes.

A JAPANESE CLOG-MAKER.

Having donned our slippers, we ascend one step, which brings us to the main floor, — into the house proper. Each entire floor is one room, but is divided into several compartments by sliding doors or screens, which are tastefully ornamented and so arranged that they can be moved about in grooves that are built with the house. Each screen has a little bronze casting let into its edge which serves as knob to lift it or move it about.

The floors are covered with beautiful white rice-straw mats, about six feet long, three feet wide, and three inches thick. Soft silk, crape, and cotton cushions, about two feet square and one inch thick, filled with cotton-wool, are placed about the floor. Imitating our host, each of us sat upon a mat. A small lacquered table, containing tiny cup and saucer of finest blue-and-white porcelain, a bowl of sweets, and a cut of sweet rice cake, similar in appearance and taste to sponge cake, was placed before each of us. These little tables were about one foot high and one foot square, with a shelf half-way between top and bottom.

On the eastern side of the room was a platform of handsome oiled wood, raised about five inches above the floor. Upon the centre of the platform stood a handsome blue-and-white vase, filled with chrysanthemums; and suspended upon the wall, behind the vase, was a "kakemono," a silk scroll, handsomely embroidered with the Imperial flower.

A JAPANESE HOME DINNER.

In a few moments a large brazier, containing a kettle of boiling water, was brought in and fixed in a place prepared for it, in the centre of the room. A handsome metal box containing tea leaves was handed to each guest. We placed a pinch of the leaves in our tiny cups, and they were filled with the boiling water. Placing a sweet in the mouth and sipping the delicious tea, with broken morsels from the rice cake, was the mode. All the while our host and hostess were doing their best in polite, flowery, honorific Anglo-Japanese to entertain us, and render our visit pleasant.

JAPANESE DOCTOR AND PATIENT.

These people have no stoves. When it is cool they depend upon thicker clothing for the body, and the coals in the brazier, for warming hands and feet. When it becomes very cold, they make a good charcoal fire in the brazier, place a wooden frame about it, spread a heavy quilt over all, and sit or lie on a large, heavy cushion, with their feet towards the brazier, pulling the quilt up around their bodies, thus keeping warm while reading or chatting. Often they begin the cold winter evenings in this fashion, while telling blood-curdling stories of murderous robbers, or of the deeds of valor of some native hero.

The floors of the kitchens are made of plain oiled boards, which can be raised, like trap-doors. Under these the family stores of charcoal and other articles are kept. A large brazier is placed near the middle of the kitchen

Kobe, Japan

where the family cooking is done; and near by is a clay furnace, " hetsui," containing the large iron rice-boiler which is so necessary in every Japanese family.

The walls are decorated with numerous utensils for culinary purposes, but there are neither chairs nor tables. Food is prepared on a short piece of board that is supported on two legs, — " mana-ita."

Charcoal and wood are the fuel in general household use. There is plenty of coal in the country, much of it of excellent quality; but it is too expensive for ordinary household use.

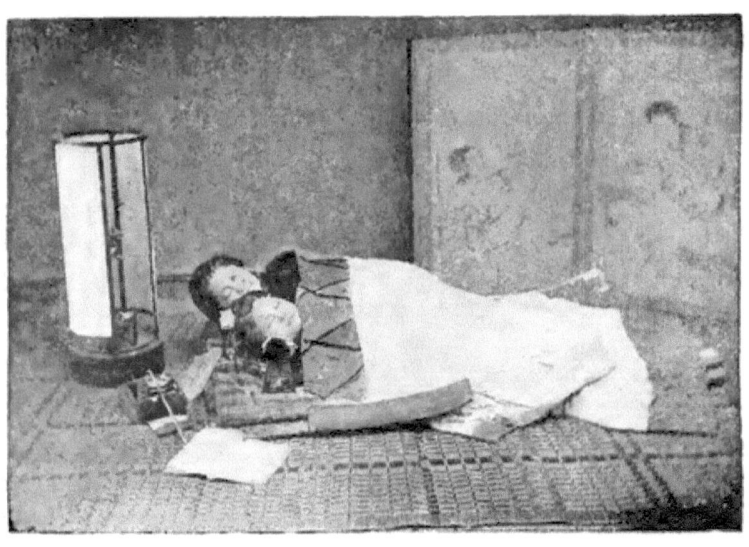

How They Sleep in Japan.

The sleeping-rooms, on the second floor, are similar in appearance to the room in which we were entertained. A closet, with sliding door, is built on one side of the room, and serves as receptacle for beds and bedding when not in use. The beds are large quilted mats of silk, or cotton goods, about seven feet long, four wide, and three inches thick, and are spread out upon the white mat-covered floor.

The head, which is always elaborately dressed, is supported by a little cushion that serves as a pillow, and is fitted into a wooden frame resting upon the floor. A small cabinet for cosmetics and a pair of metal mirrors complete the furniture of the room.

There are no people in the world who indulge in bathing more frequently than the Japanese, and their bathing arrangements are very simple. A large, unpainted tub is

THE FAMILY BATH, JAPAN.

placed in some secluded spot in the house or garden, and nearly filled with water of a temperature that would almost turn a lobster red. Kimono and clogs quickly removed, and the natives spring into the tub, and scrub and rub and knead to their heart's content, the operation being repeated two, three, and often four times a day. There are public baths in all cities for both males and females, where a little tub of hot water and a place on the cemented floor (where they can rub and scrub and douch) can be had for less than half a cent.

Kobe, Japan

MAKING THE TOILET, JAPAN.

JAPANESE GIRLS AND WOMEN

The life of a woman in Japan is unique, and very different from that of her sister in the United States. Her birth into the world is heralded for several weeks in advance by a gaudy flag or streamer from the housetop. When she is seven days old, her head is shaven, with great ceremony, and kept partially so until her sixth year. During her infancy she is carried about strapped to the back of an older sister, or perhaps her grandmother. When she is large enough to take care of herself, she plays in the open air at shuttlecock, gazes at the acrobats, and romps in the temple-grounds.

She is by instinct modest and polite, and does not know what disobedience or rebellion means. Her education is on the lines of etiquette, ceremonies, poetry, the language of flowers, and obedience to men. At fifteen she has developed into a well-knit woman,— a rosy-cheeked brunette, with dark, velvety eyes,— and is as bright as the sunshine.

She dresses according to her station in life. If she can afford it, she wears a kimono of silk or crape, which is held about the waist by a cord. Over the cord is placed a long sash, or "obi," ten inches wide, and about twelve feet long. This sash is wound about the waist, and made into a great bow at the back. It is made of silk woven with threads of gold, and forms the chief ornament. Her black tresses are subjected to frequent baths of rapeseed oil, and by the aid of decorated pins, combs, and pads, are formed into mounds and waves. She sleeps by resting her neck on a wooden pillow, "ma kora," and is enabled to keep her hair in good condition for several days. She goes to flower shows, the theatre, and to festivals, but she is always accompanied by her father, and knows nothing of flirtations. Her friends are all of her own sex.

THE HAIR-DRESSER IN JAPAN.

The Japanese take little note of affection, social position, or money when marriages are discussed, the all-important point being consideration for perpetuating the family name. No greater misfortune could befall a couple than to be childless, and this is the cause of the great number of divorces in Japan. An old maid or bachelor is almost unknown. The girl is not consulted, and has no voice in the selection of her future husband.

THE SICK BABE, JAPAN.

Marriages are arranged by the middleman, or "nakado." He interviews the relatives of both, carries on the courting, is master of ceremonies at the marriage, and acts on all matters of discord between husband and wife. He settles all family matters, has power to grant divorce, and arrange the settlement of property. He brings the young people together for the first time. The girl must submit to an inspection, and if she is satisfactory to her future husband, the matter is settled. If not, the man leaves, and the engagement is off. When the engagement is made, there is an exchange of presents of clothing and flowers.

On the day of the wedding the girl covers her face with rice-paint, rouges her lips, and dresses in white garments, — the color for mourning, — emblematic of her death to her father's family. All of her property is sent to her mother-in-law, and after her departure the house is thoroughly cleaned, indicating that she is no longer of the family.

In old times, the father's parting gift was a short sword, with the admonition to the girl to commit suicide, "harikari," if she failed to please her husband. The wedding takes place at the home of the man's family, to which the girl has been escorted by the "nakado," where she changes her mourning kimono for one of colors presented by her future husband. The house is tastefully decorated with flowers, and in one corner of the room two wooden figures are dressed as an old man and woman, being intended to signify long life for the bride and groom.

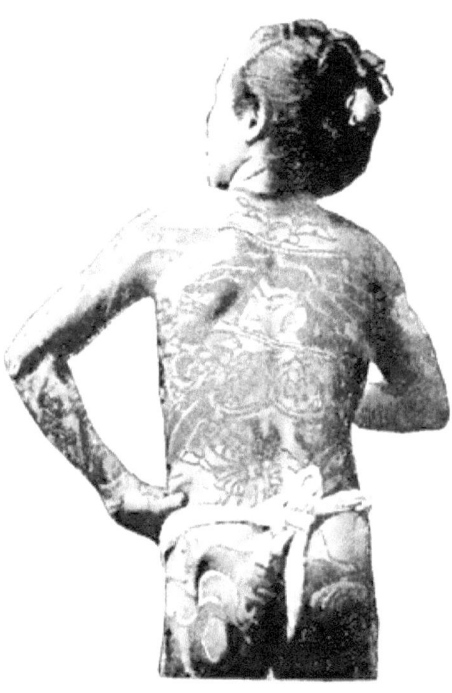

A TATTOOED JAPANESE.

Religion and law have very little to do with these weddings. They partake of the nature of an agreement, and can be terminated at any time by mutual consent. The man kneels at one side of the room, where he is joined by the bride, the "nakado," and members of the families. They kneel, facing each other, and the man hands the bride a cup of saki, from which she sips and returns it to him. This ceremony of drinking is repeated nine times to the accompaniment of music from an adjoining room, and this means that henceforth the husband and wife — for they are now united — will drink from the same cup, whether it be of prosperity or adversity. The relatives now enter, and a feast follows.

JAPANESE COOPER.

When the guests have departed, the bridal chamber is sought, and nine cups are again emptied. The husband is then served by the bride, who makes low obeisances, and by all means in her power indicates her belief in her husband's superiority. From this time the husband's power is supreme, his will is law.

After these ceremonies the woman blackens her teeth, shaves her eyebrows, and does all in her power to render herself as unattractive to other men as possible; but this practice is rapidly dying out. From childhood she is taught perfect obedience, first to her father, then to her husband

and her husband's family; and if she becomes a widow, then to her son. She is tender, gentle, and womanly, but there is no romantic homage to her. She has limited privileges, and demands no rights.

The railway terminus is at the boundary line between Kobe and Hyogo, and extensive car-buildings and repair-shops are on the grounds. There are Protestant and Catholic churches in Kobe, and an excellent club, recreation-ground, and three first-class hotels in the foreign settlement.

The population of both towns is about one hundred and sixty thousand. The foreign residents of Kobe number about six hundred, not including the Chinese, who number one thousand and twenty.

Five daily papers are published, three of which are in the English language, and two in Japanese.

The harbor is commodious, and affords safe anchorage for vessels of large tonnage. Tea, rice, camphor, vegetable wax, copper, matting, porcelain, and curiosities are the most important articles of export.

The value of the import trade is about $26,501,670; that of the exports, $17,314,595. There are 23,679,977 pounds of tea shipped from this port, the whole of which goes to the United States and Canada.

PICKING TEA LEAVES IN JAPAN.

CHAPTER IX

OSAKA, JAPAN

TWENTY miles of railroad travel over a finely made road, through a scenery varied by gardens, villages, and forests, delights the eye, and brings us to Osaka. This, the second city of the Empire, is situated on the Ajiawa River, about five miles from the sea, in the province of Settsu, and is an extensive manufacturing centre. Its houses are well built and close together, and the streets are well laid out, regular, and beautifully clean. Three hundred bridges span its canals, and it has been called the "Venice of the East."

Osaka is thoroughly native, and is not influenced by the foreigner. It is a pushing, driving city, and has been likened to some of our rapid growing cities of the West. The Imperial mint is located here, and its coinage is not surpassed by any in the world. The porcelains of Osaka are well known and admired throughout the world. Its bronzes are of the finest, and they are deservedly famous. The silk shops display the richest goods that can be produced. Some of its mills send out beautiful patterns in rugs, druggets, and carpets, and others produce cotton cloths that

JAPANESE CABINET-MAKER AT OSAKA.

rival the texture of India lawns. The iron-works are deservedly famous, and the ship-building yards send forth the steamers whose shrill Calliopes make the early mornings and the nights hideous about Kobe. Osaka is so much of a manufacturing centre that it will be well for the political economists and manufacturers of the world to remember the artistic tastes, mechanical genius, deft fingers, and cheap labor of Japan when making their calculations for the future.

The city is the seat of the Provincial government, and its

scenes are similar to those of the other great cities. The pageantry of the court, the handsome equipages of the officials, the great throngs of people, in native and foreign dress, the sedan chairs, the jinrikisha and street cars, and the soldiers in red and blue uniforms, make a picturesque foreground for the gay, open shops which line the streets.

Osaka was the capital and military camp of the Tokugawa Shoguns. For more than four centuries they shaped

JAPANESE POTTERY AT OSAKA, JAPAN.

the country's course, and made its history, from this city on the Ajiawa; and it was here they met their fate, and played the last act in the drama of usurpation, by surrendering to the Mikado, in 1868.

The castle of the Shoguns was erected by Hido-Yashi, in 1583, and is one of the finest specimens of the ancient feudal castle to be found in Japan, rivalling the palace of the Mikado at Tokio. It is now garrisoned by troops of the Imperial army, and is the military headquarters and arsenal of this district. The arsenal, situated in the castle-grounds, contains vast quantities of military stores and arms.

The Haku Butsu, "great bazaar," is filled with specimens of almost everything made in Japan: antiques, lacquers, screens, porcelains, embroideries, gold and silver and bronze work. Side by side are the newest and the oldest, beautiful things and grotesque, rich goods and common, — all attract the natives, who delight to stroll through the roads and enjoy its sights.

The Temroji temple and pagoda are fine specimens of Japanese religious architecture, and the little dingy island hotel is a comfortable place to rest in after tramping over the great city.

The population of Osaka is 500,324 souls. Its imports are $4,840,507, and the exports are $1,000,601.

From Kobe to Nagasaki, through the Inland Sea of Japan

We sail in and out as we thread our way among the islands which dot the Inland Sea of Japan, — the beautiful water which connects the Pacific Ocean with the Eastern sea. Terraced hills, dark valleys, bamboo-combed ridges, line its shores, and behind them great black mountain ranges, whose peaks are lost beyond the clouds; while here and there cities, towns, villages, and temples add their beauty. Queer, square sailing-junks and little fishing-boats are passed, and the sea and sky lend enchantment to the scene, as the white ship speeds on her way, with steam and great spread of canvas, with the starry banner at her peak, — a thing of beauty on the beautiful water.

We pass from the sea through the beautiful but treacherous Straits of Shimonoseki, the "Gibraltar of Japan," where fortress on fortress, bristling with guns, terrace the hills, where the busy garrisons are adding strength to the strong-

Entrance to Nagasaki Harbor. Papinberg in the Distant Centre.

Osaka, Japan

holds, and the huge black piles of coal await the coming of the iron and steel monsters. Between these grim hills, the treacherous waters curl and twist and turn, forming dangerous eddies and whirlpools; but having safely passed through them, we hug the shore while keeping well inside of outlying islands until we reach Papinberg, at the entrance, where we feel our way through the long narrow channel to Nagasaki.

JAPANESE SAMPAN FERRY.

The scenery all the while is varied and attractive. A fine pebbly beach extends inland to terraced hills of waving rice; bamboo-combed mountains are in the distance; and neat little hamlets of tiny native huts lie about the valleys and hillsides.

NAGASAKI, JAPAN

Nagasaki is situated on the southwestern coast of the island of Kiushiu. The harbor is about three miles long, and its greatest width is one mile. It is land-locked, and is one of the most picturesque harbors in the world. To compare it with another is absurd, for there is but one Nagasaki. The city is very old, and was the most important trading port of Japan in the early days of foreign intercourse. Near here, in 1637, were enacted the scenes attendant upon the extinction of Christianity in Japan. The celebrated island of Papinberg, at the harbor's entrance, is the spot where thousands of Christian martyrs, rather than renounce their

UP THE MOUNTAIN STREAM, NAGASAKI, JAPAN.

religion and trample upon the cross, suffered themselves to be thrown over the high cliff into the sea.

The native city is about two miles long and one mile wide, extending along the water-front, and following up the hills until they become too steep, where it loses itself in straggling summer-houses, tea-houses, and pleasure-houses among the gravestones, and the little terraced rice-fields. From this elevation a beautiful panorama of hills, valley, and sea is spread out before us; and the "sampans," with their covered cabins, appear like white gondolas gliding through the waters of the beautiful harbor.

THE HILLSIDE GRAVES.

Osaka, Japan 163

After the Christian religion had been crushed out, and the foreigners expelled, the Dutch were granted the privilege of trading with Japan. On the departure of their vessel for Holland, they were compelled to leave hostages for its return. The problem of taking care of these hostages arose, and the governor looked about the city, strolled down to the water's edge, and, opening his fan, said, "Make

AN OLD STONE BRIDGE, NAGASAKI, JAPAN.

an island like this." This was done, houses were built for the accommodation of the hostages, and, that they might be *safely* kept, the windows were secured with bars of heavy iron. Thus the Dutchmen found themselves prisoners on the fan-shaped island of Deshema.

The O'Sueva, or Bronze-Horse temple, stands upon a hill behind the city, and is approached by a wide roadway of huge stone slabs, spanned at intervals by great stone torii, behind whose columns stand massive stone lanterns.

The roadway crosses the mountain torrent by a fine old stone bridge, — a piece of engineering said to be several hundred years old. The roadway is lined on both sides by little shops and booths which extend almost to the temple.

The temple is situated in a large courtyard which contains a life-size sacred bronze horse, colossal stone lanterns and a sacred font, the whole surrounded by a dense grove of old trees, where the natives congregate to enjoy the beautiful surroundings and scenery.

At the entrance to the temple stand " Gog and Magog " in gigantic, barbaric hideousness, seeming ready to strike down any intruder. The temple is a mass of dingy columns supporting a tent-shaped tiled roof, and enclosed by wooden walls. There are three altars, each having a Buddha with different attributes. Before each is placed a grated box, to receive offerings, and a bell-cord is so located that the devout can call the attention of the god required.

A trip through the korausha, or bazaar, gives an idea of the wonderful artistic and industrial life of the people of this section of the Empire. Here we see beautiful cabinets, tables, and boxes of various styles and design, made of natural colored woods, — almost incomprehensible boxes, which, turn them as you may, you cannot open unless you know the secret; embroideries in gold and colored silks; magnificent old brocades of gold and silver threads; stuffed birds, so natural as to cause surprise; lacquer boxes and tables and trays, that rival, in decoration and color, the temples of the Shoguns; handsome and grotesque bronzes; old and new tapestries; beautiful ornaments in glass and gold and silver; carved ivory and wood in many designs; porcelains and pottery; fruit and flower stands, where one may find his favorite rosebud or chrysanthemum. The crowds of shock-headed men, gayly dressed women, and shaven-headed babies trip along good-humoredly, and add to the beautiful scenes. Chatting together or singing on the way, they seem to go through life in a merry, happy way, living close to nature, as their religion teaches,

JAPANESE TOY PEDLER.

gathering the sweets as they go. Contracted brows and sad faces are only seen on the gods and temple guardians.

The ancient Dutch prison-houses on the bridge-guarded island of Deshema are historically interesting, though now they have been converted into storehouses where beautiful porcelains from Hizen, Hirado, Arita, and Imari can be seen. Here are shown unique designs and decorations, — the finest porcelains in Japan.

Tortoise-shell work is a thriving industry of Nagasaki. One may stroll along the " Curio " street and see scores of busy artisans sawing, cutting, carving, and polishing, while fashioning this beautiful shell into the many designs that please foreign taste.

There are several shops on this street where there are exhibitions of fine specimens of ancient swords, axes, spears, and armor, inlaid with gold, silver, and bronze; old porcelains in blue and white, and in varied colors; and old brocades and silks, worth more than their weight in gold. Lacquered ware, cunningly inlaid with mother of pearl and gold, grotesque articles in porcelain, ivory, and rare woods, together with bronzes, old and new, are some of the productions of these patient people.

The fishing interests of Nagasaki are extensive, and many

FISH AND FRESH PROVISION SHOP, JAPAN.

tons of fine fish are caught, dried, and salted for the market. Hundreds of little fishing-boats go outside to deep sea soundings, where they remain until they secure the catch they desire, or are driven in by bad weather. A short trip outside of the harbor, at night, soon brings us in sight of the great fleet, — a scene of enchantment. As far as the eye can reach we see the little reddish-white lights of the fishermen, twinkling as the everlasting roll of the sea gives them undulating motion that sends weird rays through the surrounding blackness.

Nagasaki Harbor at Noon on a Fourth of July.

The feast of lanterns is held in October, after the harvests. For days preparations are being made, and the festival is talked about. Cakes and cookies and sweets, and all the mysterious things the Japanese mother can devise to tempt the appetite and gratify the palate, are prepared. In the mean time, the male portion of the community is busy with preparations; houses are decorated, lanterns, flags, and transparencies are purchased or im-

ARTISTS DECORATING LANTERNS.

provised, wagons are decorated, and "floats" arranged. When the night arrives, the people are in a fever-heat of expectancy; houses are illuminated; a great torch-light procession with beating drums, ringing bells, decorated wagons and floats, banners and illuminated transparencies, marches through a section of the city, and pandemonium reigns amid this good-natured throng of men and women.

After going over as much of the city as possible, the procession is so timed as to arrive at the head of the harbor about midnight, when all who have had relative or friend lost at sea or anywhere drowned, launch a miniature sampan made of rice-straw, gayly decorated and filled with provisions. A bright light is placed inside of the little sampan, so that the spirit, whose name is painted in a conspicuous place, can distinguish it. Many of these little craft are stranded and burn upon the beach of the long harbor, while many others float out to sea to hunt the lost spirit whose earth-name is borne upon its frail bow.

After launching these little boats, the people re-form in family groups, and with lighted lanterns and a store of provisions wend their way up the hills, amongst the graves, where they feast with their dead. They believe that the spirits are present and enjoy the feast with them. The feast lasts for two nights and days, and when it is ended refreshments are left at the graves so that the spirits can feast at their pleasure.

After another trip through the "Curio" street, where we inspected the beautiful specimens of armor and arms, old porcelains and silks, reminders of the last Shoguns and their faithful henchmen, and watched the cunning artisans fashioning beautiful designs in tortoise-shell, we strolled up the hill to the Shinto temple. Turning from the street into a flight of wide stone steps, which is flanked on each side by heavy retaining walls, we mounted the thirty or more steps which brought us under the torii and into the temple courtyard, — a large terrace bordered on all sides with fine old trees. A stone well for ablutions is fixed in the centre of the court, and numerous elaborately carved stone lanterns are scattered about in artistic disorder.

The temple is of plain, old unpainted wood, as the teachings of the Shinto faith require, and is more impressive from its great size and its surroundings than for architectural beauty or decoration. Massive pillars of bright wood, capped with heavy green-bronzed heads, give support to great girders and lintels with curious bronze ends ; and little birds fly about, and chirp from their nests between the rafters which support the black tiled roof.

A FUNERAL PROCESSION IN JAPAN.

The matted floor is soiled from use and age. The shrineless altar, with its sacred white papers and the great metal mirror overhead, adds to the beautiful simplicity of the interior. A couple of bonzes, priests, in elegant robes, were moving about in preparation for some event.

As we were about leaving the temple we met a procession of white-robed natives, two and two, each man bearing a massive bouquet of artificial flowers. Body-bearers bore a beautiful white-wood box which was about thirty inches square, and the same in height, with a slanting cover upon it like the hipped roof of a house. A body had been placed in this box in a sitting position, with the knees under the chin, and the head pressed forward. This coffin, or box, was placed close in front of the temple altar, while the persons composing the procession formed a triangle about it, the vertex of the triangle being towards the entrance, and the sides extending towards the chancel rail. One of the priests pulled the bell-rope to call the god, then all present engaged in silent prayer. The ceremony lasted for about half an hour, and there was no sound except the ringing of the bell, the clapping of hands, and the chirping of the little birds under the roof. One of the priests then clapped his hands three times, when all bowed low; the procession re-formed, and the body was borne out of the temple.

When the procession reached the great porch of the temple, one of the priests opened a little wooden cage and set a beautiful white dove free. The freed bird circled round and round, each time widening its circle, until it had about completed the third, when it started off and upward, almost in a straight line, and was soon lost to sight, emblematic of the flight of the freed spirit.

COFFIN AND FUNERAL ORNAMENTS, JAPAN.

The little company now resumed its march, slowly and reverently moving up the hills to the spot where the remains of their friend were to be hidden from the sight of men.

A drive around the beautiful harbor brings us to the old native fort whose guns were always pointed towards the devoted island of Deshema, lest the poor Dutch hostages should forget their captivity and endeavor to enjoy the freedom of the neighboring hills. Lotus-fields and beautiful flowers are beyond. Charming scenes are through the vale to the right, and the Russian village that skirts the harbor is in the valley through which the terrible typhoon sweeps,

A JAPANESE COUNTRY HOUSE NEAR NAGASAKI, JAPAN.

and where we meet the odd-looking half-breeds who resemble neither Japanese nor Cossacks.

Turning inland, we dismount, walk up a very steep hill to view the surrounding country and harbor, and are greeted by a magnificent sight of mountains, hills, valleys, and clouds of wonderful shapes and colors, with the smooth, mirror-like harbor at our feet. Near us is the new residence of the kenshaw, or governor, imposing in size, of the Russo-Japanese style of architecture, situated on a commanding bluff at the head of the harbor, and surrounded by a handsome garden, which is also the official weather signal station, where the approach of typhoons are about as well foretold as rains are foretold at home.

We visited one of the public schools, situated on a hill near the kenshaw. The schoolhouse is a rectangular building, light and airy, externally having the appearance of an immense conservatory, as it is almost entirely made up of windows, doors, and roof. It is about two hundred

IN THE RICE-FIELD.

feet long, one hundred feet wide, and two stories high. It stands in a courtyard about as large as two of our city blocks. The interior of the building is divided into corridors and class-rooms, each of which is fitted with little tables, seats, and blackboards.

To give some idea of the appreciation of the schools by the people, our driver informed us, with a great deal of pride in his manner, that *his* children attended this school.

Further on, we left the hills and re-entered our vehicle, crossing two of the fine stone bridges that have spanned

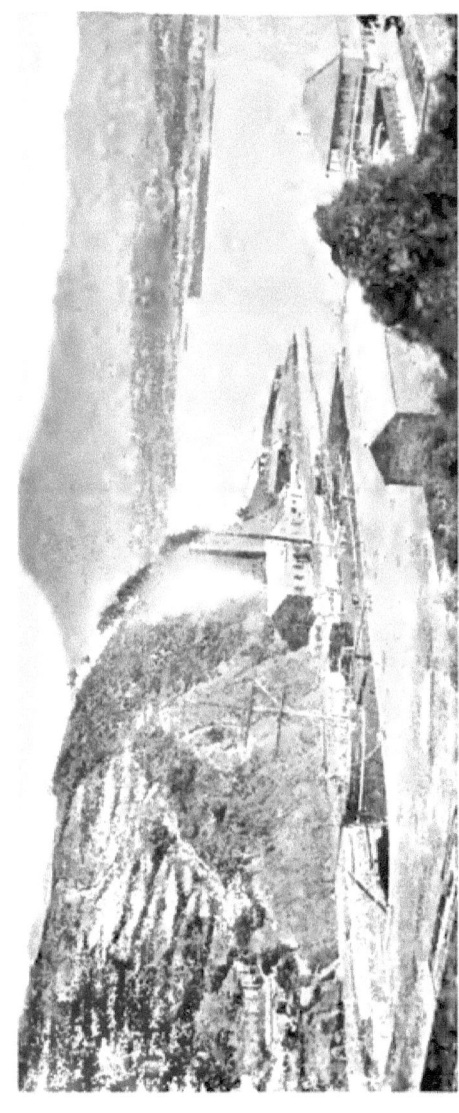

this mountain torrent for centuries. Then we went up the road, which leads along the falls, to see the crazy old mill whose race passes over one wheel and under another, as it furnishes power from the flowing waters, to grind the people's rice.

Crossing the city, we meet groups of men and women returning from their daily toil of gathering twigs from among the trees on the hillsides, and behind them groups of charcoal-venders, who have their little crossed piles of coals swung from bamboo poles, borne upon their shoulders,— every one of them having a pretty little nosegay, or bouquet in hand, or on the burden, so dearly do these people love flowers.

Pushing on up the hill, amongst the graves, we reach a favorite tea-house, where we stop awhile for rest and refreshments. Having exchanged our shoes for light slippers, we pass over the white-matted floor to the verandah beyond, where we enjoy the beautiful scenery while awaiting the preparation of our luncheon. Soon the Honorable Miss Bamboo and the Honorable Miss Chrysanthemum make their appearance, and, falling upon their knees, exchange the compliments of the day, and receive our orders.

After a time the luncheon is spread before us in American fashion, and with sharpened appetites we proceed to make our honorable waitresses stare at the way the good things disappear. Stare, did I say? I did not mean exactly that, for no one stares in Japan except the great-eyed babies; but as the Japanese, when compared to us, have such butterfly-like appetites, we think they ought to stare when we are enjoying our luncheon after a hard day's tramp.

There is a fine dry-dock of stone with extensive manufacturing and repair shops on the western side of the harbor. The dock and works were built by the Japanese government, but they are now the property of a private corporation. The dock is 483 feet long (inside of caisson, at top), its length on blocks is 375 feet, its breadth of entrance at top 89, and at bottom 77 feet, its depth of water on blocks at spring tides 27 feet 6 inches, and neap tides 22 feet.

Nagasaki has an abundant supply of good water, which is supplied to the people by means of hydrants on every block. The reservoir holds nearly 100,000,000 gallons, which pass through three filter beds and a supply reservoir before its delivery to the people. A railway is being constructed from Kumamoto to Nagasaki, a distance of one hundred miles. It is now open as far as Moji, about five miles distant.

The coal mines at Yackashema, an island which lies about six miles southeast of the entrance to Nagasaki, are very interesting. They now extend out under the sea, and a trip to them, including the descent of the shaft and the exploration of their vast passages, is an experience never to be forgotten. There one sees the little brown, blackened Japs, picking, wheeling, trucking, and sending the coal to the surface, with their tiny safety lamps, like Liliputian head-lights, to guide them, and one feels a realizing sense of being so far under the sea. When the fresh air is reached, and one's feet are fixed upon the greensward, the sensation is one of great relief.[1]

We devoted an afternoon to a trip to the crematory, which is located on the top of one of the highest hills behind Nagasaki. Our guide was a little superstitious, and, when he learned our destination, he refused to go with us; so, United States fashion, we went without him. Not

[1] There are several very productive coal mines near Nagasaki, of which the Yackashema mine is the most important, the production being over 300,000 tons in one year; that of the Nakamashema mine is 125,509 tons, and the aggregate production of the various mines in the locality is about 800,000 tons.

Osaka, Japan

being able to find the road, we concluded that "all roads lead to Rome," and struck out across the country, over rice-fields and terraces, climbing over parapets, and at times going a long way around to avoid the flooded rice-fields. The tramp was particularly fatiguing, as the mercury had taken a sudden jump up into the nineties for our benefit. Tired out, but undaunted, we finally reached our destination, and found the place well worth the visit, but, I must confess, a little mournful.

JAPANESE BULL CART.

The building is a massive brick structure, with a tall chimney of the same material, and it is situated in a barren courtyard. A little Japanese summer-house, with white awnings and massive black characters, stands to the right of the entrance, and a great pile of cord-wood is neatly lined up behind it. There are no trees on the premises, no sounds; not even the note of a stray bird breaks the awful stillness of this Dives-like inferno, man's device to cheat time and rob the worm.

We entered through a large central doorway which opens into a wide hall that extends across the entire breadth of the building and meets two other halls which extend to the rear. The hallways are lined with furnaces, so placed that their backs form the base of the great one-hundred-and-fifty-feet-high chimney. The furnaces extending across the front hall are reserved for the rich, while those opening into the side halls are on one side designed

"THE OLD MILL" AT NAGASAKI, JAPAN.

for the middle classes and on the other side for the poorer people. The furnaces are rectangular iron boxes, built in with the brick work, with an opening in the back end near the top of each, and each furnace door is fitted with a regulating damper.

When a body is to be cremated, the religious services, if any, are held in the hallway. A known quantity of cord-wood is spread over the bottom of the furnace, then the body is placed upon an iron truck, the truck is run into the furnace over the wood, the wood is ignited, the door closed, its edges made tight with luted clay, and in one hour the body is reduced to ashes. The door is then opened, the truck is drawn out of the furnace, the ashes are carefully gathered from the truck and placed in a vase, the top of which is sealed and marked. At this point my companion became nervous, and imagined all sorts of horrible things, and it was with great difficulty that I could quiet him, and get him into condition to make our downward journey.

Our descent was pleasanter than the ascent as we tried a road which led us directly to the Bund, and we were soon on board of our ship.

The climate of Nagasaki is mild in winter, and healthy at all seasons of the year. It is hot in summer by reason of the situation of the town on a plain surrounded by high hills.

During the last few years the foreign trade has steadily improved. The chief articles of import are cotton and woollen goods. The principal exports are coal, tea, camphor, rice, and dried fish.[1]

The "Rising Sun," a small English weekly paper, is published here, and also two native papers.

There are Protestant and Catholic churches, mission houses and schools in the settlement, which is just south of the native city.

Moji, Japan

Moji, an important fishing village, containing about five thousand inhabitants, is situated on the opposite side of the island from Nagasaki, about five miles distant. It is now

[1] The value of the import trade of Nagasaki was $3,000,133, and that of the export trade $3,482,226. Coal is the chief article of export, amounting to nearly one half of the whole export trade.

The population of Nagasaki is 60,860. The number of foreign residents is 1,006, of whom 671 are Chinese.

reached by a broad new pass cut through the mountains, in a country justly celebrated for its beautiful scenery. Formerly, the distance was about eight miles by a narrow country road that wound upwards and over the mountain-tops. Thousands of men and women were employed in removing this great mass of earth and rock with tiny shovels and baskets which hold about a peck of earth. The pass through the mountains is about one hundred feet wide and about one mile and a half long, and the banks are more than three hundred feet high. The road-bed has been so carefully made that it is as hard and smooth as a well-made city street, and the whole roadway to Moji, about five miles in length, is in the same condition.

MOJI, JAPAN.

At every step and turn in the road there is something to attract and to admire: terrace on terrace where the beautiful rice bows its head to the gentle breezes; the bamboo groves and little shrines; the torii and temples;

the old mill in the deep ravine; the swift-running, mad mountain stream, now swollen to river proportions, with clear, sparkling waters rushing on and down to the sea, turning this wheel and that, as it grinds the rice or spins the

HILLSIDE GRAVES OF THE MARTYRS, MOJI, JAPAN.

cotton; the quaint little tea-houses, with their wistaria arbors shading the road, and the peaceful smile of the old hermit of the mountains as he welcomes you to rest in his little black hut.

Moji is built around a semi-circular bay, its houses and huts occupying the level ground between the beach and the hills beyond. Here one sees native life uninfluenced by foreign fashions; and the male portion of the population being absent on their fishing excursions, the village appeared to be inhabited by women, children, a few old men, and the crowd of squeak-voiced curs that were continually snapping about our heels.

The beautiful ride, the varied architecture, the picturesque old inn at the entrance of the crescent bay, the little fishing vessels, tossing about in unison with old ocean's swell, and the magnificent scenery about us, — all make Moji a charming place to visit.

CHAPTER X

CONSTITUTION AND GOVERNMENT OF JAPAN

THE government of Japan was until recently that of an absolute monarchy. The Mikados were the supreme heads of the Empire, and the source of all honors and power. They were encouraged to live in seclusion and pleasure (their persons being considered too sacred for ordinary mortals to behold), while the Shoguns, the military commanders, assisted by the Damios, or feudal lords, superintended the active administration of affairs.

Several attempts were made by restless Mikados to depose these usurpers, but their efforts were not successful until 1868, when the present reigning Emperor overthrew the power of the Shoguns in a short, sharp war. They surrendered their lands, retainers, and incomes to the Mikado, who granted them one tenth of their incomes and required them to reside in Tokio.

The reigning monarch, Mutsu-hito, meaning "Honorable Gate," was born at Kyoto November 3, 1852. He succeeded his father, Komei Ieune, in 1867, and married Princess Han-ko December 28, 1868. The Empress was born April 17, 1850, and is the daughter of Prince Itchije.

The present Emperor is the one hundred and twenty-first descendant of an unbroken dynasty which was founded 660 B. C. By the ancient law of succession, the crown devolves upon the eldest son of the Emperor, and, failing male issue, upon his eldest daughter. Disregard of this law of succession has frequently occurred, and this was one of the chief causes that brought about the dual system of government in Japan. Women have frequently occupied the throne.

The power of the Mikado was formerly absolute, but in 1875, when the Senate and Supreme Judiciary were established, the Emperor declared his intention to form a constitutional system of government. The Emperor has always been the spiritual as well as the temporal head of the Empire.

The official religion is the Shinto faith, — "the way of the gods;" but there is no interference in religious matters, and all religions are tolerated in Japan. In 1877, the Ecclesiastical Department was reduced to a bureau under the Interior Department.

The Emperor acts through an Executive Council, which is divided into nine departments, the head of each being a great Minister of State. The departments are those of Foreign Affairs, the Interior, Agriculture, Justice, Finance, Education, the Navy, the Army, and the Department of Communications.

The new Constitution was proclaimed in February, 1889, and in 1890 the first Japanese Parliament was chosen. It is composed of a House of Peers and a House of Representatives. The House of Peers is composed of three distinct classes, — Hereditary, Elective, and Nominative Members. The House of Representatives consists of three hundred members, who are elected by ballot, for a term of four years, but in case of necessity the term may be prolonged. The Emperor selects the members of his Cabinet, or Council, and they are not responsible to the Parliament.

For administrative purposes, the Empire is divided into three Fu, or cities (Tokio, Kyoto, and Osaka), and forty-three Ken, or prefectures, including the Loochoo Islands. The island of Yezo is under a separate administration. The governors of these Fu and Ken are called Prefects.

Constitution and Government 187

They are all of the same rank, and are under the control of the Interior Department. Their powers are limited, and they are required to submit every *unprecedented* question to the Department for decision. All judicial proceedings come under cognizance of the local courts and the Supreme Courts, the latter being presided over by a Chief Justice in the capital.

Yori-touri, a general of great ability, founded the Shogunate in 1184. It continued through several dynasties, and exercised the executive authority. The administration was shared by the two hundred and fifty Damios, or feudal lords, who were supreme in their own dominions so long as they remained loyal to the Shogun.

The great Tokugawa family was deposed from its usurped authority in 1869, and the rank and powers of the Damios fell with it. In 1884, the nobility were re-established, and the most distinguished military and civil officers who took part in the Restoration of the Emperor were admitted to its ranks, — Prince, Marquis, Count, Viscount, and Baron replaced the ancient titles.

ANCIENT JAPANESE WARRIOR.

The revenue of Japan is $85,980,081. The total expenditure is $85,978,078, — about two dollars per annum for each soul in the Empire.

The Japanese Army

The army of Japan consists of the standing army, the reserves, and the militia. The standing army, when on a peace footing, is composed of 61,976 men, and when on a war footing, 245,310 men, which can be increased to one million. The Imperial Guard is composed of 5,336 picked troops, who do duty at the capital.

The Empire is divided into six military districts with headquarters at Tokio, Nagoya, Sendai, Osaka, Kumamoto, and Hiroshima. Four regiments of infantry, one regiment of cavalry, two batteries of artillery, one regiment of engineers, and one regiment of transport corps are stationed at each headquarters, and camps of instruction are established in fifty-six other places.

The army is organized on the French system by officers specially selected by the French government. The Emperor looks after the army and navy with jealous care. At the manœuvres, which are held every year, the Emperor spends days in the saddle, or on board ship, familiarizing himself with the condition of the troops, insisting always on the best in personnel, equipments, material, and movements. His tastes and the tastes of his people have always inclined toward outdoor exercise, the use of warlike weapons, a chivalrous bearing, and the cultivation of qualities which develop warriors.

The Navy of Japan

The navy of Japan comprises five steel coast-defence vessels, ten composite corvettes, two iron-clad frigates, six steam sloops-of-war, — five of steel, one composite, — five steam gunboats, three torpedo-catchers, four seagoing torpedo boats, and thirty-five torpedo boats, whose numbers are being increased by vessels built in Japan and in Europe.

The steel coast-defence vessel "Itsukushima," built in

France, has a displacement of 4,278 tons with engines of 5,400 horse-power. Her armament consists of one 65-ton and twelve smaller breech-loading steel rifles. One sister ship built in Japan, and one built in France, have similar power and guns. The iron-clad frigate "Fuso" has a displacement of 3,779 tons, with engines of 3,932 horse-power. Her armor varies from 7 to 9 inches in thickness. Her armament consists of four 15.25 and two 5.5 ton breech-loading steel rifles, so placed as to command every point of the compass.

The iron-clad corvette "Kongo" has a displacement of 3,000 tons, with engines of 2,500 horse-power. A belt of armor 4.5 inches thick extends around her, and her armament consists of 124-pounder breech-loading steel rifles. The "Hiyei," a sister ship to the "Kongo," has similar displacement, power, armor, and battery. The steel cruiser "Tsukushi" has a displacement of 3,000 tons, steams 16 knots an hour, and her armament consists of two 25-ton breech-loading rifles.

The "Naniwa" has a displacement of 3,700 tons, steams 18 knots an hour, and has an armament of two 25-ton breech-loading steel rifles, besides a number of machine guns. The "Takachiho" is a sister vessel to the "Naniwa," and has equal displacement, speed, and battery. The "Yoshino" has a displacement of 4,200 tons, with engines of 5,500 horse-power, steams 22 knots an hour, and has an armament of two 25-ton breech-loading steel rifles, machine guns, and three torpedo tubes. The steel cruiser "Chiyoda" has a displacement of 2,400 tons, with engines of 2,500 horse-power. Her armament consists of one 25-ton breech-loading steel rifle, machine guns, and three torpedo tubes.

Japanese sailors are bold and venturesome, and the mechanical genius of the people fits them for the guidance and management of the great fighting machines of these times.

CHAPTER XI

POPULATION AND INDUSTRY OF JAPAN

THE area of Japan is estimated at 156,604 square miles; and the population, according to the census of 1890, was 40,453,461, of whom 20,431,097 are males, and 20,022,236 are females.

The Empire is divided, geographically, into four departments or islands, — Henshiu, Kiushiu, Shikoku, and Yezo. The first three are subdivided into eight great divisions containing sixty-six provinces, and Yezo is divided into eleven provinces.

The Japanese ports of Yokohama, Kobe-Hyogo, Hakodate, Nügatee, Nagasaki, and the cities of Tokio and Osaka are open by treaty to foreign trade[1] and residence. They each have a designated settlement where foreigners may reside. Some of the treaties were revised in 1889. The new treaties were to become effective in 1890, when the

[1] The following table shows the total value of the principal classes of goods exported from Japan, in yen, or Mexican silver dollars, as:

Books and Paper	$269,979	Silk and Cocoons	$32,175,892
Coal	4,749,734	Skins, Hair, Shells,	
Drugs, Dyes, &c.	2,506,116	Horn, &c.	279,718
Grain and Provisions	10,923,467	Tea	7,033,050
Matches	1,843,637	Clothing, &c.	5,372,413
Metals	5,409,773	Duty free Goods	6,247,764
Oil and Wax	639,483	Foreign Produce, &c.	789,219
Porcelain and Earthenware	1,287,027	Total	$79,527,272

Population and Industry of Japan 191

whole of Japan was to be thrown open to foreign commerce and extratoriality, — which is very distasteful to these clever people — was to be abolished. On October 19, 1889, the Japanese Minister of Foreign Affairs was severely wounded in the capital in an attempt upon his life, incited by the agitation of treaty revision, and the work was then suspended. The revised treaties had been signed by the United States, Russia, and Germany, but they were not ratified. Negotiations were resumed, and the United

The imports from various foreign countries are classified by the Imperial Bureau of Revenue, also in yen, or Mexican silver dollars, as:—

Arms, Clocks, Machinery, &c.	$3,990,611	Lime and Manufactures of	$326,159
Beverages and Provisions	886,930	Metals and Manufactures of	5,140,893
Books and Stationery	609,990	Oil and Wax	4,971,781
Clothing and Apparel	755,519	Silk Manufactures	535,377
Cotton, Raw	8,199,251	Sugar	7,811,307
" Yarn	5,589,290	Textile Fabrics, Miscellaneous	393,390
" Piece Goods	3,502,127	Vessels	674,270
Drugs, Medicines, and Chemicals	2,225,767	Wines and Liquors	430,111
Dyes and Paints	1,218,202	Woollen Manufactures	5,481,938
Glass and Glassware	379,075	Sundries	2,521,639
Rice, Beans, &c.	6,106,537		
Hair, Horns, Ivory, Skins, &c.	1,177,101	Total	$62,927,268

The total shipping from and to foreign countries for the year 1893 was:—

	Entered.	Tonnage.	Cleared.	Tonnage.
Steamers	1,358	1,906,698	1,231	1,604,995
Sailing vessels	1,006	156,605	1,167	154,325
	2,364	2,063,303	2,398	1,759,320

Of which 1,262 steamers and 19 sailing vessels entered, and 1,280 steamers and 19 sailing vessels cleared in the coast trade; of these, more than one half were Japanese employed in foreign trade.

States and British treaties were revised and signed in 1894.

Railways already completed and in course of construction will soon make a line of communication from the extreme north to Nagasaki in the south, branching off to the important cities in the east and west. In 1892, the Parliament enacted a law authorizing the government to construct lines of state railways connecting all the important cities and towns in the Empire, and to issue bonds to cover the cost.

Tokio, Kobe, Osaka, Yokohama, Nagasaki, and Hakodate are now connected with each other and with the United States, via Europe, by lines of telegraph and cables. There are more than seven thousand miles of telegraph wires, connecting all the important towns in the Empire.

Japan is a member of the Universal Postal Union, and for the past eighteen years has managed the international as well as domestic postal service. The telephone, electric lights, steam mills, and street-cars have been introduced into the capital, and the first three into nearly all the large cities of the Empire.

THE RELIGIONS OF JAPAN

The Japanese in civilization are far in advance of other far-Eastern people, and have a more liberal appreciation of Western thoughts and customs. This is due to the fact that their national religion is Shintoism. To-day, Christianity, Buddhism, and Shintoism flourish side by side, but Shintoism is the religion of the state, and gives direction to the thoughts of the Empire.

Japanese history and Shintoism date from 660 B. C.; Buddhism came through the snows of Korea, in 550 A. D.; and Christianity was reintroduced after Perry's visit. Christianity was looked upon with suspicion and a certain dread which survived the unhappy experiences of the six-

JAPANESE FIREMEN ON PARADE.

teenth century, and although these are slowly dying away, they have affected the progress of Christianity.

To comprehend Shintoism, we must examine Taoism and Confucianism, from which the Shinto faith was formulated, and study its wonderful effects upon a nation isolated from the outside world. The doctrine of Shintoism, " Kami-no-michi," or " The way of the gods," is contained in a combination of selections from Taoism and Confucianism, and is of Chinese origin. Its fundamental principle is hero-worship, the veneration of the country's heroes and benefactors, and of all ancestors, ancient and modern. When the Mikado gave his people their present liberal Constitution, he invoked the spirits of his ancestors to witness the act.

Shintoism is broad and liberal. It lends a helping hand to everything that tends to uplift the nation, and its priests and followers have always given aid and welcome to priests and missionaries of other creeds. Notwithstanding the fact that Shintoism has been the religion of Japan for more than twenty-four centuries, it was not declared the established religion until the year 1868, after the restoration of the Mikado, when a grant of $300,000 per annum was made toward the support of its one hundred thousand temples.

Shintoism and Buddhism work side by side, and the rites of either are administered as the people may prefer. Buddhism is pushing and aggressive, and had almost superseded Shintoism.

The principal deity of the Shinto faith is Mingo-no-Mikato, the ancestor of the present Mikado, who is said to have been descended from the sun. The Mikado is known as the "Son of Heaven," on account of his descent from Mingo-no-Mikato. It is said that "when the goddess of the sun made 'Mingo' sovereign of Japan, she gave him the 'way of the gods,' and ordered that his dynasty should be as immovable as the sun and moon." The goddess also gave him a mirror, and commanded him to look upon the mirror as her spirit, to keep it in the same house and upon the same floor with himself, and to worship it as he would worship her actual presence.

SHINTO PRIEST, JAPAN.

There are ten parts of the Sacred Book, Yengi Shiki, which are devoted to court ceremonies, and these occupy a prominent place in the rules of the court of the Empire. The great incarnate god is the Mikado, but everything in nature is exalted and deified.

Shinto temples are usually divided into two compartments. One contains the emblem of the deity, which may be a mirror, a sword, or a stone, kept in a sacred box within other boxes, covered with wrappings of brocades, and tied with silken cords. In the other compartment, usually the outer one, pieces of white paper cut in a peculiar shape hang from a lintel overhead. There is usually an oratory in front of the temple, with a gong hanging over its entrance, so that the devout can call the attention of his god, and before this oratory the worshipper bows and clasps his hands together while offering his silent prayer. He then claps his hands, throws a few small coins into the box for offerings, and departs. The priests sell slips of paper bearing the name and title of the god, which many of the people use as charms. The temples are generally situated in a grove of trees, and there are often additional buildings near, which are dedicated to other Shinto deities.

These temples are of the plainest architecture, without coloring or decoration. The floor is raised a few feet from the ground, and a narrow balcony extends around the entire structure. The approach to a Shinto temple is always under a torii, "bird-perch," a lintel placed across two uprights at the entrance to the grounds. Sometimes more than one mark the way to the temple. They are made of heavy or of light materials, — wood, stone, or bronze, — and are sometimes painted a bright red color. The central part of the lintel may have inscribed upon it the name of the deity to whom the temple is dedicated.

The temple of Ise at Yamato is Shinto, pure and simple, and as it is one of the most ancient shrines in the Empire, it is annually visited by thousands of pilgrims. There is no grand architecture or decorations, no sacrifices, and few symbols. The main columns of the temple are supported on heavy stone foundations, the floors are raised about four feet from the ground, and the walls are of wood. The roof is thatched, and metals have been sparingly used. The posts, rails, and fences are unornamented, and there is neither carving, lacquer, nor color, simply the brown and gray tints and the mosses of weather-stained woods, — the ancient hut enlarged.

The "torii" are the gateways, and hanging curtains of white swing for gates. The lanterns are of coarse white paper, decorated with the conventional chrysanthemum, the crest of the Mikado. The offerings upon the altar are rice, salt, fish, and flowers, and the emblems are as simple, — ropes of rice-straw and wisps, and hanging slips of white paper, each a symbol in the story of the sun goddess, being enticements from the cave to which she had retired from the moon god's violence.

The sacred mirror is never seen by mortal eyes. It is kept in a box which is wrapped in white silk and covered by a wooden cage, which in turn is covered with a silk wrapper. The mirror is in a brocade bag, and as soon as its sheen begins to fade with age, a new mirror is added without removing the old one.

The priests call the attention of the deity by a few strokes upon a gong or bell, recite a few short prayers, bow the head, and retire.

BUDDHISM IN JAPAN

There are as many Buddhist sects in Japan as there are Christian denominations in the United States. They all believe in the teachings of Buddha, but they vary greatly in creed and forms of worship. The Tundi sect peddle medicines and charms to protect against all the ills flesh is heir to, — to cure rheumatism or the cholera, to keep birds out of a rice-field, or His Satanic Majesty out of a house, — and they sell earth to make the muscles of the dead flexible, so that the limbs can be doubled up and placed in the doghouse-like coffins which the Japanese use. This sect has thousands of temples throughout the Empire. The most powerful sects are the Monto, the Jodo, and the Nichiren.

The Monto teach that fervent prayer, elevated thoughts, and good works are the essentials. The Jodo sect pray without ceasing, abstain from eating flesh, and do not permit their priests to marry. The Nichirens are noisy and intolerant, and believe that all except themselves are doomed to eternal punishment. Their temples contain many deities and incarnations. Some cure babies and protect from all childhood's dangers; others cure all sorts of diseases. All one has to do, is to select the right temple and deity, bargain with the priest, say the prescribed prayers, and go away cured.

At almost every temple there is a sacred horse, some hogs, or a flock of birds. These are fed by the bounty of some deceased person who has made provision for their support, or by the faithful, who bestow a few beans or a little corn upon the creatures in hopes of receiving their reward for a meritorious act.

BUDDHIST PRIEST, JAPAN.

There are said to be about seventy thousand Buddhist temples in Japan.

The Buddhists of Japan are kind and considerate of each other and of all creatures. They believe the spirits of the departed have entered into some created form, to serve

200 An American Cruiser in the East

during the probationary period, and therefore they treat all creatures kindly for fear of oppressing some spirit. They are energetic and pushing. They publish many religious articles in the newspapers, and a movement is being made for the foundation of a Buddhist theological course in the Imperial University. Some advanced thinkers are hoping to make it the state religion, while others are formulating

JAPANESE WOOD-CARVING.
A Detail of the Temple, Sheba, near Tokio, Japan.

creeds for the union of Christianity, Shintoism, and Buddhism, retaining what they believe to be the best features of each, and forming a grand religion for all men. Many Buddhists, in Japan, believe that Nirvana does not mean a state of total spiritual annihilation, but the annihilation of all that is bad and the continuance of all that is good in man.

Many of these Japanese temples have been erected by men and women who became enthusiastic and gave their labor. Carpenters, masons, carvers, lacquerers, and laborers come from all parts of the Empire, and work for a certain number of days without compensation. Rich men contribute the materials, and women do the hauling and lifting. They even cut the hair from their heads and braid it into ropes with which to pull and hoist the great stones and beams. It is said that two hundred thousand women and young girls cut off their tresses and made them into the ropes which are used for the hauling about the temple of Higashi Hongwauji, now being erected at Kyoto, yet this magnificent pile will cost more than eight millions of dollars before its completion. Some of these temples have very large incomes, and almost any of them can raise from one hundred thousand to half a million dollars a year.

Class Distinctions in Japan

The Tokio Historical Society has made exhaustive researches from which the following extracts are taken.

"Until the year 470 A. D., all persons not elevated by official employment, nor degraded temporarily as criminals, were equal before the law. In that year, a man named Ne-no-omi rebelled against the Emperor Yuryaku. Ne-no-omi was killed, but the Emperor decreed that all the descendants of this man should be regarded as inferior persons and be reduced to servitude of a menial kind. They were divided into two parties, one being detailed to serve the Emperor, and the other a provincial governor."

"In 486 A. D., Karabukmo-no-Sukune rebelled, and when captured the Emperor ordered that he and his descendants should look after the Imperial tombs."

"In 693 A. D., the Emperor Jito decreed that if a man was unable to pay a debt, and if the sale of his property did not realize sufficient money to meet the obligation, he should become the slave of his creditor."

"Down to this time (693 A. D.) all foreigners who came into the country were classed amongst the *semmin*, inferior people, and unless redeemed by relatives or friends, were slaves for life. The Emperor Jito changed this law, and decreed that foreigners should be classed amongst the *ryomin*, superior people, and be exempt from servitude. For several hundred years the distinction between the two classes was very great, but under the Kamakura and Ashikaga Shoguns it was almost obliterated."

JAPANESE HOMES.

"In 701 A. D., the 'Yaiho' laws were published, and *semmin*, or inferior people, were classified as follows: (1) *ryoko*, guards of the Imperial tombs; (2) *kwanko*, government slaves; (3) *kenin*, domestic slaves; (4) *komihi*, slaves of officials; (5) *shinuhi*, slaves of private individuals."

"The first two classes were householders and consisted of rebels or their descendants. The work of guarding the Imperial tombs was regarded in those days as disgraceful employment, as all work connected with the dead was considered to defile. The slaves of classes 2 and 4 had precedence of all others, as it was not considered degrading to work about cultivated people, even in the capacity of slaves. The slaves in class 2 were mostly rebels, but they were over sixty years of age. Those of class 3 were too poor or helpless to become householders or to take care of themselves, generally poor relations, and were compelled to serve the persons upon whom they depended for their support."

" Of course, there was a certain disgrace attached to this loss of freedom, but it was preferable to many other forms of servitude. In all classes except 3 it was punishment for crime or violation of law. In class 3 it fixed the mutual obligation of master and servant, between persons who were charged with the support and care of others who were unable to care for themselves, and in this connection we must remember that institutions for the care of the poor were unknown. Classes 4 and 5 were composed of prisoners taken in war and criminals and their descendants. Class 5 furnished slaves for the market, as it was strictly forbidden to sell a member of the other four classes."

" Men and women of class 5 were bought and sold, and their personal liberty depended upon the disposition of their owners. But the Japanese have always been a kind-hearted people, and the hardships to which their slaves were subjected were no more than always exists between master and servant."

" Slaves were forbidden to marry with the other people, and the slaves of one class were prohibited from marrying the slaves of another class. The punishment for a violation of this law was fifty stripes and annulment of the marriage. The slaves who guarded the Imperial tombs were under the control of the Imperial Household officials."

" Before 691 A. D., the sale of people belonging to the *ryomin*, or superior class, was common, but the Emperor Jito issued a decree in that year specifying the cases in which the sale of persons should involve degradation in social rank.

If a peasant was sold for the benefit of his elder brother, he was not degraded, but if he was sold for the benefit of his parents, he was degraded, and a person sold to discharge a debt did not lose his rank as *ryomin*. In the case of traffic in slaves, a written bargain had to be prepared and submitted to the authorities for approval."

JAPANESE TRAMPS.

"A curious document bearing on the sale and prices paid for slaves in Japan was recently discovered. It gives an account of the sale of certain persons in Mino. There were three males and three females. They realized a total of 4,900 bundles of rice-plants. The ages of the three males were 34, 22, and 15 years, respectively. The two elder slaves brought 1,000 bundles each, and the younger 900. The ages of the females were 22, 20, and 15 years, respectively. The two elder ones realized 800 plants each, and the younger one 600. Various marks of identity are described, such as red spots on the left cheek, freckles, etc."

"If they became sick within three days after the sale,

the sale was null and void. In case of runaways it was customary to pay a reward amounting to five per cent of the value of the slave, if he or she were captured within one month, and of ten per cent when a year had elapsed between the runaway and capture."

"Slaves might become free and enter the *ryomin*, or superior class, under certain conditions: in case of persons who had been stolen and reduced to slavery illegally; when a master died without an heir and his house become extinct; when given their freedom by their master. Official slaves became free when reaching 76 years of age, or too ill to work. Freedom was often obtained after a few years' service by those who had been reduced on account of their association with rebels, but not owing to any prominent part they had taken in opposing the government. Slaves occasionally obtained their freedom by displaying great proficiency in some art or accomplishment, and were sometimes released by the will of the sovereign. In such cases there was usually some special object in view, such as the encouragement of agriculture."

" There are no reliable statistics, and it is not known exactly how many slaves there were at any given time. But it is believed that they amounted to about five per cent of the whole population, and that the number of female slaves was slightly in excess of the males."

" The early Tokugawa Shoguns were much given to social classifications. They not only revived the old distinctions between *ryomin* and *semmin*, which had nearly died out, but also divided the latter into a number of minor classes. At no time in the history of Japan was the list of persons officially designated *semmin* so large."

It was: (1) " *Chori*, originally the name given to the head of *Eta*, but in later days used as a synonym of *Eta*. (2) *Eta*. (3) *Hinin*, an outcast, one who is too low to be regarded as human; originally applied to criminals, now extended to beggars. (4) *Yamaban*, mountain-keepers. (5) *Kawara-mono*, beggars who are required to bury criminals. (6) Ordinary beggars. (7) *Shiku*, persons who dance before shrines. (8) *Miko*, a witch, one who tries to appease angry spirits. (9) *Maimai*, a male dancer who uses no music. (10) *Gaunin*, a mendicant friar. (11) *Sodekoi*, a class of mendicant priests, who wear long-sleeved koromo and beg with a wooden bowl, — " sleeve beggars." (12) *Ombo*, persons employed in the burning of bodies. (13) *Niugyo-tsukai*, puppet showmen. (14) Actors. (15) Brothel-keepers. (16) *Zato*, blind shampooers. (17) *Sarugaku No*, performers. (18) *Onyoshi*, diviners. (19) Plasterers. (20) Makers of earthenware. (21) *Imonshi*, moulders. (22) *Tsuji-mekura*, wayside blind beggars. (23) *Saru-hiki*, men who exhibit monkeys. (24) *Hachitataki*, priests who obtain money by beating a metal bowl and reciting passages of scripture. (25) Stone-cutters. (26) Umbrella-menders. (27) Ferry boatmen. (28) Dyers. (29) *Teubotate*, the keepers of archery grounds. (30) Pen-makers. (31) Ink-makers. (32) *Seki-mori*, barrier guards. (33) Bell-ringers. (34) *Shishi-mai*, persons who dance with masks for the amusement of children. (35) Makers of rain-coats. (36) Keepers of bath-houses. (37) Watchmen. (38) *Mikawa mausai*, beggars who acted as mummers at the New Year. (39) Jugglers. (40) *Yashi*, showmen. (41) *Inn mawashi*, professional dog-trainers. (42) *Hanashika*, story-tellers. (43) Serpent-charmers. (44) *Nazo toki*, expounder of enigmas. (45) *Chikaramochi*, professional athletes. (46) *Kogo nuke*, persons who crawl through a narrow basket without being hurt by the drawn sword attached to it. (47) *Kitsune-tsukai*, trainers of foxes."

Why some of these occupations were deemed ignominious, and why some were not so classed, is unknown, but it is certain that every irregular method of obtaining a livelihood was considered a degradation. Begging was abhorred.

Population and Industry of Japan 207

All connection with dead bodies was supposed to defile. Even pen-makers, who used the hair of deer, and ink-makers, who used the bones of horses and cows for hardening their ink, were condemned. Occupations were often considered ignominious on account of their associations;

A COOLIE.

archery grounds were often used as meeting places of loose character, hence they were despised.

During the time of the early Tokugawa Shoguns, the control of *semmin* of all classes was intrusted to Dauzaemon and Kurnma Zeushichi. The powers with which these two men were endowed enabled them to establish a kind of judicial government. All the misdemeanors of *semmin* were dealt with by these chiefs, as the Shoguns considered it beneath the dignity of ordinary court officials even to pass judgment on the outcasts of society. The reign of the Dauzaemon family over the *Eta* and other classes of outcasts dates from the time of the Kamakura Shoguns. During the reigns of the late Tokugawa Shoguns, the classes of persons included among *semmin* were gradually diminished, until, at the commencement of the Meji, — the present era, — the government was memorialized on the subject, and as a result even the *Eta* and *Hinin* were placed on an equality with their fellow-men. The Japanese have never taken kindly to class distinctions, and I cannot show these facts more forcibly than has been done in the preceding historical sketch, and in the following from the "Japan Daily Mail:" "In no country do a man's circumstances count for so little, provided his personal character merits esteem. A nobleman's carriage standing in front of the humble home of a highly valued friend of its owner is a sight no less common than significant, and is an abundant proof that the assumption of our modern wealth-worshipping world, and all the senseless minor class distinctions of fashionable society, are adjuncts of a civilization which in many of its characteristics is infinitely inferior to that which Japan, sitting at the feet of nature, has succeeded in developing."

JAPANESE ART

The Japanese have been artists, and have given their imagination full play from the earliest ages of their history. Their manners, customs, and dress are æsthetic, and their houses, lacquers, bronzes, porcelains, and household utensils, — in fact, almost everything they own or make, from the hut to the temple, from the bow of a coolie to the sword of the Damio, — are artistic.

Population and Industry of Japan 209

MAKING UMBRELLAS IN JAPAN.

There are no Cupids, no Venuses, and no Apollo Belvederes, but there are elegant forms, and shapes in every material worked by man. There are dragons, monsters, landscapes, and flowers, and many nameless forms that are elegant products of the imagination. The Japanese are a nation of artists in conception and finish, and the whole people are appreciative of art, to the extent, at least, of good taste and form. Their art and architecture are different in style from those we know in Europe and America, and must not be measured and criticised by the old rules and standards.

As our fathers raised the tree-trunks, placed lintels across them, and fitted a roof over all, ornamenting and decorating them until they developed into the various orders, simple and complex, that we know in Europe and America, so the Japanese have advanced from the cave and tent to the hut, and have developed this until it has expanded into the gorgeous splendors of the temples at Nicka, Sheba, Uyeno, and other places, at which artists, architects, and cultured men and women from all lands marvel and wonder.

The Shoguns were patrons of art; and there can be no doubt that the seclusion of Japan from foreign intercourse kept that art in pure channels, and caused artists to work for art's sake alone, by curtailing the demand for the rapid reproduction of their work for commercial purposes.

The elegant simplicity and taste displayed in their houses are nowhere excelled, and no people are better housed. Their dress, in design, material, and decorations, is the most artistic worn by man. As a rule, their art wares are named from the locality in which they were made, or from some artist who made his reputation by their production.

Perhaps the oldest art-workers in Japan are the wood and ivory carvers. These artists ply their sharp cutting tools, and produce the most natural, lifelike representatives of whatever design is born in their fanciful brains. This may be the ancient warrior, the boatman, wrestlers, the musüme, vines, flowers, birds, or monsters, — but all are faithfully reproduced, perfect models, and works of art.

Their artistic wood and metal workers almost kept pace with each other; and specimens of the beautiful productions of these old masters — specimens that are older than the Christian religion — are still to be seen. Both woods and metals are lacquered; but that finish is usually put upon wood.

One of the most important operations is that of thoroughly seasoning the wood, which these clever people do to perfection. After this, the various pieces are fitted together, and the grain of the wood is filled in with a paste made of powdered stone. After the joints have been made, and are firmly set in place, the edges are rubbed smooth with a fine, flat stone, and the whole article is coated with a composition of finely powdered burnt clay

Population and Industry of Japan 211

and varnish. When dry, it is again smoothed over with the stone. The article is then covered with silk or fine paper, which is pasted on with great care to prevent creasing, and receives about five coatings of the clay and varnish, each coat being allowed to become thoroughly dry before the next is applied. The surface is then made perfectly smooth by rubbing with stone of a very fine grain, and the lacquer is laid on with a thin, flat brush of fine hair, —

JAPANESE WOOD-CARVER.

human hair being preferred for this purpose. Each coat is thoroughly dry and hard before the next is applied, and the final coat is laid on with the utmost care, with cotton-wool, and is almost rubbed off with fine, soft paper. When thoroughly dry, the article is polished with deer's horn ashes, reduced to a fine powder and applied with the fingers. So far, we have only finished the background.

The decoration, in gold, silver, mother-of-pearl, or a variety of metals, is now to be added, and the metallic powders used for this purpose are numerous. The compositions differ in size and shape, and are distinguished by various names, and the powders are used to produce various effects according to the knowledge and skill of the artist.

Nashiji is the decoration most frequently seen. It is made by covering the article with particles of ground gold-dust, until it resembles gold stone, and great skill is required to distribute the particles evenly. This is covered with several coatings of fine transparent lacquer, often exceeding a dozen in number. This decoration dates from the fifteenth century. It is either made of pure gold-dust, gold and silver dust mixed, or of silver-dust alone.

Giobu-Nashiji also dates from the same century, and has small squares of gold-leaf instead of the powdered metal. Similar work is made in mother-of-pearl, each piece being applied separately with thin, pointed bamboo sticks.

For Togi-dashi, ground and polished metals are used, and the design is laid in a thicker lacquer, and is emphasized by a fine, white powder and then gilt, the brighter pieces being raised above those of the lower tone by means of a stiff lacquer and gold-dust. When this has become dry, the parts which are to be gilded are covered with lacquer, and then thickly dusted with gold; this, when dry, is again thrice lacquered and thoroughly hardened. The surface is then rubbed until the gilt design is shown. Great care is required to avoid injury to the gilding during the various manipulations. After the design shows through the glaze, the article needs to be polished.

In Hira-makiye, the design is not raised above the general surface, the design and effects being produced by shading or softening the metals, or by touching up and toning mother-of-pearl or colors, when the most beautiful effects are produced.

The Tsui-shiu (red) and Tsui-koku (black) lacquers

are carved out of thick coatings of lacquer. Guri-lac is formed of many layers of colored lacquers, through which the designs are cut to expose the layers. Chiukiu-bori is made by incising the design in fine lines into the body of the lacquer, with a graver, and filling the lines up with powdered gold.

Some of the greatest of Japanese artists have been workers in lacquer. A list of articles of this ware would

JAPANESE LACQUER WARE.

include entire suits of Japanese furniture used by the princes and nobles, — boxes, stands, trays, decorations for temples and houses, and hundreds of other forms. A suit of furniture includes two tauser, or stands, on which the tray and nine boxes are placed. The boxes include large ones for holding papers and books, incense and game boxes, a sloping reading-desk, and a writing-desk, picnic boxes, fan boxes, and oblong letter boxes.

A letter was often placed in this box and borne to its destination by a servant. Frequently the servant's mouth was bandaged so that he could not breathe on the box, and much stress was laid on the fashion of the cord around the box, and the manner of tying it. If the recipient of the letter was inferior to the sender, he retained the box as a memento; but if he was an equal, he returned his answer in the box.

An Inro was a necessary part of every gentleman's dress. It was made fast to a netsuke by a silken cord, and strung through his sash. It was used for a seal box or for perfumes and medicines.[1] An Inro is made of metal, wood, crystal, bark, ivory, shells, and lacquered wood, and usually has four trays, each one fitting into another with great precision.

Many of these articles in lacquer are extremely interesting and valuable specimens of Japanese art. Marvellous harmony of design and coloring are often combined with a minuteness of detail that causes us to wonder at their completeness; and frequently a few rough strokes, dashes of a single color, are so graphic that a beautiful picture is produced, — a story is told. Hokusai and many others have made their names famous by their works in lacquer.

In a country where civil wars and feuds were of frequent occurrence, and a stain, of any kind, upon one's good name could only be wiped out by suicide with one's own sword, the sword was brought to great perfection.

Where the art instinct was universal, and jewelry for personal adornment unknown, the sword was regarded

[1] Seals have been in common use in China, Japan, and Korea for ages, and formerly took the place of a signature. They are made on small blocks of ivory, wood, or metal, on which is engraved the owner's seal. This is placed on a pad of vermilion ink, and stamped in one or more places on any document used.

Population and Industry of Japan

with deference, was subject to carefully prescribed rules of etiquette, and was handed down as the most precious heirloom; it became the dearest article of personal adornment. Artists manufactured and decorated the sword and lavished their skill upon it. It is said that they attained such perfection in the blade that for temper it was unrivalled in the world, often performed marvellous feats, and acquired such a thirst for blood that its owner was prohibited from wearing it. Ornaments were lavished upon it, and these were executed in every variety of metal, and in designs so distinct that it is extremely difficult to find two exactly alike.

To wear the sword was a privilege to which only the lord and his vassal, the "Samuri," were entitled. In the sixteenth century the fashion of wearing two swords came in. The "kantana," about three feet long, was for offence and defence, and the "waki-zashi," about two feet long, was for the "hari-kari" (suicide). A lighter sword than the "kantana," but of the same size, and called the "chisakantana," was used for dress and court purposes.

In full dress, the color of the scabbard was black, with a tinge of green and red. The fittings and mountings of these weapons are as follows: the guard, or "tsube," a flat piece of metal that is either square, circular, or oval in form; a short dagger, "kokatanka," which is fitted into one side of the scabbard; and the "kogai," a smaller dagger, or metal skewer, which is fitted into the opposite side of the scabbard, and is left as a card in the body of an adversary killed in battle; small ornaments, "menuki," placed on each side of the hilt to give a good grasp; the cap, "hashiva," of highly ornamented metal, and held upon the head of the hilt by a silken cord which is passed through opposite eyes; an oval ring of metal, "fuchi," which encircles the base of the handle, and through the centre of which the blade passes; the "kurikata," through which the "sagewo," or cord for holding back the sleeves while fighting, passes; and the "kejiri," or metal end of the scabbard.

Doctors and inferior officials wore the "aikuchi," a dirk without a guard, and the "jintochi," or two-handed sword, and the "mamori," or stiletto.

As a rule, the artists confined themselves to particular decorations, although some artists made several parts of the weapon, and others completed the entire sword.

As famous armorers and workers in metals, the Miochiu family have been celebrated since the twelfth century, and they have received marks of the highest distinction from royalty for their work. They made the famous eagle that is in the South Kensington Museum, and the sixteenth-century dragon is their work.

In the fifteenth century the Goto family appeared as workers in metal, and their work has always been held in great esteem. They were attached to the Shogunate, and always produced work of the highest quality. The successors in the family were always chosen from those who displayed the greatest proficiency in the art of metal-working.

In the sixteenth century, Kaneiye, Nobuiye, and Melada introduced damascening, chasing, and inlaying with the "tsube," and Kaneiye is considered to have been the creator of artistic swords.

At the beginning of the seventeenth century, the country entered upon an era of peace which extended over a period of about two hundred and fifty years. The sword-guard was then adopted for dress purposes and to adorn the sword. From this time we see changes in the character of the metal used, and the decorations employed. At Osaka, damascenings of gold and silver were used in the iron. Kaneiye incrusted his work with copper, and enamels were introduced by Douin and Kinai, whose beautiful pierced "tsubas" provoke the admiration of all who examine them.

At the beginning of the eighteenth century, there were three great schools of these workers in metals,— the Nara, the Yokoya, and the Omori. The Nara school was composed of a large number of artists, and was started in opposition to the Gotos. The Yokoya school joined with the Omori, and became famous for its pierced and gold "tsubas," with their battle-scenes. Teruhide was famous for his

AN INSTRUMENTAL CONCERT, JAPAN

waves and imitation of gold stone, and may be considered as of this school.

The armor, spears, and pikes, in elegant design and workmanship, kept close behind the sword, and there are some fine specimens by famous artists in metals.

The Japanese still lead the world in the perfection of their bronzes, and they have two great schools of their beautiful art, the "Shakudo" and the "Shibuichi." Their difference consists in the treatment of the metals, but the designs may be said to be similar. The metal used in the finest work is "Shakudo," — black, with an almost imperceptible shade of blue, — and is composed of ninety-five parts of copper, two to four of gold, one to one and five tenths of silver, and traces of lead, iron, and arsenic. Shibuichi is of a lighter color, bears a slight resemblance to steel, is hard, of a fine texture, and is composed of fifty to seventy parts of copper, thirty to fifty of silver, with traces of gold and iron. The precious metals are used to produce different effects. In the Shakudo, the gold gives the rich purple tint, or "patina," as it is called. In the Shibuichi, the silver causes the metal to assume its beautiful silver-gray tint under certain atmospheric conditions.

In making these beautiful articles, the designer has the shape formed in clay, — a mere core, — whether vase or other form, after which he makes his designs for decoration. These are made of wax, and are arranged upon the model with wonderful skill as they are evolved from his fertile brain. When the article is sufficiently decorated, the whole is covered with clay which fills in, under, around, and over each leaf, quill, or whatever the decoration may be. This is a difficult operation, requiring great deftness and skill.

When covered, a huge, ill-shapen mass of clay is all that appears to represent the imagination, brain, and handi-work that has been expended. After the mass has become hardened, it is carefully turned about in a fire to melt out the wax decorations that have been imprisoned within the clay, leaving the hollow spaces that correspond with leaf or flower, monster or sea. The molten bronze is poured into this hollow space. When cooled, the outer clay covering is broken away, and the inner core dug out, leaving the beautiful form ready for the finishers.

The finishers carve, touch, and retouch, and polish with chisels, hammers, files, and scrapers, producing the delicate outlines and the high polish of the finished piece. After this has been done, the article is touched with chemicals to produce the desired tint, and the artist receives the criticisms and congratulations of his friends.

Shippo ware of the Japanese, Cloisonné of the French, is the most beautiful production of pottery. The Japanese created this fascinating ware, which is a combination of metal work and enamels, and for contour, color, and wonderful finish is without a rival in porcelains.

The little brown, shock-headed smith pounds the copper into shape upon the beakhorn of his rude anvil, and dovetails the meeting edges together. He then places the vessel upon his rude little furnace of live coals, spreads over the flux and solder, and furiously fans the lurid, green-gold flame that melts the solder and brazes the vessel. Satisfied with the perfection of this work, he removes the blackened article, and again hammers it to a finish upon the rude little anvil. The designer now takes the article,— vase, plaque, or whatever form it may be,—and outlines the thousand delicate and intricate designs that are to be delineated upon the rough metal forms.

A second artist in metals now clips silver and brass wire into tiny pieces, and bends and fits them into the many shapes required by the design. These almost microscopic curves, elbows, angles, and circles are cemented over the outlines made by the designer, and stand up from the body of the article like filigree work. When the outlines are all laid on in cement, the article is taken once more to the furnace, and the wires are fused, thus securely fastening the outlines to the body, and making it one complete thing. If the work was now polished, it would be a beautiful work in filigree; but the article is passed to an artist who is skilled in the mystery of enamels, who fills in the multitudinous little crevices between the wires with beautiful colors.

After another firing the article is handed over to the

polisher, who polishes the rough surface. Gradually the rough surface disappears, here and there a smooth place appears, until finally — it may be after hours or days of polishing — the article is seen in all its perfection of design and colors, reds, yellows, greens, and browns encased in tiny threads of gilt and silver, — a thing of beauty and a joy forever.

It is said that from the earliest ages in their history whenever a Japanese died, his wife and one or more servants committed suicide, and the remains of all were interred together, so that he might have company and consolation upon his long journey in the land of spirits. In the year 2 B. C., the Mikado Suinin issued an edict abolishing the cruel rite, but the old fashion was persisted in. Nomi-no-Sukune, an officer of the court, devised some clay images, and succeeded in having them interred with the remains of the Empress who died in the year 3 A. D. This set the fashion, and Japanese ceramic art was born. From this time, images superseded the cruel suicides, and artists sprang up, each endeavoring to make his images the truest to nature. The originator, Nomi-no-Sukune, was decorated Hoji, or clay-image-artist, and Japanese art branched out in new directions.

The Satsuma is recognized as the " Royal porcelain of Japan." It is of creamy color, and has a peculiar crackle finish. It is made by most skilful potters, and is decorated in beautiful designs with colors and golds. The decorations are outlined in black, after which bright pigments and pure gold are beautifully worked in. About the year 1600, the Prince of Satsuma invaded Korea, and while there became interested in pottery. He induced a few potters to settle in his domain, and they became the originators of this beautiful ware, under the patronage of the Prince. This ware was never offered for sale, but was

Population and Industry of Japan 221

brought to the highest degree of perfection attainable, and was presented, as a special gift, to whomever the Prince chose to honor. For many years it was only used by the Mikado and nobles. The Korean potters intermarried with the Japanese, and their descendants are still working this Satsuma clay-bank, and producing the royal ware in cream, crackle, and gold.

JAPANESE ARTISTS DECORATING PORCELAIN.

In 1670, a disciple of the famous decorator Tauyu decorated some pieces of colored enamel faience for the Prince of Taugen. The designs were more elaborate than the customary decorations of this ware, and the few pieces that remain, known as the "Satsuma-Taugen," are among the rarest specimens of old Japanese pottery. They are cream crackle decorated with brown figures, and are of the Kano school.

Satsuma ware lost favor in the seventeenth century; but the celebrated decorators, Kuwabara and his kin, produced a hard, close-grained ware. They adhered to the cream-color with finely crackled glaze, and their paste was as dense as ivory. They decorated in enamelled diaper and dragons and flowers; and Satsuma regained its old place. In 1785, it was further improved by Yanasuke, an artist of great fame, and the ware of his time is considered to be the finest ever made.

Modern Satsuma, made since the visit of Commodore Perry, is decorated in Kyoto for the foreign markets; and while it is beautiful, with decorations of saints, warriors, and deities, it does not compare with ancient products of the kiln of the Prince of Satsuma. There are thousands of specimens of modern Satsuma, but there is nothing more rare than a piece of the old ware. It is well to note, in searching for the old ware, its extreme solidity, its graceful and restrained decoration, its ivory-like surface, the sharp, hard edges, the perfection of gilding, the accurate outlines of its enamels, and the brilliancy of its delicate coloring.

The Hizen ware is fine, and beautiful, and gorgeous in decoration. Great quantities of it found its way to Europe through the Dutch intercourse, but it was considered second and third rate ware in Japan. The shapes were not Japanese, but were made to suit the taste of the purchasers. Huge vases and bowls and the varied sizes of plates were not in accordance with the artistic taste of old Japan. The finest wares were made in the kilns of the princes, where the best manipulators and decorators were employed, and products of these kilns were bestowed as princely gifts. The choicest works of blue and white and of Kakiyemon and Keuzan were rarely seen outside of Japan until within the last twenty years.

In 1530, Shousui of Ise learned in China the process of decorating porcelain with blue. He returned to Arita in Hizen, bringing with him a small store of raw material, which he worked up into small articles, and he became famous as the father of Japanese porcelain. Gorobachi and Gorohichi followed in his lead, and carried on the work until the material was exhausted and the manufacture ceased.

About 1608, Naboshima brought Risanpei, a Korean potter, to Arita, where he found the feldspar which was suitable for the manufacture of porcelain. Blue-and-white porcelain was made, but it was about fifty years before the discovery of the art of using vitrifiable enamels, which require a second firing over the glaze, at low temperatures.

Porcelain, in Japan, was first decorated over the glaze about 1650. This process was introduced by Takuzayemon, who learned it in China. Takuzayemon was neither potter nor artist; but Kakiyemon, a good potter and a bold artist, learned the secrets from his friend, struck out in new directions, and produced decorations in colored enamels which created a new school in Japanese porcelains. He attained a degree of perfection, both in material and style, that have never been surpassed. His ware has a fine, hard, white base, and gives a clear, bell-like sound. It is decorated with bamboo and plum blossoms, or with corn sheaves and flowers, and sometimes with fluttering birds.

At Imari, blue-and-white decorations under the glaze, at a single firing, are still produced, and some specimens rival the finest work of the Chinese.

Kameyarna and Hirado kilns produced beautiful blue-and-white porcelain in the eighteenth century.

Mikawa-uchi ware was presented by the Prince of Hirado to the Shogun and his private friends. The paste was finely powdered, strained, and bleached, while the glazes were delicately prepared. The white is clear and the blue is soft, very different from the intense blue of the old Chinese ware. The delicacy of the design, execution, and perfection of the firing, are not approached by any porcelains in the world.

Kutana ware, another celebrated porcelain, originated with Saijiro at Kutana in the province of Koga. In 1658, the Prince of Koga sent Saijiro to Hizen to study the art. Soon after his return to Kutana, he discovered a clay from which was produced the exquisite decorations in red, green, yellow, violet, silver, and gold, which made the ware famous. After the death of Saijiro, the ware soon lost its reputation, as his pupils could not maintain the master's style or finish.

Towards the end of the seventeenth century, Morikage took charge of the work at Koga. He introduced freedom and boldness in design, and soon made the ware famous. His products vary in subject, and are in rare tints of green, yellow, and violet. After Morikage's death, the pottery again deteriorated in quality, and the base became dark, almost black.

In 1814, the process of decoration in red was rediscovered by Yoshidaya, who produced beautiful wares in that color and gold. These soon became famous, and bear the artist's name. In 1878, Zingoro produced a more brilliant porcelain by substituting gold-leaf for the powder, and using cleaner color. Seto, in the province of Owaii, produced commercial pottery for several centuries, but it was not until 1801 that Tamekichi commenced to make porcelain. The products of these potteries are beautiful, and may be seen all over the Empire. A beautiful ware in delicate blue and white is produced at Kiyowezer, near Kyoto. It may be recognized by its coarse paste and its dark-blue decoration.

The Japanese devoted their genius as artists to faience, into which they introduced the most subtle and surprising effects by delicate shades of color, and quaint forms. Their love for artistic pottery dates back to the ninth century, since which time their amateurs have cherished the richly glazed Seiji ware, which was copied from, and

Population and Industry of Japan

excelled, the Chinese work. The early Shigaraki ware is rough, is skilfully made, and has a beautiful glaze; the Soma ware has an impressed horse; the Takatori ware has a bright lustre. Other varieties are the old Banko and Higo wares, the Yatsushina, and the Kiuezan, with its rich raised blue enamels, the Oribe, with mottle glaze, and the old Iube or Bizen ware, with its reddish-brown glaze, one of the oldest Japanese wares, dating back fully five hundred years.

Kakiyemon, Niusei, and Keuzan are the three celebrated names in the history of Japanese porcelains. They flourished between the years 1624 and 1652, and during these years Japanese decorative, ceramic art was at its height. Niusei worked at Kyoto, and his products were the cream-colored wares of "Awata." The ware is made of a hard paste, has a very fine, uniform crackle, and is enamelled on a buff ground, with floral decorations in green and blue tints heightened with gold. This work laid the foundation for a great school in faience which has come down to our times. Kyoto was filled with potteries which followed the style of Niusei, but these products do not equal his in glaze, crackle, or enamels.

Kirko-Zau, who was a follower of Niusei, in the next century, brought the Awata products to great perfection, and introduced a raised, dark-purple enamel in relief. The work of this artist is fine, with uniform crackle; clear and finished in design and execution, while the Awata ware of the present day is thin, cold, and dry in glaze, and the enamels are not so perfect.

Keuzan was no less famous than Niusei. He was a bold, dashing painter, and originated a new style of free-hand decorations in birds, flowers, grasses, and delicate landscapes. He flourished between the years 1663 and 1743, and his style still influences all the Japanese, European, and American decorative pottery. Free-hand floral decoration on china was not known before his time. Keuzan was a poet as well as an artist, and he did not hesitate to indite verses upon his landscapes. His work has the rough boldness of a masterful artist, a leader, not a follower in style; and his productions are amongst the rarest and most precious products of the Japanese kilns.

In writing of this Japan, where everything is so artistic and beautiful, I could not persuade myself to neglect the introduction of these few lines on its leading art works, — works which have had great influence over the lives and happiness of its people, and necessarily modify their intercourse with the outside world

A CHINESE CART.

CHAPTER XII

A TRIP TO THE NORTHWESTWARD

AT about half-past six on an overcast morning in May, which was Sunday, we left our anchorage and stood out of the harbor of Hyogo, Japan, bound for Chefoo, China. As we passed the flagship we gave the "flag" a steaming salute, having the marines drawn up in line, at a present arms, on the poop deck, and dipping the ensign. Our course was through the beautiful Inland Sea of Japan as far as the Straits of Shimonoseki, then heading to the northward and westward, across the Yellow Sea to Chefoo on the Shantung promontory. We had not gone very far on our way, perhaps twenty miles or so, when the weather became thick and foggy. We kept on blowing our steam-whistle at intervals, and steaming along at a slow rate of speed.

At about nine o'clock there was a bump, and we soon realized that the old ship had struck a sand beach which had not respect enough for us to keep out of the way. We were soon surrounded by natives in sampans, who were attracted by the novelty of seeing a great ship so near their little village. On investigation, we found ourselves to be in front of the village of Akashi, Japan. After some good hard backing of the engines, the ship was gotten out of the sand into deep water, when the anchor was let go and we remained until about noon; when, as the weather had cleared somewhat, the anchor was raised and another start made. We ran along until darkness set in, when we anchored for the night. After all was quiet about the ship, and " Jacky " was snugly stowed in his " dream-bag," lost to the world, perhaps dreaming of his home and loved ones, the ship's bell rang out the alarm for fire, which soon brought all of us to our feet. Hammocks were quietly triced up and stowed, and all hands were at their places for fire quarters. We soon discovered that it was only a drill. It is always a relief to know that there is no actual fire, for there is no more trying position than that upon a burning ship at sea. After running out the hose and starting the pumps, the retreat was sounded. When everything had been secured, the crew went off to whisper about the "old man," and once more to try the soft side of a mattress; but these whisperings were short-lived, as in a few minutes the rattle was sounded for "general quarters." Hammocks were again made up and stowed; lights were put out in a very unceremonious manner; the magazine was opened, and powder and shell were passed upon the deck; while the great guns were "cast loose" and loaded. Two rounds were fired from each gun, when "secure" and "retreat" sounded, and every one repaired to his "downy couch" and endeavored to make up the lost sleep. Early the next morning the anchor was raised, and we picked our way among the islands. On the second day we passed through the interesting Straits of

Shimonoseki, where the gallant McDougal forced his way in the "Wyoming," in 1863; not without a hot fight, for the Japanese were well prepared for him, and bravely contested his passage inch by inch, but the brave Yankee skipper won the fight; and the "Wyoming" passed into the Inland Sea.

Later, the Japanese government paid a heavy indemnity for the benefit of the families of the killed and wounded in this affair; but still later, this sum, together with the accumulated interest, was returned to the Japanese, who appropriated the whole amount to the erection of the breakwater at Yokohama, which protects shipping in that harbor from the effects of typhoons that sometimes sweep up the Bay of Yeddo.

The Straits of Shimonoseki are well surveyed and marked by beacons, lights, and bearings; but as the tide runs very strong, and there are whirlpools and eddies, it is safest to go through at a good rate of speed and in the daylight. The surrounding hills are well fortified, and they are still being terraced and strengthened. There is a strong garrison stationed on the hills, above the city. Shimonoseki is not one of the open ports, and foreign vessels do not stop here unless they are in distress.

At about nine in the morning we stood to the westward; and when the vessel was well clear of the land, the engines were stopped and the propeller was disconnected. The entire morning was devoted to sail exercises, tacking and wearing ship; and while the men were aloft, many of them busy on the yard-arm, a dummy, that had been quietly prepared, was pushed out of one of the cabin ports, and soon the cry was raised of "Man overboard!" The men tumbled down from aloft, while the head sails were thrown aback, lifeboats manned and lowered, and the "dummy" was brought on board, much to the disgust of the junior watch, who had the deck and was under the impression that it was really one of the men who had fallen overboard. This ended the drill, and the vessel was soon again steaming to the northwestward on her course.

As we proceeded on our way, the wind freshened and the sea increased, until by night we had about as much of each as was wanted, — and a little more than was comfortable, for the ship rolled and pitched to such a degree that it was very difficult to hang on, and impossible to keep on one's feet without being lashed to some fixed part of the ship. It was deemed expedient to " heave to " for the night, the engines turning just fast enough to keep steerage-way and prevent the ship from falling off into the trough of the sea. By daylight, the wind quieted down, and we had a smooth sea, with just breeze enough to blow the smoke away; but the thermometer indicated 90° in the shade, with a mucky, sultry atmosphere that was anything but pleasant. The speed of the engines was increased to about the full, and the ship sped on at a good rate until night set in, when the weather became so thick and foggy that we could not see about the decks, and it was impossible for the lookouts to see for any great distance from the vessel. There was no alternative but to slow the engines and feel the way, keeping the steam-whistle blowing, at intervals, to warn the people on any other vessel in our vicinity, while we were compelled to avoid several ugly, jagged rocks which show their horrid " fangs " above the surface of the sea, like very monsters guarding the approaches to fair Korea.

About noon of the next day we entered the Yellow Sea, the sea which separates Japan from Korea. As there are no rocks until near the coast of China, at Shantung, two hundred and eighty miles distant, in spite of the thick weather, we pushed the ship, and arrived off Chefoo on the sixth day after leaving Kobe.

CHEFOO, CHINA

Yantai is the port to which the name of Chefoo has been applied. As a matter of fact, Yantai is in the vicinity of Chefoo, but has no connection with it. While the town was in possession of the French troops, business men crowded there and settled about the camps under their protection; and as there was no fixed plan of settlement, many of their houses were surrounded by native buildings, hence they now have disagreeable neighbors, and what should have been one of the pleasantest places of residence in the far East has been marred by the undesirable surroundings.

The later foreign settlement has grown up along the seashore, where there is a fine sandy beach. For miles beyond the town, stretches a gently rolling country, and back of this the hills rise into mountains, and render the landscape interesting and varied.

In consequence of its wonderful climate and beautiful beach, Chefoo is the summer resort of many foreign residents of China. Here, as all over the East, the houses occupied by foreigners are built of sun-dried bricks, covered with plaster, and painted in some pleasing color. The doorways and window openings are usually trimmed with stone, and the roof is covered with tiles. The houses are of large proportions, have spacious verandahs on every floor and side, are situated in commodious, well-kept gardens, and have an air of elegant comfort that is not seen elsewhere. As a rule, the furniture and fixtures are products of Eastern art, and are poems and marvels in woods, metals, stones, porcelains, and silks. There are six commodious churches of various Christian denominations, and a fine club-house where everything necessary for the comfort of man can be obtained.

In the older settlement, and on the beach, are fine hotels,

which for appointments and comfort cannot be excelled in the Eastern world. There are many fine shops, where goods that have been imported from every part of the world can be obtained, from " Murray's canned corn " to the trappings for a lady's saddle-horse.

My guide and I, mounted in sedan chairs, made a trip into the country and through the native city. The guide, Ah-Sin, did not speak very good American, and I had some difficulty in making him understand my Chinese; but as my principal need of him was to point out the roads, we managed to get along fairly well. He was very patient with me; indeed, I do not remember any creature more patient than a coolie, who is paid for an afternoon's ride in a sedan chair while guiding a " foreign devil."

On our way to visit the native city, we passed out of the settlement into the broad country, which is traversed, here and there, by little paths not more than a yard in width. Each path has a narrow ditch running parallel with one side of it, and these little paths are the highways of this section. Coolies with heavy burdens upon their backs, and little Chinese ponies, laden with provisions, or great timbers, or some heavy piece of machinery, were led by their masters towards the distant mountains. All about these paths are little gardens, where vegetables are grown to sell to the residents of the settlement. My curiosity was aroused by the sight of grave-like huts in one corner of almost every garden spot. They looked like places into which these poor people might crawl and die; but they proved to be the homes of the lonely gardeners, and near each one of them there is a little well from which they draw water to supply their thirsty plants.

As it is a dry, rainless district, irrigation of the land is necessary; and this is accomplished by raising water from the wells and pouring it into little ditches, whence it runs about the land. Many of these poor people seemed to be continually lifting basketfuls of water out of these holes in the ground, and pouring it into these earthen gutters.

After yielding two and three crops in a year, this land is still as productive as almost any well-kept garden in America. After the Japanese, the Chinese are the finest agriculturists in the world; they are patient, hard workers, and never tire of turning over, cleaning up, and manuring the land.

The United States Consul at this place has interested himself in introducing California fruits to the farmers of the country, and, by so doing, he has varied the products of one class, and added to the table luxuries of the other.

All about these hills, we see schools, missions, and churches, — monuments to the good women and men who have left their kin and friends in Christian lands to teach these people how to live and die, and for what to hope.

Having reached the gateway in the mud wall of the native city, we were received with much shouting and considerable bustle, of which the guide came in for only a small share, as his rank did not count for much; but my importance seemed to be increased by having the servant with me. Ah-Sin explained the situation to the mob, and after the expenditure of some "cash," we were permitted to proceed on our way in peace.

After passing through the city, we found the streets and roads — narrow, crooked, unpaved, and dirty — receptacles for the abominations of the place. The poor, rickety huts are made of mud, which is piled up and allowed to dry in the sunshine, after which a thatched roof of straw is placed over it. The best houses — but there are very few best among them — are built of sun-dried bricks, and the walls look as if in any excitement or crowding they would fall to the ground. There is not a shop in the miserable town equal to the poorest of the thousands to be found in the business portion of old Canton.

The day was sultry, and a great many native gentlemen of leisure were taking their siestas on the roadsides, dressed in their birthday clothes, as is the custom in this part of the world. We could not find anything in the wretched little shops to serve as a memento of the visit, and as a last resort we offered a price to one of the gentry for the pipe he was smoking. He evidently thought the offer too good to lose, and closed the bargain by surrendering the pipe, which we brought off in triumph.

This section contains the most unskilful mechanics that we have seen in the East. The boats and sampans in the harbor are clumsy, rough, and heavy. We saw some carpenters, "wood-butchers," at work in the town, doing the very worst with a piece of wood that was ever seen, hacking, chopping, and botching it to such an extent that it was a pity the poor wood could not cry out in protest against the rough usage.

As we passed along we saw the native process of making bricks. Two or three coolies pour water into a hole in the ground, two or three others scatter straw over the water, while others jump about in it for the purpose of mixing the mud and straw together. I cannot imagine why they do not let their great fat hogs do this, unless it is because they prefer to have the fun themselves. When sufficiently mixed, the mud is scooped up in basket-shovels, and carried to other men who place it in wooden frames ("moulds") the size of the proposed bricks. These men press the mixture into the frames; it is levelled up, and then placed in the sun to dry. No attempt is made to smooth the bricks; on the contrary, they are roughened, we were informed, for the purpose of making them hold to the mud-mortar.

We visited the only temple that we could find in the place. It is nearly in the centre of the city, a mean old structure well on the road to ruin. Some "sing-song" men were performing in its front courtyard, one old fellow doing a first-class bass; and as he had a very large audience, there can be no doubt that the performance was, according to native taste, fine.

Everywhere we heard comments upon the dryness of this climate, and I am free to say that I believe it is one of the dryest climates in the world, but it is said to have the healthiest climate in China.

In the long winters when the Pei-ho River is frozen over, the mails and merchandise for the more northern cities are landed at this point, and conveyed overland to their destination. The harbor is commodious, and there is sufficient depth of water for vessels of large draught. It is exposed, however, to strong gales, which prevail at certain seasons of the year.

Very important fortifications have been constructed by the Chinese authorities at Port Arthur, Wei-Hai-Wei, and on neighboring hills, for the defence of the place.

The population of Chefoo is about thirty-three thousand, of whom about six hundred are foreigners. Its trade is principally in beans and beancake, of which enormous quantities are sent to the southern ports of China. The total value of the trade of the port is about $17,000,000. Large quantities of fine fish are caught near by, which are salted for the market.

Wei-Hai-Wei

Wei-Hai-Wei, the most important stronghold and arsenal in China, is situated on the southern shore of the Gulf of Pichili, about twenty miles to-the eastward of Chefoo. It is an old walled city among the hills, whose inhabitants are well-to-do producers of silk and workmen in the arsenal.

The city is of great size, including within its walls many cultivated fields. The wall is dilapidated in places, and many of its gates are closed. The western gate is in general use. There are several famous temples among the hills in the northwestern corner of the city.

Large quantities of silk are made from wild silkworms, which are fed with leaves of the oak shrub that covers the surrounding hills.

Wei-Hai-Wei has a naval college where young men are educated to become cadets in the Chinese Imperial Navy. It has a commodious, well-sheltered harbor, formed by mountain rocks which extend into the sea, and almost meet a large island which lies across the northeastern side of the harbor and protects it from the winds. This harbor will accommodate a large fleet, and affords good shelter from typhoons. It can be entered in the winter when the other ports are closed by ice. Its forts and earthworks are located on almost every rock and hill, and bristle with Armstrong and Krupp guns of heaviest calibre.

Wei-Hai-Wei contains the most extensive arsenals and shops in the Empire for the manufacture of war material, and is believed by the Chinese to be impregnable.

CHEMULPO, KOREA.

CHAPTER XIII

A TRIP TO KOREA

WE sailed from Chefoo on the afternoon of the 7th, and dropped our anchor on the Korean coast in a hurry in full sight of some of the ugliest rocks that ever confronted a seaman. The run across the Gulf of Pichili had been as pleasant as could be desired, as there was no wind, and the sea was as smooth as a mirror; even the almost ceaseless long-swell of old ocean was gone.

The sun shone brightly by day, and the sunsets were ever to be remembered for their greens and golds and grays. Quiet and gorgeous tints blended into a beauty such as no artist could reproduce. The nights were as near perfection as those that mortals dream of, but seldom realize. The moon, about half-full, shone out resplendent in a silver sheen, deepened by the clearness of the heavenly vault; and Jupiter shone amongst the lesser planets and stars, like a globe of fiery whiteness. Early the next morning a great rainbow spanned the heavens, while its ends were in the sea and reminded us of the old saw,

> "Rainbow in the morning, sailors take warning;
> Rainbow at night is the sailor's delight."

But as we have all gotten away from the "unlucky Fridays" and other superstitions of the sea, this beautiful rainbow only impressed us by its brightness and symmetry of form.

Later in the day, after the men had finished their hard-bread and coffee, the ship's decks were cleared, a target was anchored about one thousand yards from the vessel, and we had target practice with great guns. All being in readiness, the ship was gotten under way and steamed back and forth and about the target. The guns were loaded with powder and shell and fired at the target. Observers were stationed on certain lines and in the ship's maintop to note and record the line and effect of each shot. Many of the shots were excellent, and all were good.

After luncheon there was exercise with machine guns, rifles, and revolvers. As each man's name was called, he stepped in front of the line, fired his piece at the target which had been brought nearer to the vessel, and fell back in place. Some of this work was most excellent. After these exercises we anchored the ship for the night.

The next morning we started for Chemulpo, Korea, where we arrived at about five in the afternoon, anchor-

A Trip to Korea

ing in the outer harbor about three miles from the town, and about two miles from Roze Island, as we were afraid to anchor in the inner harbor, where the rise and fall of the tide is nearly thirty feet, and sandbars make the navigation uncertain.

CHEMULPO, KOREA

The town of Jeuchuan, or Juisen, known to the Japanese as Junsen, is situated at the entrance of the Satee River, a branch of the Han, and about east of Roze Island, on the west coast of Korea, in the province of Kuing-Kei. The town has grown in a few years from an insignificant fishing village to a place of no mean proportions. Many substantial buildings, in the European style, have been erected, and the town is rapidly rising into importance as a commercial centre. The roads are rough and badly kept, in many places merely bridle-paths.

The British and Japanese consulates occupy commanding positions and are creditable to their nations.

The rice-cleaning steam-mill, an American enterprise, is very interesting and well worth a visit. Situated on the side of a hill, in the centre of the settlement, it stands as an engineering curiosity, — Yankee boilers with Japanese coal, run by a Chinese engine, to clean Korean rice. Here steam has displaced the ancient man-power, it is true, but the work is thoroughly done, and the owners are satisfied with the profits.

On a commanding hill to the right of the settlement, overlooking the native town, is the temple which commemorates the peaceful landing of the Japanese. It is surrounded by tea-houses of the better class, and is near the little Japanese cemetery. With the waters of the Satee and Han on the one side, Roze Island for the background, and amid the beautiful plains, valleys, and hills of fair Korea, no more delightful situation could be imagined.

The temple is made of a fine grained wood, resembling our cedar, and carved in places, while its square pillars, beams, and lintels are held in place by framing that is supplemented by massive bars and angles of bronze, which give support to the heavy tiled roof. This temple has no doors, and the chief feature of its decorations is a large painting of the " Landing of the Japanese and their reception by the Koreans." This fine picture shows Japanese disembarking from their vessel, while others are landing on the shores of Korea, and are being received by white-robed Koreans. The leader of the Japanese carries a copy of the treaty between the two nations.

The tea-houses are exquisitely neat, and the entertainment at them is all that could be desired. Beautiful views may be enjoyed from the verandahs, as well as from the neat little cemetery on the side of the hill.

There are two hotels in the settlement, the "Stewart House," which is conducted in the semi-foreign style by a Chinaman, whose name the house bears, and the Japanese hotel, " Dai Butsu." The proprietors are accommodating, and it is well to know one of them before making the trip to Seoul; either one will make all arrangements for the journey and secure accommodations at the tea-house in the capital.

Jeuchuan, the sub-prefectural town, is situated about ten miles distant from the port of Chemulpo. The rising town of Mapu, on the main road to Seoul, is about seventy-five miles distant from Chemulpo, or about thirty miles from Seoul.

The land forming the Japanese settlement was sold by public auction in 1884, and land sales in the general foreign settlement took place in November of the same year.

Chemulpo is governed by a Municipal Council composed of the foreign consuls, one Korean official, and three representatives who are elected by the land-holders. Two foreign and one Chinese policemen, in European uniforms, do duty in the settlement, under the direction of the Council.

The settlement has been neatly laid out with broad roads, which, in rainy seasons, rival for mud the war-time roads of old Virginia. The lots are all improved with substantial buildings, and the roads are planted with fine shade-trees.

The approaches and the river (Satee) have been surveyed by the British and Japanese, and the charts of late dates are entirely reliable. The navigation of these waters is dangerous from the many sandbars, washings of the rivers, the frequency of sudden dense fogs, and the absence of lights and beacons. The outer anchorage is accessible to the largest vessels, but the holding ground is not reliable, and vessels are liable to drag their anchors when the wind is strong on shore. The inner harbor is accessible to coasting vessels of light draught as far up as Mapu.

An overland telegraph from China to this port, and connecting Seoul and Ping-yang, is in operation.

The climate of Chemulpo is healthy and similar to that of Baltimore.

The foreign population is about three thousand, of whom about twenty-five hundred are Japanese. The native population is estimated at about three thousand people, who live in mere huts built on the lowland marshes. Their settlement is most miserable and unsanitary, and altogether is the filthiest place in which I have ever seen human beings crowded. If the Japanese succeed in teaching these poor people cleanly habits, they will have done a noble work for humanity.

The ascent from the boat-landing into Chemulpo is by

an inclined roadway of massive granite blocks, for about fifty rods, the road having an inclination of about 18°. As the tide falls, it leaves the inclined road covered with mud and slime, which frequently makes the ascent somewhat dangerous and at all times filthy.

Landing here, and travelling over an unkept road full of hollows and hills, with no approach to straightness, does not impress one very favorably with Chemulpo. A tramp through the native settlement should be made in old clothes for the filth, stout boots for the mud, a cigar for the smells, and a stout stick for the curs, — for all are dangerous; but the life one sees on such a trip is very interesting and well repays for the risks taken.

The roads through the settlement are about eight feet wide, broken and filthy. They are lined on both sides by mean little huts, one story, eight by ten feet in height, and made of any old materials the unfortunate natives are able to gather. Some are made from old dry-goods boxes, some of mud, and a very few of sun-dried bricks plastered over with mud, — anything that will give shelter, hold the mud plastered over them, and carry the straw-thatched roof intended to keep out the winter's snows and the summer's rains. The interiors of these cabins are as filthy and unkept as the exteriors. Dogs, pigs, and fowls share the "kang" and house with the family; in fact, they are part of the family. Except for the flowing white robes, there are no evidences of cleanness in the place. The only water we could discover was in the little tubs containing the fish for sale, and in the green pools along the roadsides. Every cabin has a compartment called the "kang," a sort of room, with earthen floor, under which a fire is made. Here the members of the family resort to secure warmth, and in the evenings mats spread upon the floor form the family bed.

There is a shop of some description in front of every cabin, for the sale of fish, vegetables, charcoal, or notions;

or it may be a cook-shop, where the vilest messes that ever ruined the stomach of a human being are concocted. Great rolls of underdone rice-flour, swimming in a pool of boiling fish-oil; an unnamable mess of green stuff, pork, and fish made into stews, and chalky-looking loaves of rice, with shellfish and oysters. These shops give the roads the appearance of long, filthy bazaars, and the snowy-robed Koreans look very much out of place, as they crowd through the filth.

These cabins have yards in the rear, enclosed by wicker fences, made from the branches of bushes. In some few cases attempts are made to do truck-gardening by raising a little green stuff and a few cabbages, but there are no fruits or flowers; indeed, I doubt if the Koreans care for flowers. Many of these yards are uncultivated, and contain abominations of the foulest sort. How the people live and flourish amidst such surroundings is beyond my comprehension.

When one has run the gantlet of the dogs, the urchins, and the smells, and reaches the end without having been bitten, or ditched, or having contracted cholera, it is a relief to roam over the hills to the little Japanese cemetery, and gather the beautiful wild flowers that may be had for the taking, or to visit one of the tea-houses on the hill beyond, from whence we frequently watched the fishermen and the beach-combers gathering oysters, crabs, and other gifts of the sea, when the tide was out. Sometimes we took pictures of the quaint scenes about us, pitched quoits upon the tea-house green, listened to the mandolin-like strains of the sweet samisan, or were entertained with tales of daring and war by a bold Korean warrior, who, when his tales were finished, politely invited himself to partake of our refreshments.

The common people are innocent and inquisitive, child-like and bland, with no intention of being impertinent. They will smooth down your clothes, and inquire about the materials of which they are made; ask to see your watch, and require an explanation of its mechanism; and your pockets must be turned out and the contents explained.

I gave one of these people some sour drops. I happened to have with me; he thought them a species of amber beads. When I explained to him that they were edible and sweet, he ran off, but soon returned with a crowd of slipshod females, who were all very importunate for a supply of the novel sweets. In a short time my little stock was exhausted, and it was interesting to see the disappointment depicted upon their countenances, as they went off empty-handed. I afterwards learned that these ladies looked upon me as a magic-man, in league with the spirits.

The Executive, the Senior Watch, and I called upon the Governor to pay our respects. We were met at the boat-landing, the foot of the inclined roadway, by a Chinaman who was to act as our guide. He had mustered three dilapidated sedan chairs for our use, and four coolies to act as bearers for each chair. We were in full-dress uniform, and the "conveyances" seemed ridiculously out of keeping with the importance of the occasion and our good clothes; but the visit had been prearranged, and there was nothing to do but go ahead.

The chairs were made of bamboo basket-work, with long poles projecting out before and behind on each side, for the bearers, and there was a canopy over the top to protect the rider from the weather.

The Senior Watch had the most dilapidated rig of the three; and as his bearers were as inexperienced as the others, he seemed in imminent danger of being tumbled out on his head. The best chair in the lot fell to me; but as my bearers had not practised enough to give a steady swing to the chair, the ride was very uncomfortable. We were accompanied all the way by a rabble of idlers who thoroughly understood and enjoyed our discomfiture.

After having been borne up the inclined landing, and through the foreign settlement and skirting one edge of the native village, we started up a very steep hill, which put our stability to the test, but we reached the palace entrance in safety, and were thankful. The great outer doors of the palace courtyard were opened with much ceremony. Some twenty officials came out to meet us, and there was a great deal of bowing, chin-chin-ing, and good American

A DELEGATION OF KOREANS VISIT THE "ALERT."

handshaking, as we dismounted from our rickety old bamboo cages. As soon as we pulled ourselves together, as it were, we were escorted through the courtyard, up a flight of broad steps, and into the audience-chamber.

His Excellency and suite, in their official robes, were already present to receive us. We did not need a special presentation, as we had entertained the Governor on our vessel; and he reached out to greet us — more in American than Korean fashion — as soon as we entered the room.

After more greetings and handshakings, we were all seated, and enjoyed a pleasant chat with the Governor and the other Korean gentlemen present.

Presently cigars were served, the servant cutting off the ends and lighting them for us. Later, wine and cake were brought in, all the while the conversation flowing on in pleasant channels. We inquired after the health of His Majesty the King, and expressed the hope that it might be a thousand years before he would be called upon to ascend on high to ride the celestial dragon. When we took our leave, we were escorted to our chairs, the Governor insisting upon seeing us to the outer gate, and again shaking our hands.

The audience-room, in which we had been received, was about thirty feet long and twenty-five broad, with a very high ceiling. It was fitted in the European fashion with a handsome velvet carpet, made near Boston. Lace curtains, with heavy silk trimmings at the windows, a handsome mahogany table, placed lengthwise of the centre of the room, and chairs to match, made it a beautiful audience-room.

When we entered the room the Governor stood near its centre. He was clad in a long robe of dull blue silk, with square breast-and-back pieces embroidered with birds of gay plumage. He wore the ear-hat of the Korean noble, with a long strand of heavy amber beads, like a chin-strap, but reaching down upon his breast, and his shoes were of embroidered silk with pointed toes.

When we reached the native village on our way back to the landing, our attention was attracted by wailing sounds from some one apparently in deep distress. We dismounted from our chairs and hunted for the cause of these outcries, which we soon found to come from a professional mourner, who, in shrill, high-pitched tones of voice, was announcing the virtues of the deceased person lying before her. These

A Trip to Korea 247

poor professionals come from the lower walks of life and are generally objects of pity. They cultivate the funereal expression and the loud, shrill voice that adds horror to the otherwise dismal surroundings, and inspire feelings that make the " Westerner " wish he were as far away as pos-

KOREAN MOURNING COSTUME.

sible. Of course, these professional mourners, like stone-cutters with epitaphs, add virtue to virtue for the fee, and deem the facts of the case to be no concern of theirs.

We learned, through our guide, that the deceased was the father of a numerous family, and had been a very worthy blacksmith's helper, who was cut off in the flower of his manhood. His good deeds and virtues, as narrated by the mourner, were innumerable; and as soon as the family ceased to pay for the mourning, the funeral would take place.

When a Korean dies, his body is prepared for interment much after the fashion in China. Placed in a strong, heavy wooden box that has more or less ornament upon it, he is professionally mourned for as long as family and friends can afford to pay for that service; and when all is ready, the box is borne to the grave by bearers, preceded by the professional mourners, who contort and howl in proportion to their pay. The relatives and friends follow, dressed in brownish-white robes, the males wearing immense, coal-scuttle-like hats of the same color, and having a long staff of natural-colored wood in hand. When the grave is reached, the box is lowered into the prepared place, or in some cases is placed upon the surface of the ground, and earth is piled around and over it. The term of mourning is three years. After this sight of distress and misery we made another start for the vessel.

When I had removed my camera from under the seat of my chair and was preparing to take a view of the poor little shops in the native village, a great crowd, but a good-natured one, gathered about us, obstructing the view. We soon learned that the people were all anxious to appear in the picture, — not that they might ever see it themselves, but they were anxious to be identified with their village.

What hovels and huts for a people to be proud of, and with which to wish to be identified! The contrast is very great between these miserable Korean cabins, and huts in the swamps, and the neat, artistic peasant homes of the Japanese upon the hillsides.

The Chemulpo Club's home is situated in the foreign settlement. It is neatly fitted with billiard, reading, refreshment, and retiring rooms, with a bowling alley in its neighborhood. Its membership is cosmopolitan. Americans,

Britons, and Japanese fraternize in its hospitable rooms and lounge away an hour or two each day.

The currency of the country is in a wretched condition, and native money is scarce. Chinese "cash" is used for all small transactions. It was usual to see shopping parties followed about from shop to shop by a stalwart coolie bearing a huge bundle of stringed cash upon his shoulders; and when it is remembered that the value of the cash is from 1,000 to 1,300 to the Japanese or the Mexican dollar (depending upon the rate of exchange), one can understand the great inconvenience of doing business.

The Korean coolie, stalwart as he is, is a study in his way. With a wooden frame which much resembles the framework of the under side of a common wheelbarrow strapped upon his back, he is prepared to bear great loads in the shape of stones, goods, or machinery. All he needs is a firm place to back against, to steady his great burden, and then he marches off with a firm tread and steady gait. They are great meat-eaters, and devour every part of the animal. Their wages are small, and they are happy if they can secure fish and rice enough to satisfy their hunger. When the tide is out they resort to the beach in great numbers, and supplement their scanty store of food with the oysters, crabs, or fish found there.

Cook-shops and booths, the latter formed by four bare poles supporting an old straw matting for awning, are scattered about the roadsides, in the business locality where these poor toilers can procure food, and may rest in the shade while eating it.

In all large business houses, the Japanese are the leading men, while the Koreans may be employed as the common laborers.

The Korean mail service is conducted in the ports by Japanese, but in the interior of the country the work is done by Koreans.

Chemulpo was opened to foreign trade in 1883. The value of the imports from foreign countries is about $3,500,000, and the exports amount to about $1,500,000, the difference being paid in gold. The total trade of the port is about $6,000,000.

SEOUL, THE CAPITAL OF KOREA.

CHAPTER XIV

SEOUL, THE CAPITAL OF KOREA

THE distance from Chemulpo to Seoul is about thirty-five miles, and the journey can be made on horseback, in sedan chairs, or in one of the two little steamers which ply on the Han River, whenever the tide serves and they are not aground; but whichever route is taken, there are always regrets that the other was not chosen. If one has resolved to rough it, for the sake of the beautiful scenery and seeing Seoul, either route will amuse; but if comfort is anticipated, the journey will be disappointing.

Both by the land and the water route, the scenery is beautiful and the eye never tires, for new and strange things of beauty and of interest are always present to awaken emotions of pleasure and surprise. The roads are rough and uncared for, — mere bridle-paths, — and if travelling by land you will likely sigh for one of the little steamers. If you have taken passage in one of these, you will find it untidy in its fittings, unreliable in its movements, and as far from comfortable as can be imagined, and you wish for the chair or horse, with all the jolting and dust.

There are no hotels in Seoul, and if you are not fortunate enough to be a guest of some resident you will have to seek accommodations in the Japanese tea-house, in which case you should be provided with bed-clothing and provisions; or if one of the little steamers happens to be at the landing, you can travel the three miles to the Han River, and make your headquarters on board for the night. In either case, you will have to superintend the preparation of your own fare, or be prepared for Japanese or Korean fare, which is not entirely to the American taste.

Having arrived at Seoul, the capital city of Korea (native name, Han-Yan, meaning " Fortress on the Han "), you find it situated in a beautiful valley, about three miles north of the Han River, and thirty-five miles from its mouth, almost in the centre of the province of Kuing-kei. The valley extends in a northeast and southwest direction, and the city takes the same general trend. There are eight gates in the city walls, arranged after the fashion of the gates of Peking. About the year 400 B. C., Ni-Taijo, the founder of the present dynasty, selected the site for a fortified camp, which afterwards developed into the present city. The city is surrounded by stone walls which average about eighteen feet in height, and the watercourses are spanned by arched stone bridges. The houses are about eight feet high, built of stone, or of mud-covered bamboo frames, and roofed with tiles or thatched with straw. Internally they may be considered clean, for the

Seoul, the Capital of Korea

Koreans have the Japanese fashion of removing their shoes before entering a house.

The city is divided into four quarters by the intersection of two main streets. The central point has been marked by the erection of a large tower which contains an old Korean bell, seven feet high. Several other important streets radiate from the tower, and they are all called " Bell-roads." Every night at half-past eight the " cur-

GATEWAY TO SEOUL.

few " is sounded by the great bell, when all men must retire from the streets, which are given over to the use of the women until half-past one in the morning, and during that time the women visit and receive visits from their female friends. While there are no men on the streets, the women go with uncovered faces, wearing the colored " war " coat about the shoulders, shawl fashion.

The King's palaces are situated in the northern part of the city, and are surrounded by about one thousand acres of land, enclosed by heavy stone walls, about sixteen feet high, and pierced with several gates. A guard of soldiers is stationed at these gates at all times, and there are special gates for people of different ranks.

An audience having been arranged, the person is conducted through the gate corresponding to his rank, then through roads and corridors, — some handsome, others mean, — until a large room, fitted in the American style, has been reached. Here he lunches and rests until the time for the audience. He is next conducted across a handsome court and up a flight of stone steps, which are guarded by massive stone dogs, carved by Korean artists. He finds himself in a large, open hall, with a massive tiled roof, supported by numerous scarlet columns. The floor is of handsome, inlaid woods. A beautiful Korean screen stands at the opposite side of the room where the King receives.

When the King grants an audience, he receives in a scarlet robe, embroidered with gold medallions on the breast and back, and on each shoulder. He wears a heavy jewelled belt about his waist, and a blue, wingless hat upon his head. No one can pass in front of him, and servants hold up his arms as he moves about. All must prostrate themselves in his presence. He begins his day at five o'clock in the afternoon, and retires at about eight in the morning.

Little two-story storehouses have been constructed, about the "Bell roads," in such fashion that the shops under them open into courtyards instead of into the streets. Whenever the King makes a "progress," these little houses are torn away. This pageant is a ceremony of very unusual occurrence, and its details are said to have been unchanged for hundreds of years. Little wooden shanties, that serve as workshops and for business purposes, have been erected in front of almost every house, not only reducing the width of the streets, but giving them a squalid appearance.

Seoul, the Capital of Korea 255

The city is very dirty, piles of filth being allowed to accumulate; and the open ditches, on each side of the roads, are often choked up with refuse.

The shops are mean, and it is difficult to find fancy articles of Korean make. The best way to obtain curiosities is to let your wants be known as soon after your arrival as possible, name a place and date where you can

GATEWAY TO THE KING'S PALACE, SEOUL, KOREA.

be seen, and you will be waited upon by merchants who deal in such wares. Fans, antique metal-work, Korean coins and mats can be obtained in this way. The prices will be high, as the articles are rare and the owners not anxious to part with them.

One of the sights outside of the city gate is the exercise of the Royal troops. They are uniformed in blue coats, plum-colored trousers, black fur hats with bright yellow tassels, and their feet are encased in half-high boots. They are armed with modern rifles, and are a stalwart, fine-looking body of men. Their movements are creditable, and they have the free, easy carriage of the volunteer rather than the stiffness of the regular. They are trained by two Americans who served in the Civil War and now hold commissions under the Korean government.

The courage and endurance of the Koreans has often been tested, and there is no doubt that they will give a good account of themselves in case of need; but it must be remembered that the whole army numbers only twenty-five hundred men.

Street life in Seoul is picturesque and novel, and no city in the world equals it for quaintness. The gateways in the city wall, the palace gates, and the marble pagoda are worth seeing as the work of this interesting people. Outside the city walls, to the northwest, the immense bowlder image of Buddha stands boldly forth in its granite grandeur, requiring some play of the imagination to decide whether it be the " Light of Asia " or some other man. But it is a work of nature rather than of art.

Passing out of the northeast gate and through a miserable-looking country, we reach the village of the Buddhist priests, where these gentry luxuriate in greater comfort than the average Korean. Through the southwest gate we are conducted to the temple and tomb of Queen Chung. The temple is filled with soiled red hangings, has a shrine of Buddha incarnated, and the whole structure is noisome with foul odors.

The pleasure-grounds, surrounding the palaces, cover an area of a thousand acres, and are very interesting. They extend to the foot of the mountains, where some magnificent views may be had. There are no modes of conveyance except sedan chairs, and a reliable guide is necessary, both to point out the way and to act as interpreter.

THE KOREAN ARMY.

PING-YANG, KOREA.

CHAPTER XV

PING—YANG, KOREA

WE left Chemulpo early in the afternoon of May 20, reaching Ping-yang Inlet late on the 22d. During the daylight the weather was warm and balmy, not unlike May-days at home; but the nights were chilly, and our progress was slow, owing to the dangerous coast and the fogs which prevailed. The steam-whistle made the days and nights dreary by incessant "tootings," which were necessary to give warning of our position and movements; and it was a relief to our strained-eyed lookouts when we dropped anchor in forty fathoms of water, and "piped all hands to rest."

Through light rifts in the fog we had occasional glimpses of the coast and the great barren rocks, jutting up from the sea, — rocks without a vestige of verdure upon them; resting-places for the gulls and sea-spawn, and breakers upon which the unwary mariner might be dashed to destruction. No lights, no marks, nothing to guide or warn in the fog or in the black storm at night when the howling winds and boiling sea, aided by the treacherous currents, might drive the ship on and on until the tale would be "missing." The memory of that region makes one shudder, and corroborates the truth of the stories that the Koreans have rendered the approaches to their country as desolate and unattractive as possible.

How different is the vicinity of Ping-yang Inlet! The scenery along its shores and up the rivers is varied and beautiful. For background, dark and gloomy hills, which thrust their peaks into the clouds, brave the anger of the storm, or receive the first kiss from the rising sun, while from their sides bright valleys of waving green extend down to the sea. Here and there a patch of woods, a cascade, or falls of silvery water which leap over or trickle down the massy sides of great rocky hills, where may be hidden gold or silver or iron or coal, — awaiting the miner's touch, — that may yet ransom Korea, and make her one of the wealthy nations of the East; villages of huts in the valleys, or near the beach, where groups of curious natives with flowing white robes and sombre hats discuss the arrival as they add variety to the already beautiful scenery.

The next morning we raised our anchor and stood close in to the land, hunting for Chelto, on the Yalu River, which we found late in the afternoon, and dropped our anchor just in time to get the full force of a very homelike thunder-and-rain storm. From an inky blackness in the heavens, lightning began to play its pranks. Soon the wind came whistling and howling, while the flashes of lightning came nearer and nearer, and sent great forked streaks among the hills and down the valleys, while the thunder boomed, and echoed from hill to hill. The rain poured down in torrents, and the clouds seemed to have opened their flood-gates. In this war of the elements, each seemed to try to outdo the other, and all were rivalled by the mad rush of the rivers, which unite here and form the Ping-yang Inlet.

After awhile, the clouds drifted away, and blue patches began to appear in the heavens, and soon we had a clear sky and twinkling stars where the angry elements had warred. Here and there along the shore, or in the dingy huts, lights sent their starlike brightness from the homes of the natives, and no sounds disturbed the peace of the " Land of the Morning Calm" except the mighty roar of the rivers, the surf upon the beach, and our bugle's " call to rest." We had finished our good-night cigars, after watching the faint flashes from receding clouds, as the lightning, loath to leave, shot forth from the dim distance like a sullen army in retreat.

In the morning we found our vessel just within the mouth of the Yalu (one of the three rivers which form the Ping-yang Inlet), opposite the town, and just inside the lines of native breastworks that mark the fortifications. The river was swift-running and muddy, sweeping like mad through a very fairy-land. The sun shone in splendor, and lighted up beautiful emerald hills, or, by contrasting shadows, emphasized valleys whose beauties allure to rest; or penetrated the dark recesses of mysterious groves, — on the very mountain-tops, — where holy men, like Moses, commune with God, and still offer blood and burnt offerings for the sins of the people.

Every time we visited the shore the tide happened to be

low, and we found ourselves more than twenty feet below the usual water-level of the little town, and our boat unable to reach land. After being carried over the muddy bottom for some two hundred feet upon the shoulders of two lusty Koreans, we were landed at the foot of the principal street ("road") of Chelto.

Chelto is situated on the right bank of the Yalu River, just above the intersection of the rivers. It contains about fifty houses, those of the better classes being built of rough stones plastered over with mud, their thatched roofs being of rice-straw. The poorer houses are made of wooden poles, stuck into the ground and laced together with basket-work. These are also plastered over with mud, and have thatched roofs. Formerly, the average Korean family was contented with a large hole in the ground, which was roofed over with straw thatching, leaving an opening in the roof for ingress and egress. These were found to afford very little protection against raids of the tiger, an animal which abounds in these northern parts. Frequently, after the visits of these creatures, whole families were found to have suffered, and in many cases funerals were the order of the day, so that to the present time the inventor of houses is considered a public benefactor, and a prayer is offered for him.

Beneath each house is a large stone under which a small fire is kept smouldering, while above it mats are placed, to be used as the family bed. Mattresses and heavy bed-covering are not required, although the thermometer often registers zero, and snow and ice are well known throughout the winter.

There are no shops in the place, it being a town of agriculturists. The residence of the governor of the province is in the vicinity. The men are stalwart, with well-formed heads, handsome countenances, just a tinge of copper in their well-turned, regular features, black hair and eyes, and

Ping-yang, Korea

graceful, free-and-easy carriage. They marry quite young, and the women soon get a worn, haggard look, which they usually retain until about their fortieth year of age, when they grow stout. Except for the "sleepy eye," they are a handsomer race of people than either the Japanese or the Chinese.

FORTIFICATIONS AND GOVERNOR'S HOUSE, PING-YANG INLET, KOREA.

They dress in flowing white robes which reach to the shoe-tops. Their loose white trousers are tied in at the ankles, and great mufflers of quilted cotton are bound about their feet, which are thrust into Chinese dress-shoes. The usual head-covering for an ordinary married man is the stiff, straight-rimmed hat of braided black horsehair, which is sometimes made of finely split bamboo which has been colored black. The usual dress of an unmarried man is the same, except that he does not wear any head-covering, and his hair is parted in the middle and made into a broad plait, which hangs down his back. When in mourning, the garb is of the same fashion, but is made of a white-brown or unbleached goods, with "coal-scuttle" helmet of the same color as the clothing. The hat covers the head, and reaches down to the shoulders, the intention being to cover the face as much as possible. The mourner must also carry a staff of natural-colored wood, which equals the individual in height.

The costume of the women is similar to that worn by the unmarried men, except that a girdle is worn about the body, which gives the costume the appearance of bodice and skirt. The women are small in stature, of good form, and are fair to look upon. While the sexes are separated at an early age, — about six years, — the women have all that can be called a domestic life in Korea. Marriages are arranged by professional "go-betweens." Ordinarily, the woman has no voice in the selection of a husband, and knows nothing of him until all the arrangements have been made, and the wife-to-be finds herself in the presence of her future husband. After the briefest ceremony, — a feast to friends, in whose presence they pledge each other in Korean wine, — the man seizes and carries off his new-made wife. These marriages seem to be as happy as those made in other lands.

Korean ladies have been famous at the Eastern courts for their grace, their wit, and their beauty. As far back as the year 1200, they were celebrated at the court of the Emperor of China, and the Pope's legate to that court reported on the "wondrous beauty of a Korean lady." Much has been written about the condition of these women; but the facts are, that they are well satisfied, suited to their surroundings and the condition of their country, and are in the full enjoyment of all the rights they know or want. When the conditions of the country change, the women may change with them, and they will get their full share of the benefits.

The Korean is a man in the full sense of the word; and because his wife is a woman, she knows how to get what she wants, and —

> "When she will, she will, and what is more of it;
> When she won't, she won't, and that is all of it."

A KOREAN YOUNG WOMAN.

The dress of the nobility is of the same fashion as that of the common people, but the materials, colors, and ornaments are different, and vary with the rank. The hat is made of fine, braided black horsehairs, with round crown, without a rim, and is held in place on the head by ribbons, which tie under the chin. The sleeves of the robe are generally of a pale blue or green color, cut long and flowing.

A KOREAN HOUSE, PING-YANG INLET.

From the sides of the hat, hanging down to the shoulders, long strands of amber beads are worn; while on the breast and back are beautifully embroidered pieces of silk, worked in natural colors. These complete the costume of the Korean of very high degree, and no swell of Europe feels his importance more than does this scion of "Choson." They do not have much furniture or many ornaments about their houses. Meals are taken, friends are received, and business is transacted in a squatting position.

At the foot of one of the streets, and near the water's edge, is an immense granary, where the rice is stored until the coming of some Japanese agent, who goes through the country and buys up the produce, particularly the rice. In nearly all my visits to the shore I had my camera with me, as it was my intention to take a picture in this interesting country at every favorable opportunity. I was here surrounded by a mob of curious men who persisted in crowding between the camera and the house I was desirous of picturing. I presented each of the gentlemen with a cigar, whereupon they all squatted down in a line on their heels, giving me the opportunity to focus over their heads and get the house, with the women, babies, household utensils, and the furnace in the yard, — a typical Korean house.

A short distance away, I took a picture of the long line of fortifications which defend the river approaches. These are made of rough stones cemented together, breast high, about one yard thick, and pierced with loopholes about

FORTIFICATIONS.

every five feet. They extend around the junction of the rivers, and up over the hills. They were made in the days of bows and arrows, and would not resist the projectiles of modern ordnance unless well reinforced by earthworks, when they could be made almost impregnable. Little did

I think, when joking with these good-natured people while taking this picture, that in a few months one of the most important battles of modern times would be fought over these walls, between the Japanese and the Chinese, — a battle whose results no man can foresee.

On our way back to the town we saw many mammoth oxen grazing upon the fields, — oxen that would put the pygmies often seen at our county fairs to the blush; while the native pony, "a natty little rig," bore his master cantering through the half-sleepy streets. The lonely merchant, half miller, half merchant, bartered his rice for a vessel of rich cream, while the good housewife wove cotton from her thrifty spinnings.

These people live very close to nature; and while the better classes are neat, clean, and as tidy as any people that I have ever seen, the poorer classes detest soap and water. A friend of mine was on the beach at Roze Island with his men, for target practice, when some half-grown urchins, inspired by curiosity, and eager to gather up the empty brass cartridge shells, came over from the fishing village near by. While they were idling around, some of our men tried to persuade them to go in bathing, but they could not be prevailed upon to do so until some small change was offered as a reward. This temptation was great, and they soon divested themselves of their scanty rags, and waded into the water, but it was only work for the money; there was no boyish fun or sport, and as soon as possible they were out of it and on their way home, rejoicing over the reward.

Korea has produced some very learned men, great artists, and workers in porcelain, but these have been among persons in the higher walks of life, who were self-educated. The common people have little or no opportunity to acquire an education. Until very recently, education for the best has been confined to reading and writing their own language, the works of Confucius, and other works of ancient China. Mathematics, even their own history, and the sciences, that have done so much towards the advancement and upbuilding of other nations, are almost unknown to them. The Buddhist priests have been their guides and instructors. The sons of nobles are usually sent to Peking to study Chinese lore.

Koreans have no domestic life, and are great tramps and gossips. Singly, in couples, and in little groups, both by day and by night, the white-robed gentry may be seen roaming over hill and plain, on their way to visit some celebrated shrine, a bit of beautiful scenery, or a sacred spot, stopping at almost every hut on the way to exchange the news and gossip. The people are good-natured and hospitable, and these tramps are always welcome to share the rice and meat, and doubly welcome when a particularly good story is told, or a bit of spicy gossip is rehearsed. The sexes are separated, and have separate apartments from an early age; and it is considered a great breach of etiquette for the face of a woman to be seen by a man.

Koreans have a great appreciation and love for the beautiful in nature. It is common to see great monumental stones that have been erected by men of means to commemorate the pleasure they have derived from the contemplation of a landscape, waterfall, or some beautiful scenery.

Their religion is founded upon the ancient Confucian of China. Their ancestors are the chief objects of worship, but they also worship heaven, and believe in spirits. They think that the air and sea are peopled with spirits, good and evil, and believe that they can hold communion with them at all times. The fifth, fifteenth, and twenty-fifth of every month are considered unlucky days, upon which they will not begin any venture.

The Koreans seem to have greater respect for the Japanese than for any other people. Their relations have been close, as the Japanese have overrun the country three or four times. They are better acquainted with Eastern

KOREAN BUDDHIST PRIESTS.

policy and diplomacy than any other nation, and are frank and honest in their dealings. The only portions of land that are of any great value are along the roads upon which the neat little Japanese houses, tea-houses, and the temple are built, where the little " musüme " pats her clogs as she waddles along, and where the Chesi makes night hideous with yells when stuffed with too much rice.

The government of Korea has a dim appreciation of the tendency of these times towards scientific progress and a higher civilization; but a very powerful anti-foreign party, with ramifications all over the kingdom, is bent upon placing all obstacles possible in the way of any change.

The Jesuits have given the Koreans a great deal of trouble in years gone by. They disguised themselves, studied the language in China, worked their way into Korea, set up their religion, and preached, making some converts. As soon as discovered, the Korean government thrust them out with fire and sword. Many were burned at the stake, others torn limb from limb, and still others decapitated. All that has been changed in the last few years, and now the missionary has permission to live in the country under certain restrictions, and is doing a good work, educating the poor, healing the sick, and teaching the people how to live and die.

Gen-san, Korea

Gen-san ("War-san," of the Koreans) extends for a couple of miles along the shores of Broughton Bay, which is on the northeast coast of Korea, nearly half-way between Fu-san and Vladivostok. Broughton Bay is a beautiful sheet of water, surrounded by green hills which are in a high state of cultivation. Gen-san was opened to the trade of the world in 1883. The town consists of about two thousand houses, with a population of about eighteen thousand inhabitants. The main street extends the entire length of the town, and into this numerous narrow and crooked lanes open. The houses are mean and dirty, resembling the poverty-stricken huts of the native settlement in the flats at Chemulpo. There is an open space near each end of the main street, where small farmers and produce dealers congregate each week for the purpose of exchanging their wares. These markets are very picturesque and interesting, and are the means of bringing together all classes of the people, native and foreign. What a Babel of sounds! Each is talking in his own language, or in some compromise between it and the others.

BROUGHTON BAY AND GEN-SAN.

The stalwart, white-robed Korean, the shock-headed obied Japanese, and the slick Chinaman in silks, barter for rice and eggs and fowls. The musüme exchanges gossip with the veiled Korean, while the Chinese maiden balances herself upon her deformed feet. The Buddhist priests "chin-chin" to each other, and walk off with a few eggs. The oxen and the ponies make friends, and the geese and fowls get mixed in their rough coops, while a Chinese urchin goes screaming down the road with a young Japanese and a Korean pulling at his pigtail.

The Japanese, as usual, have a neat, clean settlement of about one hundred and fifty comfortable houses, built in the Tokio style, and have surrounded themselves with many of the elegances of their own land. Their Consulate, in the European style of architecture, is a very large building, containing many rooms, where Japanese interests are well looked after.

The Chinese Consulate, not far from the custom-house, is situated near the centre of the Chinese settlement.

The foreign settlement is on the side of a hill, in a very healthy locality. The houses are built of brick or wood, with tiled or thatched roofs. The roads are soft, and are almost impassable in rainy weather. The Japanese and Chinese merchants carry on an extensive business in cottons, silks, dye-stuffs, and gold. There are about eighteen hundred foreign residents, of whom about fourteen hundred are Japanese. The country about Gen-san is in a good state of cultivation of produce, rice, and grasses. The soil is remarkably fertile. Mines of copper are worked to a limited extent, and gold is found in the neighboring mountains. Cattle are very fine and plentiful, and are raised for use as food and as beasts of burden.

Broughton Bay is an excellent harbor, with good depth of water and fair holding ground. It is roomy, well protected against stormy winds, and easy of access. Ice never forms to a thickness that interferes with the commerce of the port. As trade improves, the natives are attracted to the town so that it is growing in almost all directions. There is a telegraph line under Chinese management which connects the town with the capital.

Trade is carried on by Japanese steamers and junks with Japan, China, and other parts of the kingdom. The value of the foreign trade is about 1,500,000 Japanese or Mexican silver dollars. The exports are hides, beans, rice, dried fish, skins, and gold. The imports are cotton and silk manufactured goods, metals, and dyes.

Fu-san, Korea

Fu-san ("Pu-san," of the Koreans) is the nearest Korean town to Japan, only separated from Shimonoseki by the Japanese Straits. It is a walled town, located at the head of a beautiful harbor in the southeastern end of the peninsula. It is the residence of the military governor, who is in charge of the Royal storehouses for rice, which are located here. There are only a few miserable huts in the town, and these are occupied by the guards and laborers employed about the storehouses.

A short distance from the walled town, opposite Deer Island, the Japanese settlement is located. As usual, these clever people have brought their homes and habits with them, and the little town is as methodically laid out, well kept, and clean as any little town in Japan. The houses are well built (in the Japanese style), are comfortable, and have many of the little elegances with which these artistic people surround themselves.

The Japanese Consul, assisted by an elective council of land-owners, administers the affairs of the settlement.

The police are uniformed in the European fashion. There is a fairly good supply of water, and the roads are lighted at night with lamps, which burn American kerosene. There are about 5,600 foreign residents, of whom 5,370 are Japanese.

Hanging on to the outskirts of the Japanese settlement is a collection of miserably wretched, thatched-roofed, native cabins and huts, with an even more wretched population of about two thousand souls, among whom the males find employment, more or less precarious, with the foreign residents; and this is about the story at all the open Korean ports. These poor natives gather about the outskirts of the foreign settlements, live in miserable huts, and as they are mentally simple and childlike, but physically strong, they eke out a wretched existence by avenues new to them; and thus the ranks of agriculturists — which are said to be overcrowded — find relief. While working and living thus, these people learn foreign methods; and crude and rough though it be, this experience is sure of its reward when the dawning day shall burst forth into the full noon of Korean prosperity.

The harbor of Fu-san is a magnificent body of water, with sufficient extent and depth to float great fleets of the largest vessels. The climate is mild and healthy, — a very Hygeia, — a paradise for old and young, where one can live in the open air for the greater part of the year; and the place has one of the finest beaches in the East, where sea-bathing can be indulged in at all times.

The important town of Fong-nai-fu, containing about thirty thousand inhabitants, is about eight miles inland.

Japanese steamers and junks make regular trips to Fu-san. There is telegraphic connection with the capital, and a submarine cable connects the town with Japan. The trade of the port amounts to about four million Japanese or Mexican dollars a year.

QUELPART,[1] KOREA

What South Africa was to the British, what Siberia is to the Russian, so Quelpart is to the Korean, — a land of banishment and exile. This dread island is situated about forty miles to the southward and westward of the mainland of Korea, in the way of the navigator on his route from Japan to the northern part of China. The coast is high and rocky; and as there is no reliable harbor, it is dangerous to attempt a landing. Deception Bay, as its name implies, is a mere indentation on the northern side of the island, and affords neither holding ground nor

[1] Pronounced Kell-par.

shelter for vessels. The everlasting, restless, dashing sea upon its unsheltered, rock-bound shores makes the landing extremely dangerous.

Fancy scrambling upon the slimy, slippery rocks from a surf-tossed boat. Struggling up the face of the rocks and bowlders, drenched to the skin, hanging on by one's fingers, then a foot-hold, a slip-back, a tug, a pull, then a dreary prospect, an almost hopeless reach, until finally one has pulled, crawled, and worked himself up the face of the rocks for two hundred feet or more, when the lower plateau is reached. What a scene presents itself! Off yonder, to seaward, a great ship is moving about, like a monster of the deep; beyond, the heavens and the waters seem to meet and merge into one. Turning inland, the emerald and black hills and plains of the " accursed prison island " lie before one, and yonder Auckland looms up sixty-five hundred feet towards the clouds, and offers the Korean a holy place for sacrifice and prayer.

In the quiet restfulness of the place, tired nature succumbs to repose; and, on awakening, the balmy air, the delicious scent-laden breezes, the sweet songs of the birds, and the presence of a group of curious natives make one feel this to be the very " Land of the Morning Calm."

Near Deception Bay is a native settlement of several hundred huts, occupied by the garrison and a few hundred inhabitants, who live and die in this lonely place with scarcely a thought of the world without and its affairs. So innocent and ignorant are they that if they are told of the great countries beyond, or of current events of the world's history, they stare at you as if in a daze, with no sign of appreciation. They have no knowledge except of their little crops, hunts, and the affairs of the petty island.

In olden times, the island was a resort for pirates and thieves, who swarmed the neighboring seas, and preyed upon all on land or sea, but " modern appliances " having rendered such occupations, to say the least, a little dangerous, the island has been given over to more honest purposes. The government have used it as a place of banishment for offending natives, and for foreigners who have had the temerity to penetrate into the forbidden land, but whose heads it was deemed advisable to leave upon their shoulders. Here they languished out a miserable, hopeless existence until relieved by death.

Up to the foot of Mount Auckland a rolling land is interspersed with hills and valleys, while waterfalls, rippling, silvery streams, and terrace on terrace, add their beauty to the scene. The soil, rich and productive, is well cultivated in many places, while over large tracts the wild hog has almost undisputed sway. The monkey frisks and chatters from swinging boughs, while the almost helpless native smiles in innocent glee at the antics of the Darwinian specimen, and either attacks, or retreats from his hairy foe.

Until recently the government maintained a system of watchers and watch-towers on the island, as well as on the mainland, to signal the approach of suspicious vessels, and to give warning of any danger. A great fire was lighted, the smoke of which could be seen at the next station, and this signal was repeated from station to station until seen at Seoul.

The cultivation of a friendship with a few of the natives induced them to furnish us a large basket and a coil of straw rope, which facilitated the descent to the rocks below and at the same time lessened its danger.

CHAPTER XVI

KOREA

"Land of the Morning Calm, — and evening rest,
And afternoon repose, — thy life's lot seems
A dolce far niente undistressed
By labor's pain or keen ambition's schemes.
Keep thou thine ancient state; since countless years
Have thrown no wave of progress on thy shores,
Best now to stand aside, nor share the fears
Of those who surge and clamor at thy doors.
Still let thy sons, like shadows of the past,
White-clad and silent, watch the distant strife
Nor seek to know, nor long the die to cast
Which shall with knowledge mar thy simple life."

KOREA, Choson ("Land of the Morning Calm"), called Koria by the Portuguese, who were the first navigators known in the far East, and still called Korea, or Corea, by foreigners, is a peninsula situated on the northeastern side of Asia, extending southwestward between China and Japan. It is about six hundred miles long, and lies between the 34th and 43d degrees of north latitude. The Sea of Japan is on its eastern side, Manchuria lies to the north, the Yellow Sea is on the westward, and the Korean Channel marks its southern limit. It has a coast-line of about seventeen hundred miles.

Korea is a land of mountains and hills, many being from 1,000 to 8,000 feet in height. They appear snarled and tumbled about in all directions, but the trend is northwest by southeast. The highest lie towards Manchuria, and here the Yalu and the Tumun rivers are formed. Hieu-fung, the highest mountain in Korea, is 8,114 feet high, and is at the southeastern extremity of the range.

The Yalu, the chief river of Korea, and a portion of its northern boundary, has two sources, one on the southern slopes of the mountains, the other in the northeastern portion of the peninsula. These unite and form the "three-mouthed river," the eastern, central, and western. The eastern is the deepest, but has the strongest current, the central has less current, and the western is comparatively small and safe. It is about forty-five miles from the harbor of Taku. Until very recently the navigation of this branch was interdicted by the Korean government, and strangers found attempting to use it were put to death or transported to Quelpart. Its navigation, like that of all Korean rivers, is unsafe on account of many sandbars.

The Tumun is the second great river in Korea. It takes its rise on the eastern side of the northern range of mountains and flows into the Yellow Sea. The Han River, upon which Seoul, the capital, is situated, and the Ping-yang, rise in this range of mountains, and are very important rivers. These rivers are frozen over for several months in the year.

The navigation of this entire coast is dangerous, owing to the strong tides and currents among the islands and rocks and the prevalence of dense fogs. There are several deep, well-sheltered harbors on both coasts, which will be more fully noticed in the descriptions of the settlements.

Korea possesses many advantages in hills, dales, sea, and river, and, lying at the mouth of the Yellow Sea, it receives the moderating influence of the southwest monsoon, which tempers the climate and necessarily causes many productions to surpass those of the continent in similar latitudes. The climate is healthy, invigorating, and bracing in the northern part, where the winters are long and cold. The southern

280   An American Cruiser in the East

portion is exposed to the winds from the Yellow Sea and the Korean Channel, which moderate the winters and make the summers enjoyable.

The common people suffer terribly from scarcity of fuel. The mines are filled with coal, but there are no means of

His Majesty Li-Fin, King of Korea, and his Royal Highness
the Crown Prince.

distribution, even if permission to work the mines were given; and so much of the arable land is under cultivation for the food supply that there are not enough forests to furnish fuel. Their only relief is in warm clothing. The wealthy line their robes with the skins of animals, while the middle class and the poor quilt cotton-wool in their garments. Clothing made of wool is unknown to them. In the capital, a favored few obtain small quantities of surface coal, which is mixed with a proportion of mud to give it body, and is burned in open grates. It gives out a heat that is anything but satisfactory.

Korea for political purposes is divided into eight provinces, and each of these is subdivided into smaller jurisdictions, as in China. The people are of the same race as the Japanese and Chinese. In appearance, they are like the people of North China, but they are more frank and more like the Japanese in their manners. They are a brave people, and are excellent friends but dangerous foes; their history is full of the proofs of this. They have frequently fought the Japanese and the Chinese, and the French and Americans can bear witness to their courage. Their devotion to the cause of the Roman Catholic priests in their hour of trial, and their open door and hearty welcome to every comer, clearly proves their friendship and hospitality.

According to native history, a Chinese warrior named Kisbi, or Kitaze, who in 1122 B. C. was defeated and had his army put to rout by the Tartars, fearing to return to his native country with broken fortunes, led his followers down the peninsula, subdued the native " hairy " race he found there, established the political and social order, and became the first Korean monarch. His descendants are said to have ruled until the fourth century B. C. As the " hairy " people, or Ainos, were of an indolent but independent disposition, and could not be utilized in the new economy, their lands were confiscated and the owners disposed of. The present dynasty is descended from Ni-Taijo, a young soldier of fortune who succeeded in deposing the Wang dynasty. Seoul, whose native name is Han-yan (city on the Han), was selected by Ni-Taijo as his capital, and it has remained the capital city since that time. The present ruler, His Majesty King Li-Fin, is the twenty-eighth sovereign of the present line.

The kingdom is governed, under the King and three Prime Ministers, by five Departments, — those of Finance, Ceremonies, Public Employment, War, and Justice. The general administration of the government is patterned after that of China. The revenue for the support of the government is derived from the land tax, and amounts to about one million of Japanese or Mexican dollars each year. The King, though an independent sovereign, recognized the Emperor of China by a yearly tribute until the year 1895, when before the tablets of his ancestors he solemnly declared his independence of China.

The Koreans have always been able military engineers, skilled in the construction and defence of fortifications. After the lapse of twelve hundred years, ruins of their works are to be met with on all sides as we travel about the coast, from the round tower, with encircling court, to the great walls surrounding a city, — on plains, on hills, and on spurs on the mountain-side.

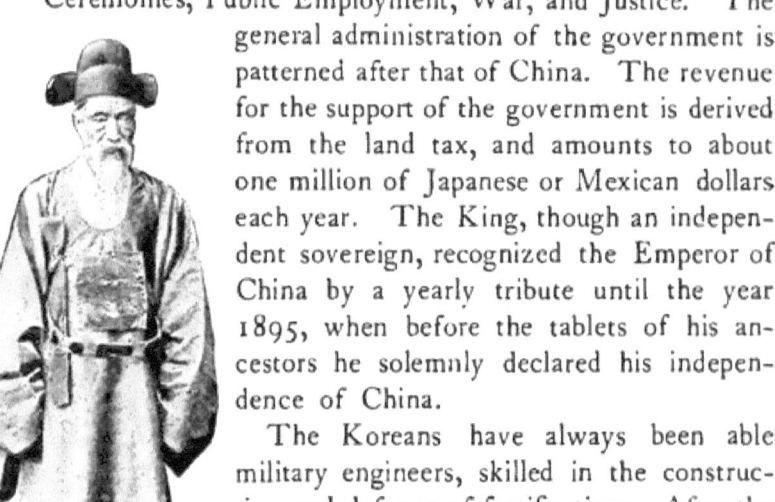

THE PRIME MINISTER OF KOREA.

Among the rugged mountains which are the barrier-wall between Korea and Manchuria, and in the valley of the Yalu, ranges a tribe of independent mountaineers who live in defiance of both Korea and China. They have frequently been attacked by the Chinese forces, but it has been found impossible to dislodge them. They are of Manchu descent and are partially civilized, are expert "medicine men," and occupy themselves in gathering and preparing medicinal roots, and in hunting for gold. At certain seasons they meet the Chinese and the Koreans and exchange their medicines and gold for products of China and Korea.

For centuries the Koreans successfully resisted all efforts to induce them to hold intercourse with foreigners, going to the extent of converting their border-land and the entire coast into a desert, in order to render entrance as dreary and as unattractive as possible, and visiting the punishment of death upon any person who had the temerity to pass the bounds thus set. At the same time, they were striving to build up a nation worthy of the country they inhabited, and they became masters and teachers in literature and poetry, in metal and art work, painting and embroidery, and for hundreds of years they instructed the Japanese and the Chinese.

They invented one of the most perfect languages in existence, — a religion founded upon the teachings of Confucius, — and their engineers were building civil and military works in the East when Rome was young. Their mastery of the arts has been lost in a great measure, and the descendant of the master has taken the place of pupil, while the descendant of the pupil has become the master. But it must be remembered that much skill still remains in Korea, as is demonstrated by their beautiful boats, which are made of wood without metal fastenings, guns, small and large, nearly all breech-loading and of most beautiful workmanship, and their artistic costumes.

The houses of the wealthy class in Korea are oblong, one story in height, built of stone or wood, plastered inside and out, and covered with a thatched roof. The door is placed near one corner of the house; near it is a boiler for cooking, and a small space for the cook to work in. The " kang," a mammoth stove of brick, stones, or terra-cotta, is built within this room, and the top of it forms the floor of the remaining portion of the house. The sleeping-rooms are at the back end of the "kang," which serves to warm them, and the fire which is used for cooking purposes also heats the "kang." The windows are small openings covered with oiled paper or scraped skins of animals, and only serve to show the inmates how dark it is within the room. The houses of the people of the better class are neat and clean.

THE "CHOSON," THE ONLY VESSEL IN THE KOREAN NAVY.

Like all Eastern people, the Koreans have great veneration for age, and a white head is a "crown of glory." The Japanese and the Chinese shave the hair from the heads of their boys, sometimes in fantastic shape; but the Koreans allow their hair to grow all over the head, part it in the middle, and wear the back portion hanging down in a broad plait. When they marry, this plait is cut off, leaving a stump about four inches long, which is turned up, flat on the head, and worn under the hat.

In the northern part of the country, the poorer classes dress in clothes made from a species of grass-cloth, woven from a fibrous plant which is cultivated extensively. This cloth bleaches as white as cotton, and is substituted for it. In the southern part of the country cotton is worn, and the people dress in white, except when in mourning, the color for that costume being a whity-brown. The wealthy wear silks, either of their own or of Chinese manufacture. The poor people use straw sandals, while the upper classes wear shoes made of cloth, or of leather, both having leather soles and pointed toes. The middle classes wear shoes made of stout twine plaited; the soles are made first, then the upper part is worked on, and it is remarkable how well these shoes wear. The hats have broad brims and cylinder tops, and are made of black horsehair or of fine woven grass. This costume is after the style of the Ming dynasty in China. The buttons are of amber, ornaments of jadestone, and the ladies affect pearls. In the northern part of the district, dishes and table-ware are made of polished cast-brass, which is rich in copper, while in the southern part the table-fittings are made of clay and porcelain. Prospectors claim that the country is rich in minerals.

All cereals and vegetables are found in abundance; grapes, apricots, peaches, plums, apples, pears, and cherries grow throughout the country; and gooseberries, currants, and strawberries are found in the northern part. The fruits come to great perfection, but owing to over-cultivation they do not have the rich flavor of corresponding fruits raised in the Middle States of our own country.

The cotton produced in Korea is of staple and fine quality, similar to the best of Sea Island cotton. Formerly, large quantities of foreign cotton cloth were purchased from the Chinese at the gates. Koreans raise no sheep, and have no woollen manufactures. The mulberry-tree is cultivated in many places, the bark being used in the manufacture of a paper which is known all over the northern part of China, and it is especially valued for its texture and strength. It is used for screens, windows, umbrellas, etc.

A KOREAN FAMILY.

Medicines used by the Chinese are produced in great quantities in Korea. Ginseng, a celebrated tonic, constitutes one of the most important articles of trade; and tobacco, of a mild quality, is grown in many places, and is almost universally used.

The elm, several varieties of pine, the cedar, several species of oak, birches, and cork-trees are common. The iron-wood, hawthorn, and the wild fig are frequently met. Chestnuts and several other varieties of nut-bearing trees are found, and the valley of the Yalu is celebrated all through the far East for its massive pines.

The Korean horse is small of stature, but of good wind and bottom. Oxen are raised all over the country in large numbers for agricultural purposes and for food; dogs, cats, and pigs are common, but they are smaller than with us. Wolves, tigers, and the wild hog are nuisances in the north, and the lives of the natives are made miserable by their raids. The eagle, pheasant, stork, and crane are common, and ducks, fish, clams, and crabs, similar to those found in our waters, abound.

The Japanese give the following account of their first invasion of Korea.

"In 192 A. D. Chin-ai, the fourteenth Mikado of Japan, was holding his court at Isuruga, Eichizen, when a rebellion broke out in Kiushiu. He marched at once to Kiushiu against the rebels, and there fell by disease, or by an arrow. His wife, Jungu Kōgē, after his death headed the Japanese army, and, leading the troops in person, quelled the revolt. She then ordered all the available forces of her realm to assemble for an invasion of Shina, Korea.

" All being ready, the Queen Regent set sail from the coast of Hizen, Japan, in the tenth month A. D. 202, and beached the fleet safely on the coast of Shina.

" The King of Shina was struck with terror and resolved to submit. Tying his hands in token of submission, and in presence of Queen Jungu, he declared himself to be the slave of Japan. Jungu caused her bow to be suspended over the gate of the palace of the King in sign of his submission.

288   An American Cruiser in the East

" She restored the King to the throne as her vassal; the tribute was then collected and laden into eighty junks, with hostages for future annual tribute. The tribute comprised pictures, works of elegance and art, mirrors, gold, silver, jadestones, and silk fabrics. The Japanese ascribe the glory of this victory to the then unborn babe who was afterwards deified as Ojiu, god of war, and worshipped as

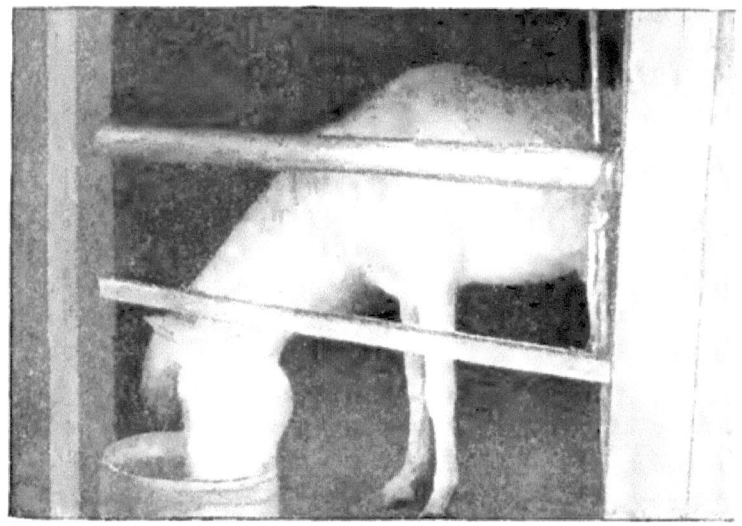

SACRED WHITE HORSE OF JUNGU TEMPLE.

Hachimiu, or the Eight-bannered Buddha. Many temples are dedicated to Jungu, the one at Hyogo (Kobe), being especially famous. And a sacred horse is always kept here ready for the commander who is to lead the forces for the defence of Japan."

I made a picture of the poor beast, and found him to be so badly fed that I doubt if he would be able to carry his own holy bones very far, if he were let out of his cage and given a crack of the whip. Just outside of his stable a small stand is erected where beans can be bought, ten beans

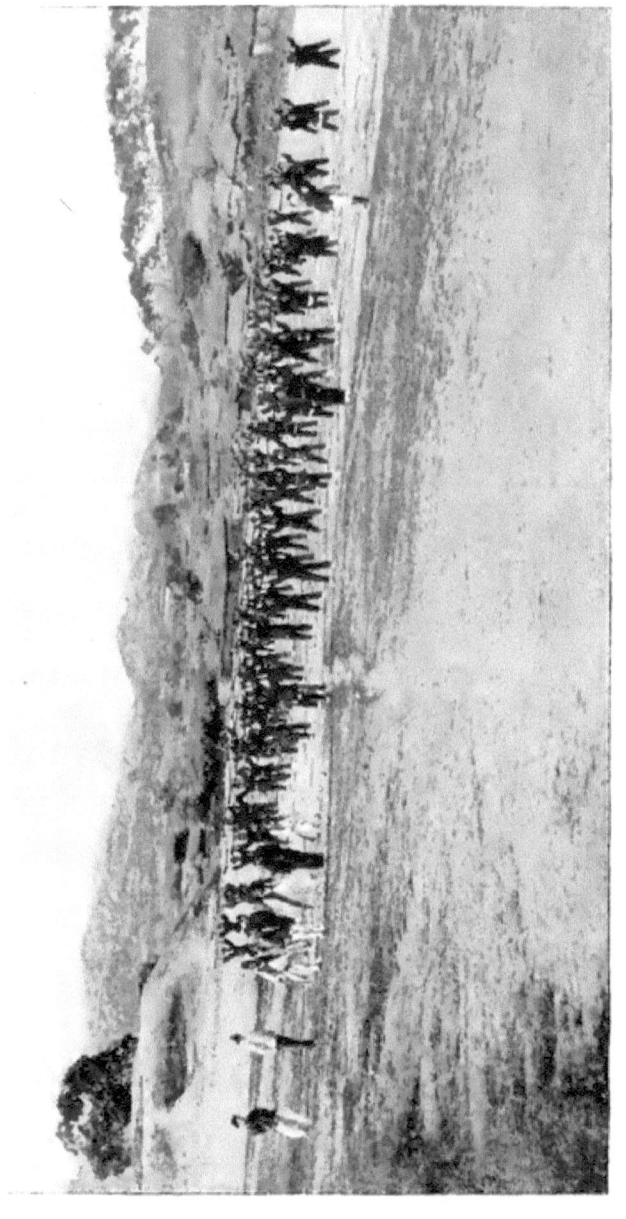

The Korean Army,—Skirmish Drill.

for a cash, — a cash being about one tenth of a cent. Whoever has pity for the poor creature buys beans and feeds them to the horse. Amongst the common people, a belief is current that if they have a question to be answered by Buddha, they can get the answer through the horse: thus, if the beans are all licked up by the horse, the answer is negative; but if a bean is left in the tub, the answer is affirmative.

Korea has been invaded by both Chinese and Japanese, but before 1894 she enjoyed such rest and seclusion that she became known as the "Hermit nation." The Chinese, Japanese, and other nations have tried to force themselves into the country at various times for the purposes of trade, but with indifferent success until in 1871, when the United States sent a fleet to Korea, and made a treaty with the country. Since that time foreigners have had the right to trade at Seoul and at Chemulpo. After the settlement of Japanese in the ports of Fu-san and Fuensen, and the better acquaintance of the natives with them, the prejudice against foreign intercourse gradually died away.

In the country districts, the men break the ground, but the women sow the seeds, gather the crops, and attend the cattle. The women also spin the cotton, weave the cloth, and fashion and make the household garments, while the men roam over the country.

Occupying one of the most varied, fertile, and beautiful countries on the face of the earth, with a climate similar to our own Middle States, the people may be called a nation of homeless wanderers. Their houses are small and mean, merely coverings to protect them from the sunshine and the rains, with bare earth-floors, or at best a mat for covering. The sexes have separate apartments, and there can be no feeling of home. There is very little that can be dignified by the name of furniture, as they have no need of chairs or tables. The heated stone slab of the "kang" takes the place of a bed, and a few brass tea-cups and a tea-pot is about the extent of their possessions in this line.

There are no newspapers, and very few books can be obtained by the poor. There is no entertainment except gossip, not even music, for they are not a music-loving people. They love to sit and contemplate the beautiful surroundings, or to wander from place to place and discuss the news.

The principal articles of import are cotton manufactures; but the amount of these has been disappointing to the foreigners who have been interested in the trade.

It must be remembered that the people are poor, very poor, and every housewife spins the cotton, weaves the cloth, and makes the garments that are worn by her entire household. This is her recreation, after her agricultural labors have been performed. She knows nothing better, and it would be a crime to deprive her of these occupations until she has been educated in other directions.

The population of Korea is about ten millions. The foreign trade is valued at about eight million silver dollars per annum. The principal articles of export are rice, hides, bones, beans, and small quantities of gold. The customs service is modelled after that of China, and is subordinate to it.

CHAPTER XVII

SHANGHAI, CHINA

CHINESE JUNK.

WITH steam and sail, and a fresh blowing monsoon at our heels, we made good speed across the Yellow Sea. For the last fifty miles or more we were in the cold, chocolate-colored waters from the Yang-tse, and on nearer approach our western horizon became a long brown line, indicating the low shores of mysterious "old Cathay."

We took on a pilot, ran near the light-ship for a while, and then stood on the course. Fantastic shapes of curling smoke hung in the heavens; masts of vessels, and the forms of trees loomed up ahead of us; fleets of bamboo-sailed junks, with great eyes carved and painted on their bows passed, and crews of pig-tailed "Celestials" leered at us as they trimmed sail or steered the dingy crafts.

The entrance of the river is dangerous, as the coast is low and mud-banks lie in every direction. The river-banks are studded here and there by walled villages, or mud-forts, bristling with great guns. The fields are crowded with round-top grave-like bakers' ovens. Here and there, the hairless water-buffalo wallows in the slimy mud, and the sad-faced coolie toils with hoe or line, sighing for a laundry in America.

We crossed the bar at Woosung, the "Heavenly Barrier," across which the Chinese sank stone-laden junks in 1884, to keep the French from ascending the river. One narrow channel was left open, and this has washed out and deepened somewhat. At certain stages of the tide, vessels drawing eighteen feet of water can cross the bar and proceed to Shanghai; but, owing to the shallow lumps and shifting channel, the navigation is extremely dangerous.

The intention was to build up Woosung thirteen miles below, and avoid these dangers by having vessels anchor there. As Shanghai had become too valuable to abandon, it was deemed best to connect the two places by rail. A railway was built and equipped about twenty-five years ago, and after its completion a syndicate of Chinese bought it out at a high price. The people who sold the road congratulated themselves on the nice way in which they had "done the Chinese," but their congratulations were suddenly turned to consternation when they learned that the new owners had torn up the tracks and thrown them and the locomotives into the river, declaring that the road had obstructed "fung-shuy," and brought bad luck to the country.

As we ascended the river, the scene became more animated: crowds of junks, painted in gay colors, but dingy with dirt and age, drifted or sailed swiftly by us; great and small junks from the coast, or great canal, laden with rice, or oil, or matting, sailed on, or hugged the river's bank, waiting for change of wind, and steamers from every quarter of the globe rode at anchor, awaiting their precious freights. Along the river's banks, paddy-fields have given place to great shipyards and dry-docks, foundries and machine-shops, marine railways and great storehouses. A little further up, and we are before an imposing city.

We now have a full view of the most important commercial city in the far East, with its magnificent buildings, steeples, and spires, unrivalled shops, hard, smooth roads, and beautiful drives. Little steam-cutters fly about between shipping and shore, the sampan with sail and scull, and all the noises and bustling of a great, busy, driving centre are present.

Shanghai is situated on the left bank of the Woosung River, a tributary of the Yang-tse, at their intersection. It is in latitude 31° 9' north, and longitude 121° 4' east, about twenty miles from the sea.

The United States, German, and Japanese consulates are situated on the river-front. The public garden, where a fine military band plays every afternoon, is just across the creek, and the business part of the city extends further up the river. The French Concession is still further up, and beyond it is the old walled Chinese city.

There is a fine club in the English settlement facing the river-front, and a Country Club a short distance outside of the city, on the Bubbling-well Road, where handsome grounds can be enjoyed, and ball and tennis indulged in. There is a fine racecourse a short distance outside of the settlement; the autumn and spring meets are events which attract crowds from all over the coast, business is suspended, and everybody attends the races. Chinese ponies are entered and run at these races. They are a stunted breed, with good wind and fair bottom. The races are well contested, and some very good time has been made, both in running and steeple-chase.

The drives about Shanghai are delightful and interesting. If one runs out the Bubbling-well Road, mounted upon a Chinese cob, or on the Sickaway, and to the "Point," and return in a dogcart, he will have enjoyed a variety of interesting and ever-changing scenes. One is impressed with the great number of Chinese graves which are everywhere except in the middle of the roads. Some are well kept, some are badly kept, and many have not even a covering over the strong box which contains the corpse. Some have so cracked, warped, and parted as to expose the ghastly bones within. Along the roads and at their terminus there are neatly kept inns where rest and refreshments may be had.

OLD SHANGHAI

Having secured the services of "a guide, philosopher, and friend(?)" in the shape of an intelligent Chinaman, we pass through the French Concession, and soon reach the suburbs of the old walled city of Shanghai. No one can say how old the city is, as the date of its settlement is lost in the obscurity of ages, and there is no known record of the people who first dwelt here. The city is surrounded by a double brick wall, about fifteen feet high, which is filled in with earth, making the whole thickness some twenty-five feet. A roadway is formed on the top of this wall, where troops can be moved about for the defence of the city. The top is reached by means of broad stone steps for foot-soldiers, and broad inclined roads for the artillery. The wall is about three miles in circumference, and is in a fair state of preservation.

There are six large gateways, each having double iron doors leading into the city, and there are other gateways in different localities inside of the city, which divide it into districts. Any or all of these gates may be closed in troublesome times, in case of fire, riot, or other commotion, or when it is deemed desirable to isolate a district. The gates are always closed at night, when each district is shut off from the other, and the whole city is closed to the outside world. The approaches to these outer gates are filthy in the extreme, and there do not appear to be any sanitary arrangements, inside or outside.

Crowds of Chinese — men, women, and children, rich and poor and beggars — were elbowing and crowding each other, in and out, through the gates of the city, and at no time did we see a vestige of that courtesy and kindly greeting that is so prevalent in Japan. Here it seemed to be every one for himself, as though his very life depended upon the business in hand. As we passed through the gateway, we were scowled at by a couple of dark, fierce-looking pig-tailed soldiers, who were guarding the entrance. We looked into the dingy little "guard-house," just inside of the gate. Opposite its entrance was a stand of banners with spears and some ancient weapons, — ugly instruments of torture for close quarters, but not such as one expects to see in the closing days of this century. These, together with a heavy revolver, completed the arms of the fierce braves who were lounging upon the mats in dirty blue-and-scarlet uniforms.

The streets are about eight feet wide, and are paved with stones, which reach from house to house. They are lined on each side with neat two-story houses, whose roofs are of tiles. The lower floors are gay, open-front shops, where wares are temptingly exposed to view. People swarm the streets in great crowds, pushing and jostling as they come and go; pedlers hawk their fish, fruits, or some odd article fancied by our Celestial friends; a monotonous song of the swinging bearers drowns the voices of the throng as some dignitary is borne along in closed palanquin. A poor coolie picks his weary way with a great beam of wood, or an unwieldy pack upon shoulders or back; the statue-like beggar thumps his little bell until you satisfy his demands; the farmer's man jogs along with balanced buckets of filth; the outrunners of some wedding or funeral procession, or the henchmen of some mandarin, make a way through the throng for their procession, or for their lord and master.

There is a great forbearance manifested in all these crowds; seldom is there an unpleasant word, and rarely any breach of the peace. In other lands a large police force would be required to maintain order in such crowded thoroughfares, but here everything adjusts itself, — the people give and take, and pass on.

The nearest approach to an evidence of friendship one sees is in the meeting of two acquaintances face to face, when each places the palms of his hands together, shakes his own hands, and each profoundly bows to the other person.

There is a little niche on one side of the entrance of every shop, where joss-sticks are kept burning for luck, and there is a shrine and a god in the principal room, before which the aromatic punt sends up its fragrance in inverse proportion to the daily sales. The little shops are filled with silks and satins, plain, in colors, stripes, and plaids; brocades of all colors, in bird and beast, and flower patterns, beautiful embroideries, in plain and natural colors, fringes, ribbons, laces, and skeins, gauzes, and pongees, that are celebrated throughout the world; and it is interesting to see the patient weavers and workers in embroidery, as their deft fingers and trained eyes guide the shuttle or needle in the manufacture of the beautiful goods.

Furs of all kinds and grades, from the almost priceless sable to the humble sheepskin, are to be seen in the shops; porcelains from the finest shapes, decorated in gold, silver, and colors, to the grotesque white lions, dragons, dogs, and apes; images of gods and tablets, gilt, lacquered, and plain, are side by side with fine carvings and sculptures. Rich furniture in polished iron-wood, teak and cherry, wonderfully carved, is enriched with colored marble panels, showing landscape or cloud effects; lantern shops, where globular, cylindrical, and square lanterns, in paper, silk, glass, and metal, old and new, oddly designed and decorated, hang side by side, show their impossible people, dragons, birds, and landscapes. If there is one art the Chinaman is deficient in, it is that of giving the relative proportions in his drawings and paintings, and nowhere is this more manifest than on his lanterns.

We see the dingy little holes of cook-shops, with their seething, black furnaces, and steaming fats, broths, stews, and fries. We see great cakes of quivering jelly, white or scarlet or brown; baked and crispy ducks, and the tempting porker; the hind quarter of a choice cur, with feet left on as a guarantee of genuineness; stewed fish and shark's fins; the head of a sea monster in eels; cabbage leaves and boiled rice, — and a hundred other similar delicacies that make up the menu of the epicure of the Celestial Empire.

Fish, great and small, dried and smoked and fresh (the latter swimming about in shallow tubs to prove their freshness), crabs and crawfish, lobsters and diminutive, coppery oysters, gold and silver fish, eels, and scores of others, from the shark to the minnow, may be seen in the tubs and on the stands. When a purchaser comes along, if needs be, a piece is hacked out and sold, and the poor quivering fish is thrown back into its tub to await the next purchaser.

Olive, nut, and tea oils, of all grades, are seen in curious wicker baskets, covered with oiled paper.

The apothecary's shop has its mysterious collections of bulbs and roots, blisters and plasters, and the thousand drugs and compounds, including charms, for which these people are as eager as many in more favored lands.

In the gay little tea-shops one may regale himself with a cup of the beverage, and indulge in a sweetcake which resembles chocolate, with little blocks of cocoanut scattered through it, but which upon investigation proves to be brown-sugar rice-cake, with chunks of pork fat.

The Chinese charity hospital is the cleanest establishment that I have ever seen in a native city. The buildings are dingy from age, but are as neat and clean as could be desired. We saw many patients who were suffering from wasting lung troubles, others with the dread elephantiasis, some bad cases of rheumatism, and some who were evidently in the last stages of consumption. We have been led to believe that the Chinese have no charities such as we have, but this is a mistake. This one, and another that I shall mention further on, are as noble as any in Christian lands, and the people who conceived of them and support them deserve honor and credit for their work, whether it be done under the cross or under the lotus.

The Mandarins' tea-garden and club-house deserve some mention. The club-house is a fine structure in drab brick, with massive tiled roof, where porcelain dragons, fish, and birds seem to be making fantastic gyrations through the masses of lotus and peony blossoms. The mandarins meet here to discuss politics and the news, while indulging in the toothsome dainties of a Chinese menu amidst the dingy scarlet hangings.

The Jeweller's Guild is a busy mart where matrons and maidens love to gaze at the beautiful wares in jade, gold, and silver. Bracelets, pins, rings, chains, charms, beads, and many quaint and odd shapes that please the native fancy are displayed in profusion.

Crossing the winding sheet of water upon a zigzag bridge that could only have been designed by a Chinaman, we reach a little rocky island and the great temple. The temple is a massive structure in dingy scarlet and gilt, with tiled roof, covered with the accumulated dust of years. Passing the hideous guardians at the entrance, we enter the temple and behold many shrines and deities. The general appearance was more that of a junk-shop, or cheap museum, than of a dignified temple. Two dressed dolls — representing a mother and daughter who were ill, and for whose recovery prayers were being said — were placed under a great bell. At intervals, a young priest, to attract the attention of the god, tolled the bell by striking its side with a beam of wood. Then he clapped his hands together, and whispered the prayer in behalf of the sick. One corner of the temple has the appearance of an undertaker's establishment, as it is piled up with coffins, large and small, which are supplied to the poor by a guild of the temple; and this I consider the second of their noble charities.

A motley crowd loiter about the outside of the temple. Old women mend rents and patch torn and worn clothing, while the owners stand or sit by until the work is finished; jugglers twirl a dinner-plate on the end of a bamboo stick, or pull yards of colored ribbons from their hungry throats; barbers shave a pate or fix a queue; dentists, with goggles upon their noses, stand ready to extract a molar, or to apply the soothing drops; fortune-tellers show their cage of little birds, one of whom selects a card from which the filthy owner will read your fortune; around the corner a beggarly crowd may be seen, intently bent upon the result of their chance at "fan-tan;" the beggar, wrapped in a piece of soiled matting, which is too small to hide his festering sores, thrusts himself through the crowd, and importunes for alms.

The little tea-gardens behind old Shanghai produce some very fine tea, and we were interested in visiting them, although the "last picking" had been done more than a month before our arrival. The tea plant yields a crop after its third year, and this is gathered in April, June, and September. The pickers, usually women and children, must have clean hands when they begin the work, and great care in the handling is required at every stage. The medium-sized leaves are the most desirable, the larger leaves being left upon the plant to gather moisture for its sustenance. Each leaf is picked separately and placed in a large basket, which, when filled, is slung on the end of a bamboo pole, and carried across the shoulder.

The leaves are spread in a clean place in the air to dry, after which they are trodden upon to drive out any moisture that may remain. They are then heaped together and covered over for the night, during which they become "heated," foment, change color from green to brown, and become fragrant. They are then crumpled and twisted by being lightly rubbed between the palms of the hands, when they are again put in the sun, or, if the weather is rainy, they are arranged in a sieve and placed over a grate of hot coals, where they are stirred about with a stick until they have all been heated alike. They are then sold to the tea merchant, who has them carefully sorted by women and children, who separate the bad leaves and stems from the good ones. The tea is scented and flavored for its particular standard or market, after which eighteen or twenty handfuls are placed in a shallow copper bowl, over a charcoal furnace. The leaves are moved about in this bowl until the required form and color is obtained, when they are placed in carefully prepared, sheet-lead, paper-lined boxes, which are sealed up to exclude the air and moisture.

The box is weighed, stamped, and marked. Samples have been retained, and the tea merchant always tastes and tests the tea before buying or selling. The tea is hurried off to market, where the first or new crop always brings the highest price.

The methods of the Chinese artisans are very curious; for instance, they do not use work-benches. The material to be worked upon is placed on the floor, or ground, and is held in place with the naked feet, while the workmen squat or climb all over it in performing the required operations. In sawing and planing they always cut on the pull, never on the push. If they are turning metal or wood, the lathe is nearly always swung in one direction for part of a revolution, and then in the other. A sculptor or carver will place his block of stone or wood upon the floor, and squat and work around it, never even dreaming of a bench; and yet these people use chairs, tables, cabinets, and bedsteads, — some of their furniture being very elaborate.

The city of Shanghai is located on a low, alluvial plain, which is intersected by numerous creeks and canals that surround the walls, and enter the city from many directions. The river, in front of the foreign settlement, is filled with steamers and sailing vessels from every part of the world, and,

A ROAD IN SHANGHAI, CHINA.

lower down, the Chinese government has an extensive arsenal, where war vessels of the largest tonnage are built and fitted out.

The municipal government of the foreign settlements is vested in a council, whose members are elected annually, and have charge of the local government and police, and of public improvements and repairs, the cost of which is raised by taxation. The settlements have many fine churches, missions, and schools.

The Tae-ping rebels held possession of the city and settlements from 1853 to 1855, during which time its commerce was nearly ruined, but it has since grown to vast proportions. The city is a very important entrepôt for goods passing into the interior of China, and for imports and exports, from and to foreign countries.

The imports of foreign goods amount to $110,000,000, and of native products fully $70,000,000 per annum. The principal articles of import are opium, cotton, woollen goods, and metals. The exports are tea and silk. Large quantities of opium are distributed to other parts of the country.

WATER-FRONT, NINGPO, CHINA.

CHAPTER XVIII

NINGPO, CHINA

COMING in from the sea on a cold, frosty morning, after contending with a fresh monsoon, one is prepared to enjoy the novel and beautiful scenes of the Ningpo River. The old Chinese fort on the point, with its great dragon-banner; the rice-fields, glistening like diamonds as the new-made ice sparkles in the sunshine; the quaint villages, with their rude cabins and picturesque inhabitants, and the thousands of toilers, moving over the great plains; the double-eyed junks, thronging the banks of swift-running, muddy waters; the strange town of tent-shaped ice-houses on the one bank; the thousands of graves scattered over the other, — all form the foreground of the picture, and the vision ends in the distant blue-black line that indicates the mountain's range. Through a dozen miles of such scenes we pass, and are opposite Ningpo when we drop our anchors in muddy waters, where junks are crowded about us.

Ningpo is in the province of Chekiang, on the Yuna River, at its junction with another swift-running stream, in latitude 29° 55' north, and longitude 121° 22' east. Its port includes the city of Ningpo, the Chusan group of islands, and the cities of Tsike, Funghai, Chinhai, and Tsianghan. The immediate surrounding country is a low, flat, alluvial soil, of remarkable fertility, cut up by a net-work of rivers and canals that are covered with junks. The river-front is lined by junks, unloading and loading their rich cargoes of silks, tea, oils, fish, and rice.

The opposite shore, as far back as the eye can reach, is built up with tent-shaped straw ice-houses, each house about twenty-five feet high, thirty feet long, and thirty feet wide at the base, and tapering to a pointed top. Early every morning thousands of men, women, and children may be seen gathering the ice, and packing it within these straw tents.

The whole plain has the appearance of a great Indian town.

Deep-sea fishing is one of the principal industries of Ningpo. The venturesome people of this place often go a hundred miles, or more, upon the sea, to reach a favorite fishing-bank. The junks are laden with ice, and the fish are packed in it until the return. Hundreds of junks and thousands of people are engaged in this occupation.

The city walls, about five miles in circumference, are about twenty feet high and are fifteen feet wide at the top. There are six double gates, and a moat nearly surrounds the walls. The moat communicates with canals which extend from the surrounding country into the city, where they form two lakes, — Sun Lake and Moon Lake. Sun Lake contains a sacred island, which is reached by several of those delicate aerial stone bridges, for which this portion of China is celebrated. The temples upon this island are the most extensive and beautiful to be found in China, the finest of them being dedicated to the Queen of Heaven.

A CORNER OF THE CITY WALL, NINGPO, CHINA.

All fishermen, women, and girls believe themselves to be under her special protection, and the people of Fuhkin consider her their guardian and patron, as she is the deified daughter of a fisherman of that place. No labor or expense has been spared in honoring the goddess, the finest ornamental stonework, the richest wood-carvings, and gold, silver, and colors, in barbaric splendor and profusion, compose and adorn her temple. The other temples, in honor of titular gods, are fine specimens of Chinese architecture, decoration, and ornamentation, but they pale in comparison with the magnificence of that to the Queen of Heaven.

Ningpo is ornamented with a seven-storied hexagonal pagoda, — "the heaven-sent pagoda," — one hundred and sixty feet in height. The outer covering has crumbled away, leaving the rough brickwork exposed. The building leans a little like the tower of Pisa, and old trees and bushes are growing from its corners, but it is an interesting and impressive monument of the past. Its top is reached by flights of rickety old wooden stairs on the inside. The view from the top of this old pagoda well repays one for the risky climb. The homes of two millions of human beings, with their hopes and fears, joys and sorrows, life and death, lie before us. Beyond the miles of tiled roofs, serpent-like streams meander through the great muddy plains, which reach to the foot of the mountains, and villages dot the shores, between which hundreds of junks sail on their busy way. At the foot of the old pagoda stairs is a shrine containing eight gods, and a priest sees that the joss-sticks and little lamp are kept burning.

The streets of Ningpo are well paved, and are wider than those of any other Chinese city that I have visited. The shops are bright and gay with native goods, but all that a foreigner is tempted to purchase are the exquisite wood-carvings, — statuettes of natives, and beautifully carved cabinets and frames, which are really worth the care required to bring them home.

The Ningpo River is crossed by a pontoon bridge which is more than six hundred feet long, and is lined on both sides with native shops and booths. It is a gay promenade where all phases of Chinese outdoor life may be seen. Behind the end of this bridge stands an old fort, dating from the days of the occupation, and near it is a monument which commemorates the event.

Outside of the city are thousands of burial-places. Some

are handsome stone and brick vaults, or mounds of earth as high as one's head. In others, the coffin is placed upon the ground and covered with matting, while in quite a number of instances the corpse is tied up in a piece of matting, and lies on the ground, exposed to the heat, the cold, and the storms. As may be supposed, all classes are represented here, the rich, the middle class, and the poor,

THE PONTOON BRIDGE, NINGPO, CHINA.

and the poor beggar lies unburied, almost uncovered, in death.

Thousands of men, women, and children crowd back and forth over the pontoon bridge and among the shops. Pedlers, with great packs upon their backs, call out their wares or spread them upon the walks for inspection. We see little shops where rice, fruit, and soups are sold, their owners shivering behind the tiny stoves while awaiting a customer. Horses, wheelbarrows, and sedan chairs add to the confusion, and the place is alive with barter and trade.

The blacksmith squats upon the ground and pulls his bellows and warms himself at his curious forge; the barber's tinkling bell announces that he is ready to shave a head, dress a queue, or put the last delicate touch upon the eyebrows of a dude; an old cobbler is mending shoes; and near by a woman is patching or mending a rent in an old garment; a crowd of youngsters are enjoying themselves with shuttlecock, striking with their heads, elbows, and heels; and the old men indulge in flying great kites made in forms of beasts and birds and gods.

The Chinese have some curious customs. Soon after a child is born, its wrists are decorated with scarlet cords to which charms are attached. These are expected to ward off the ills to which infantile life is exposed, as well as to keep off evil spirits. When the child is one month old, a barber, dressed in red, the religious color, shaves all the hair from its head except one little tuft, which is left at the crown as a foundation for the queue. A boy must be shaved before the ancestral tables, and a girl before the image of the goddess of children. In either case, thank-offerings are presented to the goddess, and friends send gifts of eggs, cakes, and sweets to the baby. These presents are done up in red paper or silk.

The ancestral tablet is a small monumental slab of wood or stone, which stands for the dead ancestor. Sometimes several generations are represented on one slab by names, dates, and inscriptions. These tablets are similar to a diminutive tombstone, and are generally lacquered in black and decorated with gilt characters. The spirit of the dead is supposed to enter the tablet, and the more frequently it is worshipped, the better the spirit is pleased. After the fifth generation, the spirit is supposed to have passed into another body, and is no longer worshipped.

Three moons after the shaving of an infant, the goddess is thanked and invoked to make the child grow up strong

A Ningpo Chinese Family.

and good. On its first birthday, the goddess is again worshipped, and thank-offerings are made to her; while the child is dressed in gay clothing, and pencils, tools, books, and various other articles are placed before it. All the members of the family and friends stand around in expectancy, for whatever is first taken into the tiny hand is believed to presage its future occupation. From this time on the child is taught to worship the gods, to bow before them, and to raise his hands when incense and candles are burned in their honor.

The boys wear a tuft of hair until the tenth year, when the queue is trained. Chinese boys are experts at top-spinning, seesaw, and quoits, and no boys enjoy the sports with more zest; but in all their play there seems to be an underlying vein of gravity and soberness that is not often seen among the young of any other country. At the sixteenth year children leave childhood behind them. Chinese girls are instructed by tutors, as there are no native schools for them, but native schools for boys are to be found all over the country.

The schoolmasters are very important personages. Parents take great interest in them, and are always on the lookout for the best. The master must not only know the doctrines of the ancient sages, but he must know how to teach. When a particular school has been settled upon for the boy, the schoolmaster is invited to a feast specially prepared for him. A fortune-teller decides upon a lucky day for the boy to enter school; and on entering the boy first worships at the shrine of Confucius, salutes his teacher respectfully, receives the teacher's instructions, and goes to his desk. Each boy has a desk so arranged that he cannot speak to the boy in the next desk, and they are not permitted to talk in school. In reciting their lessons, pupils are required to stand with their backs to the teacher. A Chinese school, during study hours, is a very noisy place, as the lessons are learned by being repeated in a sing-song manner, while the students sway their heads from side to side.

Schools are always closed on the anniversary of the death of Confucius, and for about ten days at the Chinese New Year, and the pupils are excused to keep family festivals, — birthdays of ancestors, — and to worship at tablets and at tombs.

Schoolmasters are men of literary honors who have a fondness for teaching. The incentive to study is the hope of taking literary honors, which are the only means of advancement. Even a person in the lowest walks of life, taking these honors, would rank as a gentleman, and be eligible to the highest place in the gift of the government.

The school punishments are standing with face to the wall and repeating some lesson or classic. For extreme cases, the culprit is beaten with the "broom," which means bad luck, and is considered the worst punishment the master can inflict. The responsibility of the teacher never ends; if the boy in after-life should commit some great crime, — kill his parents, for instance, — the teacher would be liable to be executed for the manner in which he taught the child.

CHINESE HOMES

The houses of the wealthy are built of drab-colored bricks, with heavy stone trimmings about the openings, and with tiled roofs, more or less ornamented, according to taste. They are composed of a number of large rooms, generally on one floor. In the crowded cities, some houses are two stories in height, but the Chinese think it is unlucky to live above the ground. The houses are very roomy, for it is customary to have several branches of the family and the servants under one roof. There are always three entrances to a Chinese house. The principal door, in the centre of the house, opens into a large reception-room, in which visitors are received. The floors are of polished woods, or concrete, uncovered by rug or carpet, and the walls are frequently hung with silk or satin scrolls, beautifully decorated with paintings, or embroideries, or inscribed with some motto from the sages. Beautiful lanterns hang from the ceiling, suspended by silken cord or finely wrought chains. Handsomely carved, straight-backed chairs, of highly polished wood, are ranged against the walls, while tables, screens, and cabinets, bearing old porcelains, marbles, and bronze ornaments and fans, are in profusion.

At the end of the room, usually facing the entrance, the altar or shrine of household gods and the ancestral tablets are placed, upon which incense-sticks and candles are kept burning, and offerings of flowers or meats are always to be found. The living room is similar to the reception-room, except that it has a large round-top table in its centre. All the inmates and guests of the house gather around this table at meal-time, when the viands — soups, broths, stews, bakes, and sweets — are served in course, each person helping himself with spoon or chopsticks as best serves his purpose.

The kitchen, "the realm of mystery," is presided over by a man, or "chef," who is well skilled in the Chinese culinary art, from bird's-nest and shark's-fin soups to melon seeds, and this domain is a wonderful, dingy place. One side of the kitchen contains a large brick furnace, with great bowl-shaped pans fixed into the top of it, the fire impinging upon the under sides of the pans. One of these is sacred to the rice; the others (there may be several, depending upon the size of the establishment) are for general uses. The walls are covered with a multitude of pots, pans, kettles, boxes, jars, and crocks, all for the use of the "mysterious king of the kitchen," who is as much of a tyrant in China as his namesake is in America. Above all this, high up on the kitchen wall, safely placed in a little shrine, regaled by the savory odors and content with a burning incense-stick, sits the little kitchen god, watching over the honesty of the cook; but the cook can get his revenge here as well as elsewhere. The god is supposed to go "top-side" for about ten days in every year, to make his report, and pay his respects to the gods and goddesses, and during his absence the cook can cheat and steal if he has the inclination.

Most houses have beautiful gardens, and many have extensive porches, where the adults of the family enjoy the beauties of the garden while indulging in the evening smoke. Nearly all Chinamen, and many ladies, smoke a mild tobacco, in tiny metal bowls with bamboo stems, or in a clumsy white metal affair.

NINGPO CHINAMAN.

The rich gentlemen are gorgeous in blue silk gowns which reach to the shoe-tops, gay silk breeches of brocaded silk, snow-white leggins, elegant embroidered shoes, and dark silk cap, with scarlet or blue button. Protruding beyond their flowing sleeves are rows of claw-like nails, polished in the highest style of the manicure's art, and their wrists are encircled by massive bracelets of the favorite jade.

As a rule, the Chinese appear to be a well-to-do people; but though some of them are very rich, many are very poor, and when poor no people on the face of the earth are so badly off. I have seen many who had nothing in the world, not even a rag between their bodies and the scorching sun, or the wintry blast. In this nude condition, they hang about the suburbs of the city, with great, hungry, straining eyes, and ferociously snatch up any little broken stuff that may support their hopeless existence. They roll in the mud to get its covering for warmth, and crawl alongside of an old broken tomb to sleep. Hundreds of thousands of the people are actually crowded off the land, and have their homes in sampans and junks. Many were born, reared, and expect to end their days and be buried from such homes.

A great many Chinese smoke opium, and the habit is a curse to the people. The "dens" where opium is sold and used are generally made as attractive as possible for the native, although I have seen many noisome, vile places of the sort. In either case, high or low, the victim resorts to the den, and, having made himself comfortable upon a low couch, places a tiny ball of opium in the bowl of his pipe, which he holds over the flame of a lamp until it becomes ignited. Reclining upon the couch, he inhales the insidious drug until overcome by the effects, and given up to dreams and visions. The victim of this habit soon loses his ability for business and his appetite for food. He cannot sleep, and he looks haggard and miserable.

In our trips through the city we saw scores of unburied bodies placed against the inside of the city wall, and on the roof of a stone vault there were three little bundles of straw matting, — the corpses of infants whose parents were too poor to give them burial. Three little bundles are as many as can lie on the top of the wall. When another is to be placed there, the inside one is pushed into the vault to make place for the last comer, and so it goes, until they all reach the quicklime and are consumed. A little coffin can be purchased for less than twenty-five cents, but there are thousands who never own such a sum.

Notwithstanding this poverty, the shops and rivers are replete with evidences of the general prosperity. Tea is successfully cultivated on the hills, and many other sources of industry abound. Two crops of rice are produced each year, and the mulberry and the tallow tree thrive. Quail, wild ducks, and snipe are plentiful and cheap in the markets.

The gods are invoked to assist in the general prosperity. A household shrine, containing the god of wealth, is placed in every shop, incense-sticks are kept burning before it all the time, and the shopkeeper frequently puts on his best robes and bows before the god, invoking prosperity and good business.

One sees crowds of boats of all sizes and descriptions. There are seagoing junks, that trade with Japan, Korea, or in the south, and the " hotel junks," that have large, gaudy houses built upon them, fitted with numerous large mats which are used as beds. These junks are brightly lighted by handsome lanterns, and are made secure to the river's bank. The native cities are closed at nine every night, and these boats afford convenient shelter for the weary traveller. The "flower-boats" are of similar size and style as the hotel-boats, but they are more elegantly found and decorated, and are used for pleasure. When a party engages a "flower-boat" for a trip up or down the river, music and dancing are furnished, and refreshments may be taken along or furnished by the owner of the boat.

Ningpo, Canton, Shanghai, Amoy, and Foo-Chow were opened to foreign trade as a result of the opium war of 1840–1842, between Great Britain and China. Ningpo has a very extensive coasting and inland trade, but foreign

Ningpo, China

trade has not developed, on account of the proximity of Shanghai.

Chinhai, at the mouth of the river, is a port of entry.

The suburbs included in the port of Ningpo are Kingtung, a walled town, containing about thirty thousand inhabitants, situated about ten miles to the eastward of Chinhai, and the nearest town to the Chusan archipelago, and Funghai, the district city of the island of Chusan, which is twenty miles long and about fifty-one miles in girth. It is mountainous, with valleys in a high state of cultivation, and has an excellent harbor. Funghai was occupied for several years after 1841, by the British, and was again occupied by the allied forces in 1860.

The population of Ningpo is about five hundred thousand natives, and about one hundred foreigners who are in the foreign Consular or in the Chinese Customs service. The population of the tributary plain is about two millions.

CHAPTER XIX

FORMOSA

THE island of Formosa, Tai-wan of the Chinese, is about ninety miles off the coast of China, from which it is separated by the Strait of Fo-kien, and it lies between Nan-hai and Tong-hai, the Southern and the Eastern seas. It extends from 21° 54' to 25° 19' of north latitude and 121° 15' to 122° 5' of east longitude, and contains very nearly 15,000 square miles. It shelters the coast from Amoy to the Yellow Sea, by warding off the typhoons.

The Tan-shan Mountains extend the whole length of the island from north to south, and have several lofty peaks and volcanoes. Me-kang-shang, or "wooded mountain," is over 12,000 feet high, Shan-chas-shan, or Mount Sylvia, is about 11,000, and Dodd's Range is fully 11,000 feet in height. The mountain range divides Formosa into three natural divisions, — the mountains, the western plains, and the precipitous coast.

The island shows many evidences of volcanic formation, and is in the curved line which sweeps along the Pacific coast of North America, the Aleutian Islands, Eastern Siberia, the Kural, and the Japanese Islands, through Formosa and on to the Philippines. Ho-san, or "Fire Mountain," sends forth steam and sulphur, and the hot springs of vapor and sulphur near Tam-sui are famous.

The streams on the eastern side are mere mountain torrents and cascades, but the western side has several rivers, the most important of which is the Tam-sui.

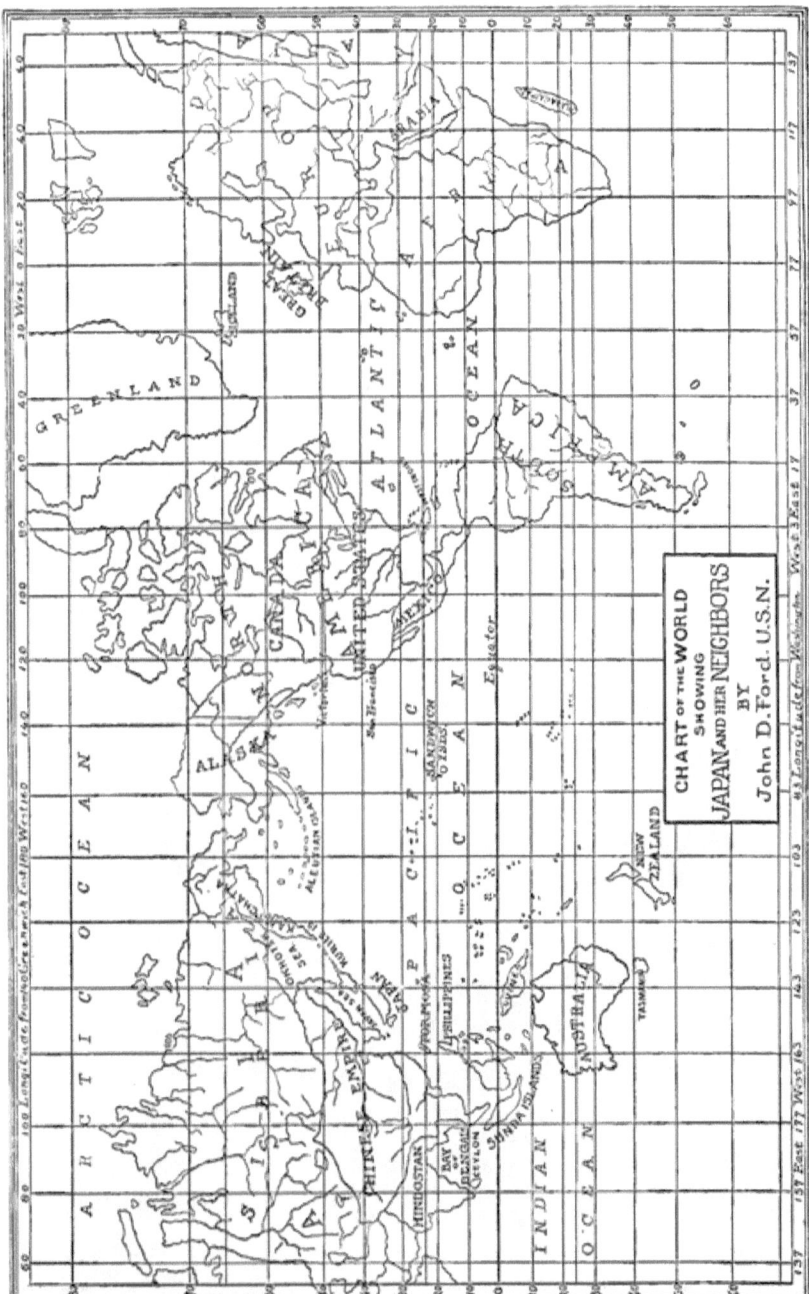

The scenery is enchanting, and it so impressed the old Spaniards that, in their delight, they named it Isla Formosa, beautiful island.

The vegetation is tropical and luxurious. The mountains are covered with dense forests of palms, camphor-trees, and aloe, and beautiful wild flowers are in profusion. The climate is tempered by the breezes from ocean, sea, and mountain-top, and the temperature averages 82° Fah. in the summer season, and about 52° Fah. in the winter months, while the rainfall is about 120 inches each year.

TAKOW, FORMOSA

Takow is situated near the southern end of Formosa. The approach to its open harbor and anchorage there is difficult for sailing vessels at all times, and impossible during the six months of the monsoon season. The water is deepest on the northern side, and the harbor must be approached from that direction.

The city is built on a point of land which juts out into the harbor, and it presents the appearance of great commercial activity. From the top of "Monkey Hill," above the foreign residences, a beautiful view can be had of the surrounding country and the harbor, where hundreds of barelegged fishermen haul their great seines, while near them the puffing exhaust of the steamer's hoisting-engines sends little clouds of vapor into the air as they whip their cargoes in or out.

The country from Takow to Poabi (the nearest settlement of native aborigines, whom the Chinese call Pepohoans, or "strangers of the plains"), is very beautiful, being filled with waving palm-trees, tall bamboos, and wild flowers, but one must be always wide awake and on the lookout for snakes in this country. It is very common to see the great yellowish-green serpents wound around the limbs of overhanging trees, or coiled up, or moving on the ground. When they stretch out their dreadful heads, and start hissing towards you, it is well to have a reliable stick in hand to be used promptly. Some of these creatures measure ten feet in length. They are fascinatingly beautiful but deadly, and, when met, the fight must be to the death.

There are many caves about this country, but in inspecting them it is necessary to remember the serpents, as these are their favorite places of resort.

The Pepo-hohans have been crowded back from their fertile plains, — the rich alluvial lands that were their ancestral homes, — and they are now settled on the mountainsides. These people are good workers, good haters, and good fighters. They still hold in loving remembrance traditions of the Dutch, who were once in possession of the land, and who were kind to their fathers until driven out by the Chinese.

The native huts at Poabi are built on terraces three or four feet high, and are very picturesque. They are made of a framework of bamboo interlaced with reeds and covered over with thick clay. A thatching of dried leaves completes the roof, and a few coatings of whitewash gives the house a neat, tidy appearance. A fencing of prickly stems extends around these huts, throwing a shade over them, and guarding the inmates against sudden attacks from an enemy. Many of the huts are built around the three sides of a square lot, with an open space in the centre where the family pass the evening together. When it is cool, a fire is made in this open space, and old and young assemble there, forming a circle on the ground. They sit together with arms crossed, smoking tobacco or chewing the betel, and talking, while their dogs are in an outer circle surrounding them. They will often sing, but they have no musical instruments for accompaniment. Their voices are harsh, unpleasing, and discordant, but the scene is enjoyable because it is novel, quaint, and weird.

Formosa has three classes of inhabitants: the Chinese, from Amoy and Swatow; the subjected natives, many of whom have intermarried with the Chinese; and the unsubdued aborigines, who defy the authority of China, and carry on wars whenever they have an opportunity. These aborigines are believed by some to be of Malay, by others, of Japanese origin. They are divided into many tribes and clans, and have several dialects. Some tribes have women chieftains, who are said to be bold fighters. These people are of medium stature, broad-chested, and muscular. They have full, round foreheads, which do not recede, large mouths, broad noses, and beautiful, full, black eyes. They have remarkably large hands and feet. Their women wear their hair in loose braids wound around their heads in turban fashion. Their dress is shabby. When near the Chinese they dress better, but are less affable,—they seem to become shy and restless. Tattooing is universally practised amongst them. They are thoroughly honest; and when they die they are buried in a sitting position, similar to the Japanese method of burial. Their furniture and utensils are all made of bamboo,—beds, tables, chairs, buckets, jars, hats, even their paper and pens. The women make a fine cloth from hemp, into which they weave colored threads, and produce ornamental effects.

Wars are common, not only with the Chinese, but between native tribes, and the heads of the slain are always preserved as trophies. Young men and boys often sleep in the "skull-chambers," in order that they may become courageous.

Many tribes show a considerable amount of skill in the arts of civilization. The houses of the village of Ka-fri-ang, for instance, are built of stone, tiled with immense slabs of stone, and fitted with comfortable sleeping and cooking arrangements, and places for storing materials of personal and household use.

The Chinese portion of the island is divided into five districts, — North Formosa, Chang-hua, Ki-ai, Tai-wan, and Feng-shang.

There are some very important towns on the island. Kelung is in the north, near the mines. Howeie has over one hundred thousand inhabitants. Fwo-tre-tia is a dozen miles from the mouth of the Tam-sui River, in the tea district, and has a population of over thirty thousand. Mengka is further up the river, and boasts of over forty thousand inhabitants. Teukchasu, a walled town in the Tam-sui district, contains a population of fifty thousand. Tai-wan, the capital, which has grown from the old Dutch fort "Zelandia," contains more than one hundred thousand, and there are many towns of ten thousand inhabitants or less; while the whole Chinese territory is spotted with villages. The entire population of Formosa is estimated at two and a half millions of people.

The mechanical force of the elements is nowhere more graphically portrayed than on this island. During the rainy season, the waters rise and cover vast beds, open up new passages across the land, and flow towards the eastern plain. Rocky heights confine the beds of the streams, and the torrents carry great quantities of soil and sand, which the currents cause the sea to deposit along the eastern coast. In this way, the port of Thai-ouau is disappearing, and that of Takow has been formed further down the coast. There are no harbors on the eastern coast; there we find mountains and the most beautiful scenery, but the west coast has the fertile plains and the ports.

The soil in the plains, of sand and rich alluvial clay, is covered with a thick vegetable mould. The Chinese inhabitants brought their mode of agriculture with them, and

OLD BANYAN-TREES.

pineapples and many plants and fruits are grown in abundance. Tea, sugar, rice, the sweet potato, millet, wheat, barley, maize, indigo, hemp, peanuts, and jute are raised in such quantities as to be among the important exports of the island.

The fauna includes several varieties of deer, wild boars, bears, goats, monkeys, squirrels, panthers, and wild-cats. The ox takes the place of the horse, and dogs are kept for hunting purposes.

The rivers and neighboring seas are well stocked with fish. Turtles, flying-fish, and coral-fish swim in the warm waters, and fine little oysters and clams lie upon the rocky beds under the waters.

Coal, sulphur, oil, and turpentine are articles of export. The principal coal fields are in the northern part of the island near Kelung and Tam-sui. This coal is highly bituminous and free-burning.

The island of Formosa was known to the Chinese from a very early date. They called it "Kilung," and its inhabitants Fung-fai, or "southern barbarians." In the sixteenth century, when the Portuguese, the Spaniards, and the Dutch were scouring these seas in quest of gold and conquest, they all happened to discover Formosa about the same time. The Dutch were a little ahead, and built the fort Zelandia, which has now grown to be the town of Tai-wan. They established a mild form of government, and conciliated the aborigine natives; but when the Tartars conquered China, some of the defeated followers of the Mings crossed over to Formosa, drove off the Dutch, took possession of a large portion of the island, and formed a government under which the natives have always been restless. In the latter part of the sixteenth century, the Chinese of Formosa acknowledged the Emperor of China, and since that time Formosa has formed part of the Chinese Empire.

In the latter part of the seventeenth century, a terrible typhoon swept over the island, throwing down the buildings on shore, and wrecking twenty-eight war vessels. Later in the same century a great rebellion broke out, and order was not restored until over one hundred thousand men had perished by the casualties of war.

Formosa is a dangerous coast in the monsoon and typhoon seasons, and until the days of steam navigation was known only on account of the dangerous navigation in the locality, the fierce winds which draw through its channel, and the large number of wrecks that were strewn along its inhospitable shores. But in these days of steam-power and a better acquaintance with the surroundings, we can stand off or on, as we please, and have no fear of the dangers that lurk about "Isla Formosa."

Shipwrecked crews used to run great risks from the cannibal natives and from the cruelty of the Chinese. In 1842 the British brig "Ann" was lost, with fifty-seven persons on board, of whom forty-three were executed at Tai-wan; and as late as 1872, the crew of a Japanese vessel shipwrecked on the coast was murdered by the savages. The Japanese government sent an expedition to punish the assassins, and a war between China and Japan seemed imminent; but it was avoided by China's payment of seven hundred thousand dollars as compensation to the friends of the murdered men, and an additional sum to cover the expenses of the expedition, after which the Japanese troops were withdrawn from the island.

Since 1877, roads have been constructed throughout the Chinese territory, the resources of the island are being rapidly developed, and Auping and Takow have been strongly fortified.

CHAPTER XX

AMOY, CHINA

RUNNING down the coast before a stiff monsoon is the very acme of sailing, and reminds us of the "good old times" we have all read of, when the time of a vessel between ports could never be predicted. If a vessel made a start, her progress would depend almost entirely upon the state of the winds. But in these days of "steam and schedules," the time of arrival can generally be calculated. If, however, one is sailing in the monsoon region, there may be delays if the winds are adverse, or his speed may be greatly accelerated in spite of "close-reefed topsails" and "the engines turning as slowly as possible."

The latter was our case on this run. We expected to arrive at early daylight, but the winds pushed us along at such rate that we found ourselves off the entrance light at about eleven o'clock in the night. The coast and entrance being well lighted, and the charts entirely reliable, we kept the lead going and ran in, anchoring for the night in the outer harbor. Our friends on shore were delighted to see the "Starry Banner" just as Key wrote, "By the dawn's early light."

The island of Amoy is a great barren rock of volcanic formation, evidently of the same chain as its neighbors Korlangsoo and Swatow. Perhaps, in past times, the great thousand-ton granite bowlders, rocks, and stones that we now see all about us, were hurled upwards in some fearful convulsion of nature; but the rains and the winds of the monsoons have washed and blown away from its unsheltered sides all deposits before they could gain a holding place among the smooth rocks.

Ages ago, so long ago that no one now knows the time, an outpost was established here to repel piratical incursions from neighboring islands. This outpost developed into a camp, the camp into a regularly fortified place; camp followers and hangers-on soon came; and when the settlement

THE DEIFIED ROCKS AT AMOY, CHINA.

was strong enough to repel hostile attack, trade began and business grew, — hence the present city.

Amoy is situated on a hill, on the south coast of the barren island of Amoy, in latitude 24° 28′ north, longitude 118° 10′ east, nearly opposite the centre of the island of Formosa. The city is about ten miles around, and is divided into an inner and an outer town, separated from each other by a chain of hills. Upon the summit of these hills there is an old Chinese citadel of considerable strength, which commands both cities, as well as the surrounding country.

Each city has its own commodious harbor, where hundreds of picturesque junks, swarming with noisy natives, can be seen, and the inclined stone landings are crowded with men and women, bearing to and from these busy water-craft burdens of rice, sugar, tea, or fish.

The inner city is protected by a network of very strong fortifications; but these are so close that in case of an attack upon them an enemy's projectiles would be sure to destroy both cities.

Amoy is the entry port of the province of Fo-kien and the seaport of Chang-chu, with which it has good river communication. Many cargoes of tea from Tam-sui and other ports of Formosa are handled here, the charges incident to the porterage and handling adding very materially to the commercial importance of the place.

The men of Amoy are stalwart, handsome fellows, who have the bearing of good soldiers. They dress like the Chinese of this section of country, but wear turbans to conceal the pigtail, which they consider a badge of oppression.

The streets of the native cities are very narrow and filthy. They are not more than seven feet wide; many of them are of less width, and there is no pretence of sanitary arrangements. To go about in them one has to be prepared to climb over and wade through the most horrid filth and abominations, and the odors are at times almost unbearable.

Granite is plenty, and can be had for the gathering and hauling. On the heights, temples, monasteries, and a few houses are built of this stone. During the prevalence of the monsoons, the climate is filled with moisture; and as stone houses are believed to attract the moisture and become damp, the people do not consider them desirable as places of residence. A great many very poor families are crowded together, more like animals than human beings, in scantily furnished, dirty houses.

Many families seem to be composed entirely of boy children. When the parents are poor, or if they do not care to rear girls, they either sell or kill them. If killed, they are usually drowned in a tub of water, and the father must do the horrid work, as any agent would be liable to be punished for the murder. The parents have absolute control over their children. Sometimes girls are offered for sale, but buyers are few. It is thought necessary that all children should marry; and parents often sell or give their girls to their friends when they are quite young, to be the future wives of the sons of the new owners. Even among the better classes, girl children are sometimes put to death, if the parents have more daughters than they care to rear.

Chinese girls of from ten to sixteen years of age wear their hair "banged" across the front of the head as a notification to the "go-between" that they are of marriageable age. The condition of a Chinese woman is fearful even to contemplate. Born a slave, she runs the gantlet of murder in childhood to die a slave, — only changing masters from father to husband, with too frequently a "she-devil of a mother-in-law" to make her life a very hell on earth. Uneducated, except perhaps in the "accomplishments of music and high-pitched discords," with no consoling resources, she works on and dreams her poor life away in stupid fancy or stolid indifference, until her time comes to maltreat some unfortunate daughter-in-law.

The boys are not treated thus, for when they grow up they can earn more money than girls, help support the parents when ill or old, and can worship the ancestral tablets, and continue the family name.

The natives of Amoy were very curious, and followed us about in crowds. If prices were asked or bargains attempted, every one in the crowd had a voice in the transaction, and if money passed, they each looked at it and expressed an opinion upon its genuineness and value; but we were not long in concluding that this was due to what might be called, "good-natured inquisitiveness," rather than impertinence. The people have a high sense of the ludicrous, and we found that the best way to rid ourselves of their undesirable attentions was to get the laugh on one of them,

FOREIGN RESIDENCES AT KORLANGSOO, AMOY, CHINA.

when his fellows would immediately discover the joke and follow it up without mercy. The person laughed at would get out of the crowd and try to sneak off, which was the signal for the greater part of the mob to follow him with jeers and shouts, and we would be left in peace until a new crowd discovered the foreigners, and gathered around us.

The consulates and foreign residences are situated on the opposite island of Korlangsoo, a large island of volcanic formation, where stones, rocks, and great bowlders have been hurled forth in some past age. The residences are commodious and elegant, and are located in beautiful gardens, enclosed by low stone walls. The roads are well kept, and some delightful tramps, together with many charming views, may be enjoyed.

The "Lampotoh Temple," above the race-course, is a fine specimen of Chinese religious architecture and decoration.

Many of the great bowlders, on both sides of the river, are decorated with inscriptions relating to local history, or with extracts from the sages.

The island was captured by the British in 1841, after a determined resistance, and is now one of the treaty ports.

The natives are expert manufacturers of a grass-cloth that is quite celebrated throughout the east. Game, fish, and fruits are abundant. Snipe and wild ducks can be had in the autumn and winter season; fine fish can be had at all times. Delicious pomolas are brought from the orchards up the river, and all the fruits of the semi-tropical zone can be found in the markets. Exclusive of junks, fifteen hundred vessels enter the port each year.

SWATOW, CHINA

Swatow is situated on the Han River, in latitude 23° 40' north, longitude 116° 42' east, and is the port of Chan-chan-foo in the province of Kwang-tung.

About the time we dropped anchor off the Consulate at Swatow we saw our colors flying on the staff of the old Chinese fort at the river's entrance, and on counting the little puffs of smoke issuing from the fort's popguns, we found that our flag was being saluted. When the salute was finished, the "Chinese dragon" was flying at our main-mast head, and the compliment was returned with our eight-inch guns. Not since the earthquake, ages ago, has old

LAMPOTOH TEMPLE, AMOY, CHINA.

Swatow had the shaking up we gave it. The great white puffs soon formed into white cloud masses, hanging about us and dimming our vision; while the reports, deep and sullen, rang out to the echo and re-echo, playing among the everlasting hills, rattling and crashing before the expanding powder waves. Thousands of frightened natives flocked to the river's side, looking on in astonishment, as the great guns boomed out the salute. They said they thought old Swatow was experiencing a series of earthquakes, and they flocked to the river's edge as a place of refuge. The old commander of the fort danced and cried, by turns, when he saw and heard how we were honoring his country's flag. After the salute, the natives were very polite and could not do enough for us.

The immediate neighborhood of the city is guarded by an ancient, quadrangular stone fort, which is armed with old two-inch, cast-iron, smooth-bore guns, mounted on ship's gun-carriages. These had been evidently obtained from some vessel in the old days. The fort is fairly well preserved, and is carefully watched by its zealous guard, who kept very close to us while we were looking through its precincts.

The houses are made of clay, with tent-shaped, tiled roofs, and many of them stand in pretty gardens surrounded by high walls. The interiors of the houses are frequently highly ornamented with dragons, beasts, birds, and flowers, the work of native artists, who are considered the finest painters in China. The houses are nearly all residences or warehouses, and we missed the gay little open-front shops that are so attractive in other Chinese cities.

Swatow is an important tea-market, and its white-metal work and curious fans are well known throughout the world. Its painters are well patronized. The people dress better than those in northern China, and the women are considered the handsomest on the Chinese coast. Like the ladies in other parts of the country, they have a wonderful way of dressing the hair, in "tea-pot," "butterfly," or plain fashion. The toes of girl babies are turned under the feet and securely bound in place to prevent the feet from grow-

WOMAN OF SWATOW, CHINA.

ing, while the rest of the body is developing. Ofttimes, the bandages are not removed for months, and the poor children suffer excruciating pains, but the treatment is persevered in. In olden times, this was done for the ungallant reason of "preventing the women from gadding about," but in these days it has become the fashion. Small feet prove that the woman cannot stand upon them comfortably and cannot work; consequently she must be a lady.

Daintily mincing along on tiny feet, or borne in state in sedan-chairs, the belles of this "flowery land" take their airing and visit some temple, or a street where they can see and be seen. Clad in broad-sleeved garments of sky-blue brocade, bordered with black, or brown, or scarlet; with wide black trousers, reaching to the ankles; with white cloth "leggins" and tiny lilac silk shoes; with thick white-edged soles; with the hair done into great, glossy black folds, representing tea-pots, butterflies, or shells; with numerous gold, silver, or colored glass pins and flowers, — they feel themselves the peers of their fairer sisters in any land.

The beautiful strip of level land which runs along the river-front of the opposite island has been utilized by the foreign inhabitants as a place of residence. Here handsome houses, surrounded by elegant grounds, with the luxuries of the far East to gratify the senses and taste, make almost a paradise on earth. Great banyan-trees clingingly spread their branches up the hillsides, and the sweet rose blends its fragrance with the geranium and heliotrope.

A tramp past the dingy little hillside temple, and a climb over the green hills, brings us into a great basin, — a very valley of death, — where we find a mass of barren rocks and bowlders that have been hurled from the interior of the earth in some past age, of which the natives have no record. For miles extends a great bowl-shaped valley of lava beds, an extinct crater, with rocks and stones and bowlders, where all is desolation and ruin, and no blade of grass or other green thing even struggles between crack or crevice to change the awful hue of nature's curse.

The views from this height are charming, — the green hills, with the great brown, serpentine rivers, meandering among them; the hills beyond and beneath; the green sea, losing itself in the great blue ocean; while the clouds, like a great canopy, cover them all.

The superstitious natives, like their brethren of Amoy, have placed inscriptions upon some of the greater bowlders and deified others; but the beating winds and mocking monsoons are disintegrating the stones, and drift the sand upon the clayey soil below, tempering it for the husbandman's use. Even now, the waving rice drinks in the dewdrops, and bathes its roots in the sweet waters, while waving "charms" ward off the poaching birds, and the air is laden with sweet odors from garden, field, and orchard. Birds chirp gayly as they roam from branch to branch, and all nature seems to smile, under the lee of this leaden old crater.

Comfortably settled in a house-boat, a junk with a cabin built upon it, fitted with a stove, some provisions, and a couple of Chinese servants, a party may sail beyond the city and keep clear of all villages. Snipe, wild ducks, and geese come onto the marshy rice-fields for food and water, and as they are gamy, the sport is fine. Oysters are large and of delicious flavor, reminding us of the Chesapeake Bay bivalves.

The rise and fall of the tide is about sixteen feet, and when the tide is out great mud-flats must be crossed in landing. These are gotten over in peculiarly shaped, flat-bottomed boats, which the native crews push in or out as they slide over the mud.

Swatow contains about forty thousand native inhabitants and about two hundred foreigners.

CHAPTER XXI

CANTON, CHINA

FROM the time of leaving Amoy until we reach the harbor of Hong-kong, two hundred and ninety miles away, we were driven by a lively northeast monsoon, which caused the vessel to pitch and roll so deeply that it was almost impossible to keep on one's feet without the aid of life lines. Under such conditions, we had great regard for the author of the old song, " A Life on the Ocean Wave ; " but when we remember that it was written on a bench in the old battery of New York, and not on the ocean wave, we must pardon the imagination and forgive the author.

The harbor between Hong-kong and Kowloon, opposite, is picturesque and novel. Beyond, are great black, fog-covered hills, dotted here and there with white houses, which grow thicker at the upper end, and form the city of Victoria. The thread-like lines indicate the Kennedy and military roads, and the cable road to Mount Austin. A great fleet of war vessels, stretching along the harbor, represents all shades of naval architecture, from the hulk, of the days of the East India Company, to the most modern steel coast-defence vessel, and all that comes between, — including the old wooden Chinese war-junk with its two-inch cast-iron gun amidships, and the speedy little steel steamers which bear the dragon flag. Thousands of sampans and junks are lined up to the sea-wall, and on the opposite side is the low, sandy Kowloon.

Steaming on, we enter the " Boca-Tigris," the " Tiger's Mouth," the entrance proper to the Hu-mun, or Pearl

River. There are some beautiful hills on both sides of the river, extending for miles from the entrance. Some are undulating, with a gradual slope, others are craggy on the river's front, and some are cut off abruptly. Every hill is strongly fortified, and bristles with great guns. Between the hills, two rows of piles have been driven, and these extend across the river, with openings in the channel about fifty yards wide, for the passage of vessels. One of these rows is composed of iron piles driven endways into the bottom of the river, with their upper ends connected by heavy chain cables. The other row is made of heavy wooden beams.

As we approached the city, the fortifications became even more extensive, and when we reached the level country we saw a great bridge, over which an army can be transported for the defence of the city. The ends of the bridge and of the obstructions are defended by fortifications, and these the Chinese call the "Tiger's Mouth."

A little further up the river, we reached a great, alluvial plain of wonderful fertility, skirted in places by native villages. Hundreds of junks sail up and down the muddy river, and one hears the din of gongs, sees the burning joss-sticks, and the gay, triangular, scarlet flags at the mast-head, for luck. Several pagodas point heavenward and the outlines of the "White Cloud Mountains" bound our horizon.

Great steel-clad, bomb-proof water batteries, the houses and huts of the people, and the hundreds of little river-craft tied to the water-front, warn us of our nearness to the city; and we drop our anchors into the dirty waters between Sha-mien and Honan, where we can get the breezes that are wafted up the river.

Canton is an immense old city and commercial port, situated on the north side of the Pearl River, in latitude 23°

7′ 10″ north, longitude 113° 14′ 30″ east, and it is the capital of the province of Kwang-tung in the southern part of China.

The scene off the city is animated, noisy, and bustling. Steamers, junks, and sampans are crowded together at anchor, tied up to the river's front, or struggle for room to move about their business. Occasionally there is a collision among these frail craft, when one, perhaps two, are cut down and sunk. A widening circle on the surface marks the spot, and is soon washed out by the swift-running current. A little driftwood on the surface tells the story of several unfortunates suffocated in the river's treacherous mud, and the Chinese world rolls on without a thought or a sigh.

Great boats go by us loaded with passengers and freight, whose stern-wheels are worked from the inside in treadmill fashion by men and boys who are stripped to the waist. The streams of perspiration flowing down the bodies of these toilers represent the cost of the trips in human blood. The neatly fitted and gayly painted sampan, which an expert boatwoman can twirl round on its own centre, flits back and forth from the shore; while little steam-cutters not only hold their own, but gain upon dignified old junks, whose two eyes may have seen storms in the Yellow Sea.

It was not many minutes before we were besieged by a hundred or more boats and sampans. There were official calls, port calls, and Chinese merchants with new goods and old, porcelains, silver-ware, ivory and silk work, and tailors with hundreds of samples of the most outlandish patterns that ever were seen, and washerwomen who were anxious to do the laundry work for three silver dollars a hundred pieces. This assemblage was one of the noisiest and most picturesque that could well be gathered on a vessel's decks. The sleek merchant in brocade silk, clean-shaven, with the address of a courtier spread out his wares and temptingly offered them for sale. The girls of the sampans, with heads dressed in the best style of the "butterfly" or "tea-pot" or in plaits, in their blue gowns and black trousers, with bare feet, but with graceful carriage, wandered about their own little boats, and added gayety to the scene.

One of the most piteous sights that we have seen here was a poor, frail craft, containing a family of lepers. It dropped stealthily down into the crowd of boats surrounding us, and the inmates importuned for the broken stuff from the messes. A little *white* fellow of about ten years managed the boat, which was a mass of old matting and filth. From its stern a handless, noseless hag, with matted hair and covered with horrible sores, was imploring succor. The man in the bow was more loathsome than the woman. His eyes were gone, the mouth was eaten away, and the face and scalp were covered with dirty ulcers. These poor people held up their withered stumps and exposed their horrid sores to excite our sympathy. They were given a lot of provisions, and the inmates of the sampans drove them off, but, much to our annoyance, they persisted in hovering about the vessel during our entire stay.

"SHA-MIEN," THE SAND-FLATS

Formerly the foreign residences were on the river-front, outside of the city walls, and just east of Canton. In December, 1856, these residences were destroyed by a Chinese mob, when the city was captured and occupied by the British and French, acting together. The city and its neighborhood were governed by a military commission, composed of officers of these forces, until late in the year 1861, when it was concluded to select a more secure place of residence for foreigners. A large sand-flat, located to the westward of the old settlement, and in front of the city, was chosen. This was made into a substantial island by building a heavy granite retaining wall around it, and filling in with soil. A canal, one hundred feet wide, was left between it and the city, as a means of protection against Chinese mobs. The two bridges, which span the canal and lead into Canton, are guarded by heavy iron gates, and there are guard-houses, where Chinese troops are kept on duty at all times. The gates are always kept closed, and are locked at night. Chinese found on the island after dark are compelled to give an account of themselves. The newmade island is about three thousand feet long, and one thousand at its broadest part, and nearly four hundred thousand Mexican dollars were expended to put it in order. A tax of forty-five dollars per acre per annum is paid to the Chinese government for its use.

Sha-mien is well located, being only a hundred feet from the suburb of Canton, where all the Chinese wholesale dealers, bankers, and merchants reside. It has a safe and commodious anchorage for vessels of about fourteen feet draught of water, but large steamers and all foreign sailing vessels are required to anchor off Wampoa, twelve miles below. It faces the Macao passage, giving a short cut to and from the sea, and the cool breezes of summer are wafted up its channel.

The residences on Sha-mien are palatial in architecture, finish, and fittings, and are surrounded with beautiful walled gardens. Their masters and mistresses are among the most hospitable people in the world. The roads about the island are broad, clean, and well shaded by trees of dense foliage. There is a handsome little English church near the centre of the settlement, while the club and the new theatre furnish the public amusements of the place.

The residents live in a state of alarm produced by the bad feeling that is always exhibited towards them by the Chinese. It is a common occurrence for Canton to be placarded with threats against the "foreign devils," and this, together with the recollection of the outrages of 1856, causes terrible strains upon the nervous systems of the foreign residents.

OLD CANTON

Having secured the services of Ah-Po, a guide, we crossed the stone bridge which unites Sha-mien with Canton. Fierce-looking Tartar guards swung open one of the great iron gates, and we entered the suburbs of the "Celestial city." A peep into the dingy bamboo guard-house, on the left of the road, revealed a double stand of barbarous pikes and spears, still useful in repelling an infuriated mob; and, lounging upon their soiled mats, awaiting a "call to arms," or to relieve the guard, were a crowd of men as piratical-looking as ever were seen.

The city is enclosed by a brick wall which is built upon a stone foundation. This wall is more than six miles around, twenty feet thick, and its average height is about twenty-five feet. Another wall runs from east to west, and divides the city into two parts, the old and the new. The old city, or northern part, is occupied by the Tartars; while the new, or southern part, is peopled by the Chinese. The houses extend along the river for about four miles, and the river-front is crowded with junks, sampans, and boats of all styles.

The outer wall of the city rises to enclose a hill on the north side, and on the other three sides it is surrounded by a ditch which extends, sewer-like, under many of the streets, while the ebbing tide is relied upon to carry off the mass of filth that accumulates in these beds. There are twelve gates in the outer wall, and four in the wall which separates the city into two parts. There are also two water-gates through which boats pass across the new city. The gates are guarded at all times, and are closed at night.

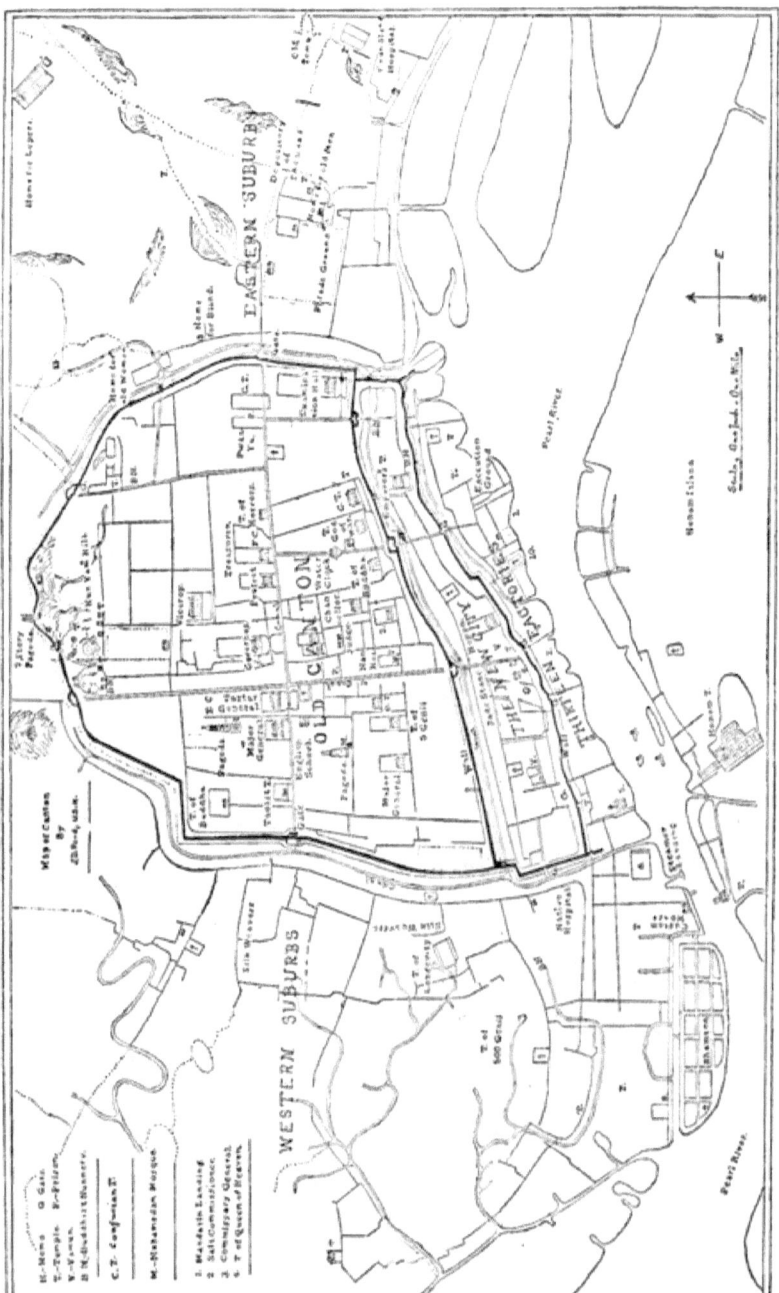

Map of Old Canton.

There are more than six hundred narrow, crooked, mazy streets in Canton, but a few straight ones lead from the gates on the southern side to the water-front. The streets are nearly all paved with granite slabs, and are well kept, for a Chinese city. The smells, filth, and other abominations that are so prevalent in the other cities are not met with here. Canton is a well-governed city. It contains 1,500,000 inhabitants.

The houses are small, usually two stories in height, with tiled roofs, and are built of drab-colored bricks, trimmed with stone or wood. The first floor is used as an open-front shop, and the rear portion and courtyard are used for storehouses; the upper floor is divided into living-rooms and chambers.

The streets are usually covered over with mattings or cotton awnings which extend from the roof of one house to that of the house opposite. The gay signs and crowded thoroughfares give pleasure and delight as we jostle among the busy throng. Every house is barricaded at night by means of shutters and great beams of wood, so that it might successfully withstand a siege.

Almost every trade and occupation has its own street or quarter in this curious old Canton. For long distances, we see shop after shop where men and boys are fashioning and coloring impossible dragons, beasts, fish, birds, flowers, and gods, in low and high relief, and the boldness with which golds and greens and scarlets are used is startling and wonderful. In another section are beautiful specimens of polished and of dull ebony cabinets, bedsteads, settles, and chairs, carved and plain, with marble, glass, or exquisitely engraved panels and finishings. In others are paper and silk ornaments for women's wear, flowers, birds, butterflies, head-dresses, porcelains of all kinds and forms, — from the wine-cup to the great punch-bowl, — in whites, greens, blues, golds, and all shades that can be imagined;

jadestones, upon which all the processes, from the cutting to the finishing and mounting, can be seen; artists, in stone or wood, side by side, working out some hideous dragon or sweet-faced Buddha; painters, who have no idea of perspective, and very little of proportion, gravely painting a twelve-foot body under a natural-size head, or a woman in the background taller than her house in the foreground, with colors and tints as absurd as the drawing; ivory-carvers in whose work we can study all the manipulations of laying out, cutting, carving, and giving the finishing polish; silk spinning, weaving, and embroidery, where wonderful effects are produced in natural and in fancy colors; shops, where paper money, artificial shoes, and food are made for sacrificial purposes, for offerings to the spirits of the dead; and as the spirits are not supposed to know better, these imitations are believed to be as acceptable to them, when offered through fire, as the real articles would be; and as the cost is much less, the custom commends itself to a practical people. We see the dog and cat restaurant, where these creatures are served in cutlets, roasts, and savory stews; fish-stalls, where great monsters swim side by side with tiny shrimp, while a stream of silvery water flows into the massive tub; wonderful little oil pictures on sheets of rice or silk; costumes of the people and punishments for the culprit; mammoth crabs and crawfish, sportive gold and silver fish, with their flat heads, staring eyes, and fan tails; mysterious herbs, drugs, blisters, potions, and charms in the apothecaries' shop, and the goggle-eyed druggist staring into vacancy. The throngs stop and glare at us "western barbarians," as we move on from shop to shop, and from street to street.

All day long the streets and lanes and alleys are filled with swarming crowds of grave and gay men and women, elbowing and pushing their way through the throng. Distinguished-looking men, whose personality would attract attention in any land, ordinary and common men, and fierce, cadaverous-looking fellows, who cause one instinctively to button up his coat and clutch his stick, — all pass, crowd, and repass in this human hive. The chattering, mincing woman, gayly decked and made hideous by powder and rouge, trips along on her tiny feet, frequently jostled by some rougher sister or impolite member of the opposite sex. The beggar slowly moves his disgusting presence from shop to shop, and drums upon his little gourd until alms have been bestowed. All are pushed out of the way, and crowded here or there, by the outrunners and chair-bearers of some low-grade mandarin who is proceeding in state. Bang! Bang! goes the gong; then a crowd in dingy scarlet with pointed hats precede his lordship, who is borne in a closed sedan-chair, over which his red cotton umbrella is held. Or it may be a wedding procession, headed by men and boys (as many as can be hired), each clad in old red coats and pointed hats. They beat gongs, play on shrill trumpets and bass drums, and are followed by bearers with sweets, roasts of duck and pig, cakes, more sweets, the bride's trousseau, fancy sedan-chairs, more gongs, and all the household furniture and utensils belonging to the high contracting parties.

If it is a funeral procession, there will be a long line of professional mourners and the friends of the deceased, all clad in dingy white garments, and accompanied by bearers with artificial money, shoes, provisions, and bundles of incense-sticks to be burned at the grave. The body is borne near the head of the line. No expense is spared on any of these occasions to make as much display as possible, and for that purpose many of these poor people pawn and sell everything in their possession. If a funeral should meet or cross a wedding procession, it is considered the most unlucky omen.

In the western suburbs we saw a large mill, where

tiny oxen were harnessed to the upper stones, and they travelled round and round, grinding rice into beautiful white flour. On the opposite side of the road there is a rival mill, where the primitive method is adhered to. Large stone mortars are planted in the ground, and over each of them a heavy wooden hammer is so arranged as to fall into the mortar. Rice is placed in the mortar; and a stalwart coolie, who is stripped to the waist, jumps on and off the end of a beam, causing the hammer to rise and fall upon the rice, crushing it into flour. This process is slow and tedious, and the poor coolies are covered with streams of perspiration; but labor is cheap here, and many Chinese prefer the hammer to the oxen-made flour.

The Guild-hall of the green-tea merchants is a handsome structure, and is highly ornamented with porcelain, carvings, and all the colors of the rainbow. The property occupies several acres of ground, upon which are a Confucian and a Buddhist temple, a theatre, and a handsome roof-garden, besides the Guild-hall, and a number of private rooms. Although the Guild-hall is a new structure, its appearance is marred by the accumulation of filth and the large number of loafing loungers who haunt its precincts.

At the entrance to the court of the Temple of the five hundred genii, we were met by an old priest who collected our fee and conducted us through a long, narrow passage, opening into a large courtyard. Here twoscore or more of young Celestials were engaged in athletic sports, which they supplemented with occasional whoops that would do credit to young American Indians. The play was rough, and the whoops were loud, but we soon passed on and entered the temple. There are several gilded images in the centre, and ranged around the walls in aisles. The five hundred colossal gods — huge men, carved, plastered, and painted in brown — sit or recline at their ease. Some have smiling countenances, others are childlike and bland, and others are hideous. Our old friend "Marco Polo" sits in a corner, crowned with a sailor hat, and seems to be at home in the company, as the curling smoke from the scented joss-stick reaches his wooden nostrils.

Some of the gods have musical instruments, and around many groups of merry, light-hearted children gambol. Upon some faces is seen the vacant stare that is, I believe, the chief aim of the devout Buddhist.

A stroll through the shops forcibly impressed us with the inferiority of Chinese lacquer-ware as compared with that made in Japan. In China, the article to be decorated is made smooth and painted red. When dry, the decoration is outlined with a stencil, after which the gold or bronze is put on over a pigment, and the article is given several coatings of lacquer. The result is, that finished work lacks the artistic boldness and brilliant finish so peculiar to the Japanese work.

We were interested in a glass-ware manufactory, where broken bottles and other pieces of old glass were being melted in little clay-lined, iron furnaces, and then worked by human blow-pipes into fancy bottles and ornamental shapes. The coloring, bunching, drawing, moulding, and other manipulations were all neatly performed by little pig-tailed fellows of not more than twelve years of age.

The Temple of Longevity is a dingy old house, where a fat, sleek, good-natured, old brown god receives the prayers and homage of all who seek him to ask for a long life. His shrine is well patronized, and the offering-box was well filled with "cash." In the public pond, we saw freaks and crosses of Chinese breeding, tiny, moderate, and mammoth in size. There were fan-tailed and tailless, wall-eyed and pink-eyed members of the golden finny tribe.

The section devoted to silk weavers is very interesting; and it is wonderful to see the beautiful fabrics produced from the rude looms used, many of which are no better made than those in use by our weavers of rag-carpets thirty years ago. The shuttles are passed back and forth by hand, and yet the texture is marvellously fine, smooth, and even, and the patterns, in stripes, checks, and brocades, are remarkable for the fidelity in repetition of design.

Just inside of the middle gate, in the south wall of the old city, we come to the court of the old temple of the "five genii," — an old pile, where the five gods hold court and receive the homage, incense, and offerings of the devout; while behind them loiters a crowd of filthy attendants, who devote their energies to smoking, sleeping, and staring at whoever enters the temple. Near by is the "Bare Pagoda," so named from the fact that its outside casing, or veneer, has fallen away, leaving its rough, time-worn old walls bare. Great patches and fissures have been made in its walls by the ravages of time and the elements, and a monster tree is now growing from its summit.

The Confucian temple, not far away, is another fine specimen of Chinese religious architecture. It is bare of gods and decorations. Little stone and lacquered wooden tablets of ancestors are set upon the altar, in the holy of holies, where the people come to worship and burn incense-sticks.

Further on, we see a fine specimen of the Chinese religious monumental order of architecture, in a good state of preservation. It is nine stories in height, and can be seen from a great distance. The view from its top includes the city and the surrounding country for many miles. Below us is the great city with its narrow and crooked streets, lanes, and alleys, thousands of tiled roofs, "bare" and "five-storied" pagodas, a few old trees, and the city walls. On the north are the hills with frowning forts upon them to awe the citizens and keep them in subjection, on the east lie the great, undulating plains, that lose themselves in the

THE BARE PAGODA, CANTON, CHINA.

"White Cloud Mountains," and little truck gardens, with their busy men, women, and boys, working about in quaint costumes. The graves, the tombs, the quiet houses of the dead, and the Pearl River, creeping like a huge muddy serpent between Canton and Honan.

After descending from the Pagoda, we paid our respects to the "Sleeping Buddha." He occupies a shrine in a dark old temple, which is no cleaner than others, but

CHINESE PUNISHMENT, — IN THE CAUGUE.

seems to be a fitting home for the "sleeping intercessor," — the eastern "Rip Van Winkle," — who must be aroused by the beating of a large drum, which is suspended in the temple from a heavy ornamental frame.

We visited the prison, which is a long bamboo shed with thatched roof, resembling an immense pig-pen rather than a place for the detention and reformation of human beings. We saw many horrible specimens of the Chinese criminal class, some being loaded with chains, some with their limbs manacled in the stocks, and others wearing the caugue about their throats, so that they could neither feed themselves, nor lie down to sleep.

The floor was covered with filthy straw, upon which the refuse of the place was dropped. The place and the people in it were extremely dirty, and the air was foul and disgusting. There was only a little hole near the top of the hut for the escape of the foul air.

Along the street, outside of the prison, long rows of rickety tables were placed, at which the natives were playing their favorite gambling game of "fan-tan." The money on the tables was mostly in "cash," — about one tenth of a cent, but in some cases it was less. They have a baser metal than the brass cash, and when they desire to use a coin of less value, they break one of these and weigh the parts in little pan-scales.

The court is near the prison, and as some cases were soon to be tried, we concluded to see the proceedings. We were ushered into the judge's retiring-room by an attendant, where we indulged in cigars to freshen up a little after our prison experience. Soon the court convened. A man in a tall, pointed hat beat a gong several times. His Celestial Honor took his seat on the bench, behind a sort of counter, a boy standing on his right, a little in the rear. Two fine-looking Chinese court reporters took seats behind two little tables (one on the right and one on the left of the court), and began making notes. A poor fellow, ragged and bruised and bound in chains, was dragged into the room by a fierce-looking jailer, who shook and pushed the poor coolie as though he were endeavoring to escape. As a matter of fact, the prisoner was as meek as a lamb. The officer made all this noise to show "His Honor" how zealous he was.

The prisoner was made to prostrate himself before the court, on one side of the room, while a witness was put in the same position on the other side, and these positions they maintained throughout the trial. While we could not understand all of the Chinese, we knew that it was a knotty case, for the boy at the judge's elbow was kept busy emptying, filling, and lighting his pipe. His Honor would take a whiff or two, look very wise, and hand the pipe back to the boy. I am not sure whether our presence had anything to do with the form of the trial or not, but I have understood that it is not usual for " foreign devils " to be

A KNOTTY CASE IN OLD CANTON.

present at the sessions of this court. This man was accused of a small theft, and was sentenced to wear the caugue, with his offence placarded on his breast for thirty days.

We next visited the "Temple of Horrors," which is very interesting as a graphic depository of the infernos, in miniature, of every creed under heaven. The spirits of some of our own ancient churchmen might stroll through the ghastly compartments and shake their sulphurous forms in glee as they beheld these miniature people undergoing every degree of torment. Some are having the flesh torn from their writhing bodies, or their tongues pulled out with red-hot pincers; others are being cut in two by slow-moving saws; boiled in oil; strangled; torn limb from limb; tortured on the rack; trodden to death under men's feet; or tossed into the everlasting pit by his Satanic Majesty, who is represented as a hideous-looking creature, in red clothes, with horns, club-feet, and a tail. This temple is in decay, and loses some of its horrible effectiveness from this fact; and if it is to continue to serve its purpose, believers in its utility must soon come to the rescue and burnish it.

The temple of the God of War is comparatively new, and is patronized by the military. It contains some fine old arms and banners, with other accoutrements and implements of war. A sacred gray horse and a half-dozen lazy priests share the beans that are contributed by the faithful; while the back part of the temple is occupied by a crowd of loungers who render the place noisome with the odor of cooking-food and tobacco-smoke.

The Mahometan mosque — a reminder of the little mosques about Cairo — is fast on the road to ruin. It was founded about A. D. 850 by the venturesome Arabians, who were in the habit of visiting and trading here. It is devoid of ornament, unless the dirty mats and "sacred spot," facing the "East," where the devout have knelt and prostrated themselves at the hour of prayer, can be called ornaments.

The examination hall is an open courtyard, lined on each side with little stall-like houses, not unlike two lines of bath-houses on some beach. Here the fate of aspirants for appointments and preferment for the district are settled. The candidates present themselves at stated times, and questions are given and answered. The papers do not bear the name of the candidate, but when finished he puts a mark or character upon them. When the examination is finished, he puts a corresponding character and his address upon a card, which he places in a receptacle prepared for it. When the papers have been examined and passed upon, the candidate is notified of the result.

The mint, a handsome modern building of European architecture, is situated outside of the eastern gate, and is operated under the authority of the governor of the province. The machinery used is of the latest design and make. Only subsidiary silver coins are made here. In design and finish, they are equal to any similar coins in the world, and are much sought after by the natives, who prefer them to the Hong-kong coins.

The Blind Men's Home, the Old Men's Home, the Old Women's Home, the Foundling Hospital, and the Leper's Village are praiseworthy charities, and do honor to the people who founded and support them.

A CANTONESE FAMILY.

Along the space between the old city walls and the lower river-front, on the site of the thirteen factories, or foreign residences, that were destroyed by the mob of 1856, a custom-house and hundreds of Chinese shops and booths have been erected; and it is here that we see the cosmopolitan side of Canton life, — the vast throngs of men, women, and children, of high degree and low; the merchant, the farmer, and the coolie; the people from the north and the people from the interior. The middle class jostle the beggar, when there is a scowl and a war of words, but they rarely come to blows. One little fellow, however, of about a dozen years, was coming along with a great basket of fish suspended from the end of a heavy pole which he bore upon one shoulder, and a lot of vegetables in a basket to balance it. The load was about as much as an able-bodied man would wish to carry. The youngster was lustily crying his wares, when he was run into by a great, awkward fellow, who sent the fish and green stuff in every direction. The boy threw down his pole and without much ceremony proceeded to thrash his big assailant in great style. A crowd soon gathered and hemmed them in, but the people would not let the big fellow strike the little one; and when the youngster had inflicted as much punishment as he chose, he quietly gathered up his wares and went down the street crying " Fish and radishes ! " while the crowd chased the big fellow off with jeers.

This section of the city is filled with little stands in front of the houses, where piles of Chinese goods are temptingly displayed for sale, — lanterns, printed cottons, caps, shoes, counterfeit Mexican dollars, porcelains, pipes, tobacco, and cheap Chinese novels. Cobblers and menders of clothes, fortune-tellers and coolies out of a job, congregate here and solicit trade; and there are restaurants and tiffin shops, where a full meal with all the trimmings can be had, in native style, from birds' nest soups, through all the stews and fries, to chow-chow dog and cat.

The pawn-shops, " the poor man's Pagodas," are massive granite towers, five and seven-storied square, shooting up from the more retired streets, where the distressed deposits the few valuables he may possess, and receives a fraction of their money value. Many people who have no homes — and there are a great many such in China — put the clothes of one season in these places on deposit until the next season, when they pay a fee and exchange the clothes. We found the floors of these towers packed with valuables and clothing that had been deposited as pledges for borrowed money. The government keeps a strict watch over these establishments, and I believe the charges are about six per cent. Whether that means for a week, a month, or a year, I could not learn.

Bankers and money-changers have little booths and stands along the thoroughfares, where they sell and exchange money, and many of them become very wealthy from small beginnings and the accumulations of many transactions. Large sums of money are made in exchange. Money is never changed as an accommodation. If a dollar is changed into cash, so many cash are deducted as the cost of the transaction, and this soon amounts to enough to be an object to these frugal people.

We were amused to see men and boys at work in a tobacco factory, cutting, or rather shaving tobacco. They were at work on large planes that were fixed in place, one end on the floor, the other elevated at about 45 degrees, with the cutting edge of the knife down. They pulled great hard bunches of the weed upwards, thus cutting it into very fine strips, resembling the fine cut used in the United States.

We visited the theatrical school-building; but the school was not in session, so we missed our chance of seeing the future stars of the Chinese Empire. The business in hand seemed to be the sale and hire of actors' and actresses' outfits and embroideries. The work was gorgeous, but we did not invest. In some of the shops in this section, we saw some beautiful filigree-work, in gold and silver, certain parts of which were filled in like mosaic-work with blue feathers of the king-fisher. Rice-paper pictures, painted fans, old and new jades, bronzes, gods, wood-carvings, china-ware, and paper-joss shops abound in this quarter, and it is interesting to loiter and watch the deft fingers of the cunning workmen as they fashion and finish their quaint wares.

Opium-smoking saloons are also to be found here, with their sickening odors and disgusting sights. Men and women are huddled about on filthy couches in all stages of the seductive intoxication, — some just falling into the dreamy state, others, perhaps, in the full enjoyment of

EXECUTION OF CHINESE REBELS.

dreams that rival a Monte Cristo; but to awaken later, and realize more horrors than were at first experienced.

In the new city, we jostle the same, never-ending stream of Celestial humanity as we stroll on, inspecting the fans, jadestone, and embroideries, the work of the gold-beaters, the rattan furniture, the ivory shops, and the French Cathedral, where Tartar troops continually guard the cross.

Outside the south gate, we stroll along the river's bank, where the same struggling, driving mass of humanity is pushing up or down the road; but the attraction for us lies in the thousands of boats that line the river's bank, — junks, sampans, and flower-boats, and hotel-like structures, gayly carved and painted in high colors, ornamented with bright lanterns and flowers (the pleasure-boats of the natives), — where feasts, music, and dancing are furnished. No expense is spared to make the Canton boats the finest that can be found on the Chinese coast.

The execution ground where condemned murderers and pirates are executed, is a sandy beach by the river's side, near the Mandarins' landing, and almost under the two temples. When an execution takes place, a company of Tartar troops, of the "banner army," form a line in the rear of the grounds. The condemned is led out to the ground, and is compelled to kneel and bend the head forward. The executioner, armed with a heavy, thick-backed cleaver, takes his place behind the condemned. At the signal he steps beside the man, and, taking the cleaver in both hands, hacks his head off. It is a barbarous sight. Sometimes several hacks are required before the head of the unfortunate is entirely severed from the trunk. One of these barbarous exhibitions suffices for a lifetime, for the scene haunts one for days, and is sometimes pictured in dreams.

HONAN

Honan, a suburb of Canton, situated on the opposite shore of the Pearl River, is the seat of many thriving industries, the most important of which is the tea trade. Many large tea hongs, where the leaves are received from the growers, and prepared and packed for their particular markets, are located here, and scenes, similar to those in other Chinese cities, are seen on every hand, —

similar open shops, with their quaint wares temptingly exposed to the passers-by. Similar crowds of impatient, hurrying human beings crowd the busy streets. In visiting the tea hongs, we see some curious processes, and learn some facts about the preparation of the fragrant leaves, whose decoctions have added so much to neighborhood gossip.

"Orange Peko" gets its fragrance by being mixed with Arabian Jessamine, and "Scented Caper" is scented with leaves of the "Orange Peko." Eighteen or twenty handfuls of leaves are placed in a large copper pan, moistened with water, and stirred by hand until sufficiently softened, when they are placed in coarse cotton bags, which are tightly fastened. These bags are then rolled about on the floor by men who hold on to wooden beams overhead, and move the bags with their feet. This rolling forms the leaves into curly pellets. When the bales are opened, the coarse leaves are separated from the fine ones, carefully fired, placed in wooden troughs, and cut up. They are then placed in paper-lined boxes, or chests, which are covered with thin sheets of lead. The paper is folded over, the lead soldered tight, the top of the chest nailed in place, and fancy paper is pasted all over it, to exclude the air and moisture. It is next carefully weighed, marked, and hurried off to market, as the first or "new crop" is the most desirable and brings the highest price.

Merchants always retain samples of their tea, and taste and test both flavor and quality before buying or selling. Tea-testing is a very important profession in the tea districts,—a fine art which requires much careful preparation. The successful "taster" must abstain from the use of all intoxicants, from tobacco, and from condiments that have a tendency to vitiate the senses of taste and smell, for on his acute perceptions and judgment the season's profits largely depend. The occupation is very trying to the

Temple of the Ocean Banners, Honan, Canton.

constitution, and is almost certain to break down the health of the taster if too long continued. Some celebrated tea-tasters have realized from $10,000 to $50,000 for a single season's profits.

The famous Har-Chwang-Sze, or " Temple of the Ocean Banners," is a magnificent pile of beautifully carved marble and stone, whose interior decorations are rich in scarlet and gold lacquers and wonderful wood-carvings. It is the finest and richest temple in this section of China, and has a hundred and eighty priests on its staff. Its patrons are fishermen and seafaring people, who come to its shrine, asking for good weather at sea and for a prosperous voyage, and who, on their return, bring the thank-offerings which swell its coffers.

Hundreds of women, girls, and boys find employment in the matting factories, where all is bustle, drive, and chatter. They prepare the straw, bleaching, dyeing, and weaving it, in rude looms, thus producing the beautiful white and figured mattings for which old Canton is so justly famous.

The green-ginger and fruit-packing establishments also give employment to thousands of these poor people, whom we saw engaged in assorting, scraping, peeling, and boiling the fruit, or root, in sugar; while others were just as busy filling, cooling, and sealing the little blue-and-white vase-like jars, that find their way to our tables with their rich delicacies.

The public flower-garden is rich in roses, peonies, and all tropical and semi-tropical flora, and the wonderful dwarfed specimens, — the rookeries, miniature streams, cascades, ponds, and waterfalls, which these patient toilers delight in producing.

From the outside, Canton appears to be a great expanse of hipped-tiled roofs, relieved by three pagodas, the square granite towers of the pawn-shops, a very few old trees, and the bamboo fire-signal stations, which rise like cages in the air. Around the northern side of the city, bare hills, thirteen hundred feet high, are almost covered with tombs and graves. The suburbs of Canton are as interesting as the city itself, and cover a space of about ten miles in length.

There are one hundred and twenty-three Buddhist temples in Canton, but they are gaudy and more noticeable for their filth than for architectural beauty.

The climate is remarkably healthy, and Canton is singularly free from fevers and epidemics; but catarrh and asthma are common. The heat in summer is oppressive, and the winter nights are treacherous. The northeast monsoon blows from October until March, after which the southeast monsoon sends up the mists and fogs. The average temperature throughout the year is about 70° Fah., and the average rainfall is about 71 inches.

The people of this old city are noted for their hostility to foreigners, and serious disturbances might occur on any day if foreign visitors would notice the insults offered to them, but by " not seeing," bad feelings are allayed and disturbances warded off. The foreign residences have, more than once, been attacked by mobs who could only be suppressed by force of arms. Canton was besieged by a rebel force in 1844-45, and it is believed that after the repulse more than one million people perished in the province.

The city is admirably located for a great commercial port, and for centuries it has been a noted place. Its nearness to the sea, its central location, the prevalence of the monsoons, and the fact that the millions of people who reside upon its tributary territory can be reached by the rivers and canals, seem to assure its situation.

The Arabs were well acquainted with the place and visited it in the ninth century, bringing their religion and building their mosques. In the sixteenth century the Portuguese came in for a share of the trade. In the seventeenth century they were followed by the Dutch, and from the latter part of the same century the enterprising East India Company carried on an immense traffic with this port.

At sunset all business ceases, the city gates are closed, and the bustling, busy streets are quiet and deserted. The general feeling of distrust and insecurity among the na-

THE WATER-FRONT OF OLD CANTON.
The Junks all in for the Chinese New Year.

tives renders it necessary to barricade every shop at dusk, and to put it in condition to withstand a siege.

The first sign of the Chinese New Year is the gathering of the junks, which come in from all directions. New scarlet flags are thrown to the breezes, and scarlet papers, having happy passages from the sages painted upon them, are pasted on bows and masts. Houses are cleaned and made bright, and the scarlet papers are pasted on walls, doorposts, and lintels. Cakes and sweets, and all the toothsome wonders of the Celestial culinary art, are produced. The coolie stops work, and the people appear in their best clothes. Settlements are made and debts are paid, so that all business transactions are settled and closed. Occasionally a cracker or bomb is exploded, like the lonely blasts on the tin horn by our urchins at home, — just to let the world know the New Year is coming. As night advances, the din increases. Sampans and boats move down and up the river, with crackers firing, rockets ricochetting, drums and gongs beating, and the whole river and plain becomes a pandemonium of glaring lights, sounds, and fires.

Suddenly a great sheet of red flame bursts forth and licks and lashes the heavens, — dense black smoke and volumes of hissing sparks curl and fly. The great guns boom, the bells ring out the fearful alarm, and the people shriek and curse and run. A lighted cracker had fallen among some waste stuff, and for three mortal hours the cruel, relentless, massive tongues of red flame snapped and roared and cracked; while through and above them, myriads of bright hissing sparks arose and danced and fell. High up in the heavens, a great bank of black smoke curled and rolled itself about, and hung like an awful pall over the doomed place. The revellers were appalled, the noises ceased, and the river regained its usual quiet. The voices of the firemen and the shrieks of the women could be heard amid the roaring flames, and the pulse-beating sounds from the great steam-pumps which were sending streams of water from the river-front. The efforts of the stalwart fellows, with their little wooden hand-pumps and buckets, and the help of the great streams from the steamers, were unavailing. Thousands of houses and their contents had gone up in the flames which were urged on by the cruel monsoon. Acres of shapeless heaps of bricks marked the spot, and ten thousand men, women, and children were

homeless wanderers on this festal night, this New Year's
Eve.

> "The world laughs with him who laughs,
> But he who weeps must weep alone."

After the lull, a bomb, a cracker, a rocket, gong, or drum, and the revelry was renewed upon the river. Bombs and rockets were sent up from boat and city, and cracked and flashed and sparkled in the air. The jolly mirth of the glad went on through the night; and the next ten nights and days were given over to feasting and drinking and joy for the glad New Year. All business, public and private, is suspended, for these days the mails, the banks, everything, is at a standstill during the holiday.

Canton has maintained her own army and navy, made and repelled attacks, and exercised all the functions of sovereignty in her own rights, in the years that are gone. The chief exports from Canton are tea, silk, sugar, and cassia, and the chief imports are cotton, woollen, and metal goods, food stuffs, opium, and kerosene.

The total value of the trade is $42,280,752, of which $22,328,632 are imports. The domestic trade is enormous, but no account of it is kept. There are 3,316 vessels entering and clearing the port each year.

CHAPTER XXII

THE GOVERNMENT AND PEOPLE OF CHINA

KUANG-SII, Emperor of China, is the son of Prince Ch'un, the seventh son of the Emperor Tae Kuang, and is a cousin of the late Emperor Tung Chi, who died from small-pox on January 12, 1875. The present Emperor is the ninth of the Tartar dynasty of Tu-tsing, "Sublime Purity," which succeeded the native Ming dynasty in 1644. There is no law of hereditary succession to the throne, each Emperor naming his successor from among the members of his own family. The late Emperor, dying suddenly, in the eighteenth year of his age, did not designate a successor, but by an arrangement directed by the Empress Dowager and Prince Ch'un, the son of the latter was declared Emperor by proclamation, of which the following is a translation : —

"Whereas, His Majesty the Emperor has ascended upon the Dragon to be a guest on high, without offspring born to his inheritance, no course has been open but that of causing Tsai Tien, son of the Prince Ch'un, to become adopted as the son of the Emperor Wêng Tsung Hien (Hien Fung), and to enter upon the inheritance of the great dynastic line as Emperor by succession. Therefore, let Tsai Tien, son of Yih Huan, the Prince of Ch'un, become adopted as the son of the Emperor Wêng Tsung Hien, and enter upon the inheritance of the great dynastic line as Emperor by succession."

The Emperor Kuang-Sii assumed the government in February, 1887, was married to Yeh-ho-na-la, a niece of the Empress Dowager on February 26, 1889, and ascended the throne on March 4, 1890.

The government of China is that of an absolute monarchy. The Emperor is spiritual as well as temporal lord and master of his people. He is regarded as the representative of Deity, "the Son of Heaven," and he alone with his ministers can perform the great religious ceremonies as High-Priest. No other ecclesiastical authority is recognized in the state, neither is any priesthood maintained at the public cost.

The Constitution, or fundamental laws of the Empire, is recorded in the Tu-tsing Huei-tien, "Collected Regulations of the Great Pure Dynasty," in which the government of the state is based upon that of the family.

The Interior Council has supreme authority in the administration of the government, and is composed of four members, two of Tartar and two of Chinese origin, with two legal advisers from the Han-lin, "Great College," whose duty it is to see that nothing is done contrary to the laws of the Empire as contained in the "Collected Regulations," and in the books of Confucius. The members of the Interior Council are called Ta-Hsis-sz, Ministers of State, and they are assisted by the Li-Pu, eight boards of government, who are under their immediate control. Each of these eight boards of government is presided over by a Tartar and a Chinese, and a censor must always be present at their meetings.

The Boards are: 1. The Board of Civil Appointments; 2. The Board of Revenue; 3. The Board of Rites and Ceremonies; 4. The Military Board; 5. The Board of Public Works; 6. The Board of Criminal Jurisdiction; 7. The Board of Admiralty; 8. The Board of Foreign Affairs.

The Tu-cha-Yuan, " Board of Public Censors," is independent of the government, and theoretically is above the administration. It consists of about fifty members, and has two presiding officers, one of Manchu and the other of Chinese birth. By ancient custom of the Empire, all the members of this Board have the right of presenting remonstrances to the Emperor. The divisibility of the absolute power takes from it much of its danger, and public opinion, backed by the protests of the censors, prevents the Emperor from violating the rights of the subject. The censors have often protested with a freedom and vigor worthy of all praise.

According to Confucius and his followers, the Empire is solely under the guidance of Heaven : " Heaven is the only master of the nation." The sovereignty is a holy mission committed to an individual for the good of the people, and it is withdrawn from him when he shows himself unworthy of the high trust. In times of revolution, the conflicts have been terrible until some decided advantage has been gained, and the people, believing that Heaven had withdrawn its smiles from its adopted son and shown the sign of a new power, have submitted to that authority without further question.

The Emperor, being the Son of Heaven, is father of his people, and has a right to the worship of his subjects. He is absolute, can make and abolish the laws, make or degrade officials, and has the power of life and death. He is the source of all power and authority, and can command the entire revenues of the Empire. The Emperor is sole proprietor of the soil and can recover possession for non-payment of taxes, or by confiscation, — for crimes committed against the state. The sovereign can transmit his power to whomsoever he pleases, as there is no law of inheritance to restrain him ; and, being the father of an immense family, he delegates his powers to his ministers, who, in turn, appoint the inferior officers of the government. This division of authority extends downwards to groups of families, of which the fathers are the natural heads, and just as absolute within their sphere.

The Emperors, after death, like the ancient Egyptian Kings, are subject to a trial, the verdict of which, coupled with their names, goes down to future generations. By this means they become known in history, and the verdict gives the estimate of their character.

The literary aristocracy is an ancient institution which has become firmly established, and gives the government all its real and direct influence. Its numbers are increased each year by the examinations. Its members are a privileged class,— almost the only nobility recognized; and it is considered to be the nerve and mainstay of the Empire, and appointments to civil officers can only be made from among its members, under well-established laws. Any Chinese may present himself for examination for the third degree. Those who are successful may take the second, which opens the way to the minor offices. Those who aspire to the higher offices must have been successful for the first degree.

The only hereditary titles of nobility acknowledged in China are those of the Imperial family and the descendants of Confucius, to whom certain prerogatives and a small pension are allowed. They have the right to wear a scarlet or yellow corselet, plumes of peacock feathers in the hat, and to have a certain number of chair-bearers, but they cannot be appointed to any office without having taken the literary degrees. For the most part, they live under the government and control of a private tribunal, which has cognizance of their behavior; and, as a rule, they live in idleness on the small allowance granted to them by the government, being too indolent to prepare for the examinations, and too proud to do any useful thing.

They spend their time in swaggering and strutting about in their tattered finery, to the infinite disgust of their neighbors.

Distinguished civil and military officers may be rewarded with the rank and titles of koung, heon, phy, tze, and nau, which about equal those of duke, marquis, count, baron, and knight. These are not hereditary, and give no rights to the son of the person rewarded, but they may be carried back to the ancestors. An officer who has been raised in rank cannot perform the ancestral rites of his family in a suitable manner unless his ancestors have been decorated with a corresponding or a higher title. For a son to have higher rank than his father would undermine the principle of filial piety, and attack the fundamental laws of the Empire.

All offices, civil and military, are divided into nine grades or ranks, — "khion-ping." These ranks are distinguished by buttons or balls, about the size of a pigeon's egg, worn on the centre of the crown of the official hat. The balls are of plain red coral for the first grade, a carved blue stone for the second, a translucent deep coral stone for the third, a pale blue for the fourth, crystal for the fifth, an opaque white stone for the sixth, and a gilt and wrought copper ball for the seventh, eighth, and ninth grades. Each order is divided into two classes, — active officials and supernumeraries, or " honorary ; " but the decorations are the same for both. All the officials included in these grades are called "konang-fu." The term "mandarin" is unknown to the Chinese, it being derived from "mandra," an abbreviation of the title "commander," which the Portuguese are believed to have applied to Chinese officials in the early days. The administration of affairs is divided into three parts, — that of the Empire, of Peking, and of the Provinces.

Filial piety is believed to have held together this nation of over four hundred millions of people for ages. Everything is done to increase the strength of this sentiment, — to make it a passion among the people that will serve as the moral support of public and private life. Every virtuous action is referred to as an act of filial piety, and every crime is treated as filial disobedience. "To be a good subject is to be a good son; to be a bad subject is to be a bad son." Every good action reflects credit upon the parents and honors them, while every bad action brings dishonor upon them. Chinese parents are looked up to as superior beings, and they are called gods by very high authority. The Sacred Edict, "Shing-gu," forbids the people to gad about to the temples, worshipping the idols and flattering the gods, but teaches them to remember the two household gods at home — father and mother — and serve them. Great stress is laid upon these in the education of the young. They are instructed in these from their earliest years, and any outrage committed against a parent is punished with death. The father has absolute power of life and death over his children.

The laws of China are severe. For small offences, corporal punishment is inflicted, generally with the bamboo, and serious crimes are nearly always punished with death. Forms and ceremonies receive close attention, and every action of life may be inquired into by the authorities. The courts are very severe upon disturbers of the peace and upon thieves. The ordinary punishments are fines, blows on the face, the bastinado, the caugue, the iron cage, exile into Tartary, and death by strangulation or decapitation. Rebels and parricides are cut in pieces, and pirates are decapitated. Punishments are usually inflicted swiftly, except the punishment of death, which must be approved by the Emperor.

Women are in a degraded condition. They are not permitted to sit at table, or to eat with men. When walking, the woman follows the man, who talks to her over his shoulder. It is said that about one woman in ten thousand can read. There are good schools and colleges for boys, but no provision is made for girls; even the birth of a girl child is looked upon as a misfortune. The wife is inferior to her husband except in her domestic position; but if she arrives at old age, her sons and their wives are entirely subject to her, and unless she has a very sweet disposition, she makes the unfortunate daughters-in-law pay dearly for her own rough experiences.

For a long time it was believed that such charitable institutions as I have noted in old Shanghai and Canton were peculiar to Christian lands and peoples, but the dictates of our common humanity caused their foundation in this country many centuries ago.

The manners, customs, language, religion, and dress of the Chinese mark them as a peculiar people, who are very conservative and dread changes of any kind. They reached a very high state of civilization ages ago, but their further progress was in some way arrested, and until very recently they actually retrograded. They were acquainted from very early times with printing, the mariner's compass, gunpowder, the circulation of the blood, and many arts, but their use of these was restricted. They do not think it possible to be wiser than their fathers were. They have very little sympathy with genius or originality, and talent is strangled by conservatism. They are a nation of classic scholars, indoctrined in old methods of the dead past, and they expend their abilities in memorizing and moralizing upon the ancient maxims. While the world has been advancing with giant strides, China has been only creeping along, — and scarcely that. Some innovations have been forced upon her, and others she has adopted in a half-hearted manner.

After their subjugation by the Tartars, the Chinese were compelled to change their dress and to wear the queue.

Government and People of China

Many patriotic Chinese preferred death to this degradation, but now the queue has become their most cherished ornament. A few of China's great men have been struggling for advancement in the lines of western sciences, and some young men have been sent abroad to study these subjects. Efforts have been made to establish banking and commercial houses with foreign connections. The old wooden war-junks are being displaced by coast-defence vessels, steel cruisers, and torpedo boats. The army is exchanging its tactics, pikes, jingals, and banners for better methods and modern rifles. The official dress is being modified. Extensive dock-yards and iron-works of various kinds have been introduced, and the printing-press and sewing-machines are working their way into the country.

Here and there, an innovation that proves itself useful and good is adopted; but the changes are slow, and so few that only a close observer notes them. A ceremonious politeness, which seems born of distrust, pervades all conditions of society, — even while the pleasantest words are spoken. A mother is called the " countenance of mercy," a father, the " countenance of severity," and a daughter, the " thousand pieces of gold." The people are vain of their personal appearance and attire. Even the coolie becomes one of the politest of men when well dressed. He swaggers, with umbrella and fan in hand, and rivals a Japanese in the profusion of his bows and in the elegance of his behavior with his acquaintances. The Chinese are quiet, orderly, industrious, and punctual, but there appears to be always among them an undercurrent of insincerity and mutual distrust.

They are a nation of born traders. Having arranged their wares in the most attractive fashion, they patiently wait for a customer, always with an eye to the betterment of their fortunes. The smallest profit is not neglected, and their greatest enjoyment is to count up the profit-and-loss account in the evening, behind barricaded doors, and to find the profit side the greater. Trade, traffic, and filial piety are taught to the children from their earliest infancy. They are given small coins and taught their value and importance. They are so well trained that it is always safe to send them to the shops, for they will never suffer themselves to be cheated. They are wide awake and knowing. The large commercial and banking houses are remarkable for their fidelity to their engagements, — their word is their bond, and may be relied upon implicitly. No matter what the loss may be, though it may bring ruin upon them, an agreement, once made, is adhered to at all hazards.

The only legal coinage existing in China are the subsidiary silver coins made in Canton, and a little round piece of copper alloy, called "tsein," and by foreigners, "cash." The tsein, or cash, have a square hole through their centres so that they can be strung together. One thousand of them are nominally worth one Mexican dollar, but their actual value varies with the rates of exchange. Frequently thirteen hundred and even fifteen hundred tsein are given in exchange for the dollar. The Mexican silver dollar is well known to the people, and they prefer it to any other money; but bank-bills of the prominent banks in Shanghai and Hong-kong are received in the large cities. The Chinese are very particular about the money they receive. As a rule, they carry little balances about with them, and weigh and test every piece of money before the transaction is closed. Some of these tsein are made of a brittle base metal that can be broken, in case a smaller denomination than one tenth of a cent is needed.

The tsein is of great use in many of their small transactions; and a few peanuts or melon seeds, a dozen fried beans, a cabbage leaf, a cup of tea, a segment or two of an orange, and many other small articles may be had for one or two of these small coins. It is with a melancholy interest that we note the thrifty housewife of some poor toiler, counting from her little string of cash the two or three required to purchase the little things, just enumerated, to provide her husband variety with his rice.

The Chinese have no division of time corresponding to our weeks, consequently they have nothing which corresponds to our Sunday; but there are numerous religious and semi-religious observances, some of which are grotesque in the extreme. As a rule, the Chinese worship at the tablets and shrines in their own homes, and only visit the temples when they feel particularly in need of consolation. Confucianism and several forms of Buddhism are the most prevalent religions in China; but the government does not give active support to any system.

The Feast of Lanterns, when every town, village, and house is illuminated with lanterns and gayly decorated in colors, is one of their most solemn observances, in which the whole people participate.

The Chinese belong to the Mongolian race. They are of shorter stature and slighter build than Americans, and are much inferior to them in physical endurance. While there are certain marked characteristics distinguishing the Chinese from all other people, it is a mistake to suppose that to know one you know them all. The dialect, manners, and customs change in almost every town; and a man from the north is as much a stranger in one of the southern or interior provinces as if he came from America. The countenance, certain national prejudices, the mode of thought, and the written language are remarkably alike, but there are great differences in dialect, manners, customs, and dress. It must be remembered that this vast country is made up of a number of kingdoms that have been separated under various rulers, and governed by their own legislation. Although they have been more than once united, they have never so closely assimilated that the different elements were not manifest.

The beginning of China's history is lost in the obscurity of antiquity with no traces of its origin. Other nations have some traditions, folk-lore, monuments, and later history which furnish data for tracing growth and progress in civilization, but unless these can be solved from the radicals of their remarkable written characters, all seems to be lost in China.

The cultured classes have always adhered to the doctrines of Confucius, while the masses have followed the teachings of Buddha. The former is an intellectual feast; the latter appeals to the senses.

Four thousand years ago, China was called Heaven, and the ruler called himself God. The business of the chief officers was to light, warm, and fertilize this Heaven; and they dressed and assumed titles corresponding to the duties of their offices. One represented the sun, another the moon, and others the planets with which they were acquainted. There was also the master of mountains, of rivers, of forests, and of fields,—a pantheon of gods. Supernatural authority was conceded to them, and the government worked beautifully,—for themselves; but the appearance of comets and eclipses, which these big little gods had not foretold and could not account for, ruined their popularity. Wars and rebellions changed this government to the feudal system, and that to the monarchy. The Chinese have had long and bloody religious and political wars.

The doctrines of Confucius balance the imperial power, and may be called the Constitution of China; while the system of examinations for literary degrees and its appointments to office has put the government into the hands of the educated, and made the unlearned subject to the learned. The Tartars, the cold-blooded men from the

Government and People of China 387

north, have frequently set this law aside; but it always resumes its sway, as the Chinese prefer the rule of the pen to that of the sword.

The Chinese have changed their forms of government, and have tried various political combinations. Their history shows about the same experiences as that of most old nations. In the twelve hundred years following the year 420 A. D., there were fifteen changes of dynasty, each accompanied by terrible revolutions, accomplished by the bloody extermination of the families dethroned.

According to the official reports, the population of China is 405,000,000, one third of the human race. This population, upon an area of 1,600,000 square miles, gives about 263 inhabitants to each square mile. The general appearance of China indicates a higher proportion of inhabitants than in any other country. The towns, roads, and rivers fairly swarm with human beings, and there are more towns and cities of hundreds of thousands and millions of inhabitants than in any other country. The laws provide for a system of registration, and severe punishment is awarded to delinquents. The population of China is arranged under four heads, — scholars, agriculturists, mechanics, and merchants. Stage-players, gamblers, beggars, convicts, outlaws, and some other classes are considered social outcasts.

The steady flow of emigration from China is a very strong indication of the condition of the country. About ten millions Chinese are located in foreign countries. They are found in large numbers in Korea, Japan, Hong-kong, the Philippine Islands, Java, the Eastern Archipelago, Cochin-China, Australia, Africa, the Sandwich Islands, on the western coast of Central and South America in the West India Islands, in Canada, and in the United States.

Without the wonderful, patient, unceasing industry one sees on every hand, it would be impossible to find the means of supporting life for such an immense population.

Labor is carefully and abundantly bestowed upon all pursuits, — agriculture, manufactures, fisheries, and trade. Villages, valleys, and plains are carefully cultivated, irrigated, and fertilized; hills and mountains are terraced, and every square foot of ground that can be made productive is brought into use. The profession of agriculture has always been highly honored in this country. Confucius and the sages have celebrated and exalted it, and the Emperor never fails to render it homage. Towards the end of March, each year, the Emperor goes in state to the sacred field, accompanied by three princes of the blood royal and a retinue of nobles. After having offered sacrifice upon the earthen altar, he lays his sacred hands upon the plough and traces a furrow. The princes and nobles follow his example and complete the field. Then the Emperor, as high-priest, blesses the work and the field. In the provinces, a similar solemnity takes place, in which the Governor represents the Emperor.

Chinese agriculture is rarely conducted on a large scale, and the simplest tools are used. In the south, buffaloes are used in tilling the rice-fields; while in the north, oxen, horses, mules, and asses are used, and it is a common sight to see a woman drawing the plough while the husband walks behind and guides it. At the end of the furrow they both sit down to rest and smoke a little tobacco. The Chinese have a passion for fertilizing the soil, and this is carried to great extremes, anything and everything being used for the purpose. Even barbers save the shavings and croppings of hair to sell to farmers for enrichment of the soil. Farmers often use the spade in preference to the plough, and weeds are exterminated as their dearest foe. They keep their places in beautiful order, and the neat appearance of their little lands compels the admiration of all beholders.

In places too dry for rice, sweet yams and hemp will

be raised, and useful trees are planted in the corners, — the mulberry, the chestnut, or some pines, according to the turpentine.

The Chinese farmer is nervous about his crop, his margin of profit being so small that he cannot afford to lose. He binds several stalks of rice together to give mutual support against the winds, he arranges little sticks, with "charmed" strings attached, to drive the birds away, and each field has such a "scarecrow" as would frighten off any crow that lives. He watches the weather, and when it is too hot and dry he covers up his plants and irrigates the land; he raises water from one reservoir to another, and by means of bamboo pipes runs it about his fields, — even up the mountain's sides. Archimedes' screw-pumps, chain-pumps, and bucket water-wheels are his implements; his feet supply the power. These water-wheels are of extreme lightness, and have little half-round buckets attached, which take up the water and pour it into large tanks, from whence it is run over the fields.

The Chinese do not know what worn-out soil is. Some places are so fertile and are cultivated with so much care and skill that three or four crops a year are regularly gathered. When the first crop is well along, the second is sowed, or planted, in the intervals between the ridges, and it is very common to see two crops in the same field at the same time.

All the cereal and vegetable productions known in Canada, the United States, or Mexico, and many that we do not know, are found in China. Barley, wheat, buckwheat, and maize are cultivated in the northern part, and rice in the southern part, besides a score or more in both. Rice is not the principal food of the inhabitants throughout the Empire. Wheat, buckwheat, Indian corn, and barley, form the daily food of the people in the northern and western provinces, while rice is extensively used in the south.

The method of preparing these cereals for food is about the worst that could be conceived. Little bunches of dough are boiled in oil, or grease, and a half-cooked paste, strings of boiled dough, and rolls of putty-like material, that would be irritating to the stomach of an ostrich, are regarded as appetizing by these poor people.

The bamboo is the most useful tree that grows in China, and there are said to be sixty-three varieties. These differ in diameter, height, distance of separation of the rings or sections, color and thickness of the wood, and in the roots, branches, and leaves. The bamboo is used for houses, fences, furniture, water-pipes, and for hundreds of useful and ornamental purposes.

The beds of rivulets, marshes, and ponds are planted with tubers, water-lilies, and lotus. The cultivation of vegetables and fruits receives great attention and is encouraged by the government. Among the agricultural products of China we find, besides rice and tea, the wax-tree, camphor-tree, paper mulberry, the tallow-tree, varnish-tree, dragon's eye, star anise and jujube, many species of orange, cinnamon, ginseng, cotton, sugar, and tobacco, — the whole range of vegetables and fruits, and a very large number of flowers.

The manufacturing industry of the country is as wonderful as it is necessary for the support of the dense population. The silks, satins, crapes, embroideries, and gauzes have always attracted attention. The porcelains have only been equalled in the last few years, and the cottons and nankeens are famous. The many useful and ornamental articles of bamboo attract attention, and the furniture, instruments, and tools are commended for simplicity. The cunningly wrought and cast metal-work of the Chinese, their musical instruments, and their art in cutting and polishing hard stones are well known throughout the world. They are unrivalled in the production of unchanging colors, but they

Government and People of China 391

are losing their originality and cunning in this direction; many specimens of antique manufacture far surpass the work that can now be done.

Owing to the pressure of the dense population upon the means of subsistence, the Chinese eat anything and everything from which they can derive nutrition. Drunkenness is uncommon in China. Tea is universally used. They have native wines, but these are too expensive for common

CAMEL CARAVAN BOUND FOR PEKING, CHINA.

use. The people are temperate in all things, and unless working hard are content with two meals a day, — the morning rice at about ten A. M., and the evening rice at about five P. M. They do not use milk, butter, or cream. Dogs and cats are regularly sold for food. I have seen dogs skinned, hanging by the side of pigs and goats. Monkeys, sea-slug, and birds' nests are aristocratic dishes, and unhatched ducks and chickens are much sought after.

An immense internal traffic is carried on by means of the numerous rivers and canals, and over the roads. The roads are mere bridle-paths and tracks, and the transportation of goods over them — on the backs of horses and mules — is a very slow and difficult undertaking. In times of crop-failure and famine, the loss of life is fearful from the difficulty of getting food supplies to the sufferers.

The densely populated portion of China is comparatively level, and is remarkably well adapted for the construction of railroads; but the Chinese, even in view of the great advantages to be thus obtained, seem unable to conquer their prejudices against these conveniences. The little railroad, only about ten miles long, connecting Woosung with Shanghai, constructed by a foreign company in 1876, was bought out and destroyed by the Chinese during the next year. The Kaiping Coal Company built a line of railway from their mines to the canal bank, afterwards extending it through Tientsin to Fungchow, near Peking. This is being extended from Tientsin to Shan-hai-kwan, and is used for passenger as well as freight traffic. Railway lines have been authorized by the goverment to extend from New Chwang to Luisi, and from Hankow to Peking, but not much beyond the surveys has been accomplished.

All the important cities of the Empire are connected by telegraph and with the outside world by cable.

The public revenue of China is about three hundred and sixty millions of dollars, and there are almost always deficits, which must be covered by extraordinary taxation, although everything is cheap and the government has no large debts. The total number of foreign residents in China is 10,149, of whom 1,526 are natives of the United States.

The principal dependencies of China are Mongolia and Manchuria, which contain a larger Chinese than native population. Thibet is also a dependency, subject to the government at Peking, and a Resident is maintained at Lhassa. These dependencies have an area of two and one third millions of square miles, and a population of about twenty-three millions of inhabitants.

The Chinese army has a total of one million men, including 678 companies of Tartar troops, 211 companies of Mongols and native Chinese (militia) infantry. The first grand division is composed of Manchus, — the troops of the " Eight Banners," who garrison all the large cities and forts throughout the Empire. The second grand division is composed of Chinese, who, when not on active duty, live in their own homes, and follow some civil occupation. With the dense population of China, and the system of registration, the army can be increased almost indefinitely in numbers.

The army seems to be uncared for. It is badly organized, drilled, and armed; and while there are some well-fortified strongholds in China, it is not possible for them to withstand successfully a determined assault or siege by any modern army.

China evidently relies upon her vast numbers, her distance from any strong power likely to attack her, and the consummate ability of her ministers; but she cannot afford to slumber thus in the face of the possibility of mobs and revolutions within her own borders, and with neighbors who are restless under restraints which, they think, hinder their development and infringe upon the rights of their subjects. Diplomacy is always more potent when supported by an efficient force.

Until the year 1884 the Chinese navy consisted of a number of wooden war-junks, and a few small steel gunboats of foreign style, which were built at the Mamori dockyard, Shanghai, and at Foochow. Since that time, the navy has been greatly strengthened. The greatest improvement is found to be in the northern fleet, which now includes ten armored steel vessels of from 3,000 to 10,000 tons, having the most powerful machinery and modern breech-loading guns. There are also many steel cruisers, and gun and torpedo boats of the latest design; but the weak points of the navy are in its personnel. The officers of many of these splendid vessels are composed of natives and foreigners, and there is very poor discipline among the crews. The foreigners are to supplement the want of knowledge on the part of the natives, who do not comprehend the possibilities of the great fighting machines, and therefore do not absolutely command them. No doubt, in case of need, there will be some splendid fighting and heroic deeds, — for the Chinese are brave men, — but there will be faulty handling and manœuvring.

Port Li (changed from Lu-Shew-kow, in honor of the viceroy, Li Hung Chang), situated on the southern coast of Shing-king, has been built up as a great naval station and dock-yard for the new fleet, and has been strongly fortified. There is also an excellent school where young men are educated in modern naval science.

Every variety of soil and climate, in every degree of altitude, are to be found within the boundaries of China, — from the heated swamps below the sea-level to the region of everlasting frosts beyond the snow-line; and in these varied climates everything for the comfort of man can be produced.

Facility of communication by natural and artificial waterways is not exceeded in any country of the world, and the mineral resources rival those of our great western States. Iron ore is found in every province, and is so common that only the finest black magnetic ore is used; while gold, silver, tin, copper, and lead are plentiful.

Sharpened by competition, the mental capacities of the people are wonderful; their higher examinations are equal to any intellectual tasks set in America or Europe. Their statesmen hold their own with any in the world, and their

Government and People of China

merchants gain ground over those of other nations. Their common people are painstaking, shrewd, and docile, and have great love of order and respect for authority. Education among the males is common, and they possess all the factors requisite for success. This people have always been the ruling race in the far East, but lost their prestige by failing to keep up with modern improvements. It is not characteristic of the Chinese to remain stationary or to move slowly, but it is the result of circumstances, — the policy of their rulers.

They have adopted some improvements that commend themselves. The Buddhist religion is an importation from India, and quite a number of Chinese are Mahometans. Nearly two thousand years ago the decimal system of notation was introduced by the Buddhists, and they changed the ancient custom of writing from top to bottom for the Indian system of from right to left. They rearranged their calendar to accord with the ideas of western astronomers, and in recent years they have republished many works by foreign authors. Hospitals and free schools have flourished for more than a thousand years, and vaccination is practised by native physicians.

Extensive arsenals have been established at various places and there is a large powder manufactory at Tientsin. The government is purchasing and building powerful war vessels of the most improved types, and is beginning to arm and drill their forces after modern ideas.

The Chinese are a progressive people. They have all the mental, moral, and religious instincts of our nature, with a keen perception of things conducive to their interests and no prejudices to prevent their adoption. Some of the statesmen fully realize the conditions, — the trend of these times, — but appreciate the convulsions, overturnings, and untold misery to many millions of people that would necessarily follow the introduction of machinery, railways, and mining, on a large scale, or any radical change in dress, diet, and mode of life, and in their wisdom they choose to move slowly.

Capital and enterprise are not lacking. America does not possess all the millionaires; there are numbers of them in China. Notwithstanding the low wages, the millions of people who are crowded off the land to live in boats, glad to get ten cents a day for their labor, China has many multi-millionaires. Perhaps the richest man in the world is How Qua, a Cantonese, who is reputed to be worth a thousand millions of dollars.

There are thousands of Chinese who would be only too glad of an opportunity to start up a new order of things if they could get the permission of their government; but it is fortunate for the people of America and Europe that the economic and political conditions of China exist there, and that changes are made so slowly. If her people, accustomed as they are to their present social conditions, modes of life, and low wages, were to open up their mines and engage in manufacturing and mercantile pursuits on a large scale, they would soon become the exporters for the world. They could undersell all other people, and at the same time realize profits of which their people have never dreamed.

To-day, hampered as they are by manual labor, rattle-trap looms, and slow methods, they do a comparatively extensive manufacturing, commercial, and banking business, and regularly declare dividends of from ten to twenty per cent in gold.

THE CHINESE LANGUAGE

The Chinese is the only primitive language in use to-day. It is distinguished by its originality, and is used by more people than speak any other tongue. It is divided into two parts, the written and the spoken. The written

Government and People of China

language has no alphabet, but is a collection of written characters, representing ideas, or objects. The original characters were signs, or rather rude drawings, — pictures which represented objects. There were two hundred and fourteen of these, some for the heavens, others for the earth, — for man, the parts of the body; domestic animals; the horse, the ox, the dog; plants, trees, birds, fish, metals, etc. As their experiences enlarged, new wants made themselves felt, the language needed to be expanded, and a new arrangement made. The forms of the rude drawings were changed, but the primitive strokes were retained; and with these have been composed all the characters. By the combinations of the original characters were formed thousands of arbitrary sounds.

Natural objects are classed under the animal, tree, or plant which was the type of the original characters. The fox and the wolf were referred to the dog, and the hoofed animals to the horse, etc. By their ingenious method, they formed real natural families. The name of every creature is made up of two parts, one denoting the kind, the other relating to the species, — indicating the peculiarities of shape, the habits, or the use that can be made of the object.

It would appear very difficult to represent abstract ideas and acts of the understanding by such a system, but the difficulties have been ingeniously met. Two pearls, one beside the other, express the idea of a friend, because it is difficult to find two pearls alike. To express anger, a heart surmounted by a slave is represented. There are great numbers of characters, the analysis of which is very interesting; but for many of the words, the characters are arbitrary. The whole number of characters amounts to about forty thousand, but less than one third of that number are used. The characters are written one above the other, in a vertical line, beginning at the right of the page.

When the words are correctly intonated and properly modulated, the speech is musical.

The Chinese language has no grammatical construction. There are some well-understood rules by which sentences are constructed and words placed in proper apposition to other words in the same sentence; but the verb has no mood, tense, person or inflection of any kind; the noun has neither gender, number, nor case; and a word is substantive, verb, or adjective, singular or plural, masculine or feminine, according to its position, or connection, in the sentence. The meaning of a passage can be determined only by close attention to the relative position of the words in each sentence, and by a knowledge of the idioms. The forty thousand written characters are expressed by about four hundred and eleven vocables; and many characters, when pronounced, have precisely the same sound to an unpractised ear. To avoid ambiguity, and as far as possible to distinguish one character from another in common conversation, the Chinese have a system of tones, so that each vocable is capable of being pronounced in six or eight different ways; and another method of clearly expressing their meaning is the combination of two words, having relation to each other in point of signification.

HONG-KONG.

CHAPTER XXIII

HONG-KONG, CHINA

HAVING taken the last picture and the last stroll through the labyrinth of crazy streets and quaint shops of old Canton, and having said good-bye to the dear friends on Shamien, we retraced our seventy-five miles of river navigation through the "obstructions," the "Tiger's Mouth," and the "Lymoon Pass," and dropped our anchors in the green waters of Hong-kong harbor, — off Victoria, the capital and chief town of the colony. We were soon surrounded by hundreds of brown, gayly decked sampans, with their picturesque crews of women, girls, and children, shrill-voiced and barefooted, who live the days through, sculling, sailing, and steering; driving sharp bargains with the sailors, and gossiping with their neighbors.

Great war vessels, merchant steamers, sailing craft, and junks crowd the harbor; while the upper end of the island is lined with junks that swarm with coolies engaged in unloading and loading, — merrily singing as they toss off great loads of rice, or coal, or some huge piece of machinery.

Hong-kong is mountainous, and shows volcanic origin in its low, granite ridges, bleak, barren valleys, narrow strips of level coast-line, and lofty overhanging precipices, where the monsoons cut and grind and burn. Here the typhoon shrieks its horrid wails as it lashes mighty ships, frail junks, and little sampans to destruction; or a pall of fog hangs between the granite hills and the sea. The prospect is wild, dreary, and monotonous, with barren, treeless hills, where no natural green thing smiles back to the sun in tender acknowledgment of goodness.

Hong-kong is one of the Ladrone ("Thieves") group of islands, so named for having been a place of resort for pirates and thieves in "the good old times." It is situated seventy-five miles southeast of Canton, in latitude 22°4′ north, and longitude 114° 6′ east. It was ceded to the British in 1841, to be used as a depot for repairing and refitting their vessels, and as a place of refuge for distressed seafaring people. It is irregular in form, about ten miles and a half long, and has a breadth varying from two to five miles, with an area of about thirty square miles. It is separated from the mainland of China by a body of water known as Hong-kong Roads, which narrows down to about one quarter of a mile in width at the Lymoon Pass.

On the southern coast, two bold strips of land extend into the sea and form the harbors of Deep Bay and Tyam Bay, and the little island of Aberdeen shelters a fine harbor which is supplied with fine dock-yards and extensive machine-shops.

Hong-kong, China

Victoria, the capital and commercial port, is situated on the northwest end of the island. It is laid out with fine wide roads and terraces. The residences occupied by Europeans are large and commodious, having, with their broad verandahs and beautiful artificial gardens, an air of elegant refinement. The houses of the Chinese are of brick, covered with mortar, and are much superior in ap-

THE QUEEN'S ROAD, HONG-KONG.

pearance to houses found in the Chinese cities; but they are not suited to the climate, being damp and unhealthy, and breeding malaria and fevers.

Society is ceremonious and exacting, and is led by the occupants of the government house, who maintain a little court after British fashion.

The city of Victoria extends for about three miles along the bay shore, and thence up the sides of the hills, where it loses itself in terrace on terrace, which are reached by winding roads, or broad flights of granite steps. Here and there a lovely villa or mansion marks the boundary, and the hotels and groups of elegant homes that comb "Mount Austin" reach down to meet the Queen-named town.

The colony is ruled by a royal Governor, with an Executive Council, composed of the Colonial Secretary, the Commander of the troops, the Attorney-General, and the Auditor-General. The Legislative Council, presided over by the Governor, is composed of all the members of the Council (except the Commander), with the addition of four unofficial members, who are appointed by the crown, on the recommendation of the Governor.

The Praya, the road along the bay-front, extends from the parade to the extreme northwest end of the town, and is lined with fine shops and storehouses, while its roadway is crowded with busy men and women. The Queen's Road is lined on both sides with fine shops, filled with beautiful and rare wares from every part of China, Japan, India, and Africa. Silks, crapes, gauzes, cabinets, ivories, lacquers, porcelains, precious stones, rare filigree in gold and silver, and cunning work in camel's hair and fine wools, are lavishly displayed to tempt the traveller; and the roadway swarms with a motley crowd of Europeans, Jews, Japanese, Koreans, Mahometans, Hindoos, Malays, Javanese, Parsees, Sikhs, Cingalese, Negroes, half-castes, and everywhere that unfortunate Chinese coolie, — the drudge, the bearer of the world's loads and burdens.

The "Sikh" policeman, in dark blue, with immense scarlet turban, stands "attention" at the corner of the road. White-robed "ayahs" and Koreans stride from shop to shop, while the pedlers cry their wares. Everybody is talking in this great Babel. "Tommy Atkins," the high private, with cap on ear and switch in hand, swaggers up the road, the observed of all observers. A picturesque group of little musümes from "Dai Nippon" chaperone

Chinese and Hindoo maidens through the mazy road.
Parsees, Chinese, and Koreans discuss money, stocks, and
the latest rumors from Seoul. The Turk and the Javanese
hold a hot discussion. The childlike and bland Cingalese
unfolds his pack, and displays beautiful emeralds, moonstones,
cat's-eyes, sapphires, and diamonds that are worth a king's
ransom, but can be purchased for a few shillings; and the

THE WATER-FRONT, HONG-KONG, IN A FOG.

small boys in pigtails toss the shuttlecock with knee, heel,
and elbow.

Victoria has most of the modern improvements. Electricity, gas, and oil illuminate its streets. A cable-car line
extends up the side of the hills, some fourteen hundred feet,
to "Mount Austin," where summer houses and two fine
hotels have been erected, and water is abundantly supplied
from a reservoir holding seventy-five million gallons. The
water-front is being extended out into the bay three hundred
feet, where a massive granite retaining wall is being built.

The intervening space will be filled in with soil, to enlarge the narrow strip of level land upon which the business portion of the city is located.

The palaces of the Governor and the Bishop, the City Hall, the Cathedral, the Museum, the Exchange, the Hong-kong Hotel, the Club Germania, the Hong-kong Club, the Botanical Garden, the Hospitals, the Barracks, the

THE PARSEE CEMETERY IN THE HAPPY VALLEY, HONG-KONG.

Government dock-yard, the parade and recreation grounds, are all very interesting to visit, as well as the fine schools which range from the primary grades to the college, and are for both sexes and all conditions. The Bowen and Kennedy roads, and the aqueducts and military roads, that almost encircle the heights, are great engineering works. The English planted on this bold, barren rock, which nature hurled up from the bottom of the sea, their roads, their hedges, their gardens, and much quiet elegance, and this is their home.

"KUHLAN, 1855"

In a gloomy spot, at the foot of the hill where begins the deep cut to the Happy Valley, stands a monument commemorative of one of the few events in which Americans and Britons stood shoulder to shoulder, and shared the dangers, death, and glory of conflict. The monument is of granite, about sixty feet high, surrounded by a handsome wrought-iron railing well shaded by four old trees, and bears the following inscription : —

> " ERECTED BY THE OFFICERS AND CREWS OF THE
> UNITED STATES STEAM FRIGATE ' POWHATAN '
> AND
> H. B. M. STEAM-SLOOP ' RATTLER,'
> IN MEMORY OF
> Their shipmates who fell in a combined attack
> on a fleet of piratical Junks off Kuhlan,
> August 4th, 1855."
>
> " KILLED IN THE ACTION.
>
> ' Rattler.'   ' Powhatan.'
> GEORGE MITCHELL, A. B.   JOHN PEPPER, Seaman.
> JAMES SILVERS, Carpenter's crew.   JAMES A. HALSEY, Landsman.
> JOHN MASSEY, Gunner, R. M. A.   ISAAC COE, Landsman.
> M. OLIFF, Private, R. A.   S. MULLARD, Marine.
>   B. F. ADDAMSON, Marine."

From that day to this, no military procession has ever passed the spot without halting, while the band plays the "Star Spangled Banner," "God Save the Queen," and a solemn dirge, in memory of the brave fellows who sleep there.

To the southward, whether you go by the deep cut, over the hills and through the valleys, or turn from the dock-yard and skirt along the Praya, the scenery is varying and grand beyond description. The Happy Valley, which is the pride of the colony, is a vast amphitheatre, with racecourse and cricket-ground in its centre, and behind the grand stand are the English, Catholic, Jewish, Mahometan, and Parsee cemeteries, with their beautifully shaded walks, clumps of palms, and strange, luxurious tropical growths and blooms, with here and there a stately pile, or stone, to mark the resting-place of some member of the silent majority.

How full these cemeteries are! It is only about fifty years since the white man unfurled his banner and took possession of the island, but in that time the "Happy Valley" has swallowed up her victims by hundreds and by thousands. The ride back to the city is delightful, but one becomes a little serious while pondering over the causes that have filled these cemeteries in so short a time.

Victoria is remarkably quiet and orderly. The streets are guarded by a force of Indian sepoys, and after eight o'clock in the evening the Chinese must give account of their movements. The mode of conveyance is by chairs, open or closed, and jinrikishas, which give employment to the coolie who is always soliciting your patronage.

Victoria has many industries, in the range of European and Chinese manufactures and art. Besides the hundreds of handiwork establishments, there is a large sugar refinery, rum distillery, a jute mill, an extensive paper mill, and an ice manufactory. Each year large sums of public money are expended for improvements, including fortifications; and the extension of military and public roads, sewerage and drainage, gives employment to large numbers of coolies. Two daily and three weekly newspapers are published in the English language, and there is one Chinese bi-daily, besides a Portuguese weekly.

ABERDEEN, HONG-KONG

The Aberdeen dry-docks are situated at the head of an inlet on the south side of the island. The entrance is easy and safe, and the anchorage is excellent. The docks are substantially built of granite. Hope Dock was opened in 1867, and has a length, over all, of four hundred and thirty-three feet; its breadth at entrance is eighty-four feet; its depth, over sill, at ordinary spring tides, twenty-four feet. Rise of tides, spring, seven feet six inches. Lamont Dock, also at Aberdeen, was opened in 1860. It has a length, over all, of three hundred and forty feet; its breadth at entrance is sixty-four feet; its depth, over sill, at ordinary spring tides, sixteen feet. Rise of tide, spring, seven feet six inches. There are extensive building and repair shops connected with these docks.

KOWLOON, CHINA

Kowloon is a vast, slightly undulating plain, on the mainland of China, on the opposite side of Hong-kong Roads, and faces the island of Hong-kong. It has been neatly laid out and built up with fine public buildings and residences, has a garrison of Indian troops, and is considered to be a suburb of Victoria, with which it is connected by little steam ferry-boats. Fine granite dry-docks and patent slips for hauling up vessels are located here. They are in close proximity to the shipping, and are well protected on all sides. The approaches to the docks are perfectly safe, and the immediate vicinity affords excellent anchorage. Powerful shears of eighty feet, to lift forty tons, stand on a wharf, alongside of which vessels can lie in from twenty to twenty-two feet of water. The depth of low-water springs in the shallowest part of the bay, in front of the docks, is thirty-nine feet.

No. 1 Dock, Kowloon, has a length, over all, of five hundred and thirty feet; breadth at entrance, eighty-six feet top, seventy feet bottom; depth, over sill, at ordinary spring tides, thirty feet; rise of tide, spring, seven feet six inches. H. M. S. "Impérieuse," of eighty-four hundred tons, is the largest vessel ever docked here. The dock can be filled in one hour, and pumped out in three hours.

No. 2 Dock, Kowloon, was opened in 1866. Length, over all, three hundred and forty feet; breadth at entrance, seventy-four feet; depth, over sill, at ordinary spring tides, eighteen feet; rise of tide, spring, seven feet six inches. The S. S. "Glenartney," of 2,107 tons, is the largest vessel ever docked here.

No. 3 Dock, Kowloon, was opened in 1866. Length, over all, two hundred and forty-five feet; breadth at entrance, 43.3 feet; depth, over sill, at ordinary spring tides, thirteen feet; rise of tide, spring, seven feet six inches. The S. S. "Douglas," of 1,373 tons, is the largest vessel ever docked here.

Patent Slip No. 1, Kowloon, was opened in 1888. Length, over all, two hundred and fifty feet; breadth at entrance, sixty feet; depth, over sill, at ordinary spring tides, eleven feet; rise of tide, spring, seven feet six inches. The ship "Napier," of 1,235 tons, is the largest vessel ever taken on this slip.

Patent Slip No. 2, Kowloon, was opened in 1892. Length, over all, two hundred and thirty feet; breadth at entrance, sixty feet; depth, over sill, at ordinary spring tides, eleven feet. Vessels can be placed on the slip in two and a half hours.

The Cosmopolitan Dock is located on the Kowloon side of the harbor, about two miles from the centre of Victoria. The depth of low-water springs is twenty-six feet in the shallowest part of the bay. The anchorage is safe, and it is better protected from typhoons than any other portion of the port. The dock is substantially built of granite, was opened in 1877, and has a length, over all, of four hundred and fifty-six feet; breadth at entrance, eighty-five feet; depth, over sill, at ordinary spring tides, twenty feet; rise of tide, spring, seven feet six inches. The Steamer "City of Tokio," of 5,079 tons, is the largest vessel ever docked here.

These docks and slips are all under the same management. The work-shops, at each, have every appliance necessary for the repairs of vessels or their machinery,— lathes, planing, screwing, cutting, punching and hydraulic riveting machines, etc., etc.,— capable of executing work on the largest scale. The shipwright's, boiler-maker's, machine, and blacksmith's shops, and the foundries, are all well equipped to execute the largest work with quick despatch. Several powerful steam-tugs are always ready for service. By the rules of these docks, vessels using their own materials and men to make repairs, while in dock, are charged fifteen per cent on the value of the labor, and ten per cent on the value of materials, except sheathing and nails, on which the charge is five per cent.

Hong-kong owes its importance to the fact that it is the military and naval headquarters of the British forces in this quarter of the globe. It is also the prominent banking-centre of the far East. It is the central port for trade in sugar, flour, salt, ship supplies, and granite, and has a larger opium trade than any other port in that part of the world.

The scenery is wild and dreary. Attempts have been made to cultivate rice and sweet yams, but even the Chinese cannot make them grow in sufficient quantities to supply the foreign residents. The orange, mango, and lichie grow in well-sheltered spots. Tortoises, boas, and several species of poisonous snakes are found about the island, and a troublesome white ant burrows into woodwork and cuts the heart out of it.

Hong-kong is not a healthy place. Malaria is given out from its decomposing granite hills, kidney diseases are prevalent, and deadly cuts and sores will not heal (surgical cases are sent abroad for cure), and catarrh is one of the nuisances of the island. The temperature ranges from 56° to 84° Fah. The mean temperature throughout the year is about 73° Fah., but is modified by the monsoons. The annual rainfall is about 59 inches.

In 1841, the population was 5,000, which has increased by emigration to about 225,000, of whom 6,000 are Americans and Europeans (including all the troops), and 219,000 Asiatics, of whom the Chinese are the most numerous. About 25,000, in addition, live in boats scattered about in the immediate vicinity. The Chinese government maintains a fleet of small revenue cutters in Hong-kong waters, to prevent opium and salt smuggling.

From Victoria Peak, — 1,835 feet high, — where the British Jack is always flying, the view is interesting and grand. On one hand stretches the everlastingly restless sea, surging and dashing against the rocks and islets of the Ladrone group; yonder, Mount Steakeuse, on the island of Lamma, two miles distant, stands 1,140 feet high; and sleepy old China is grand but mysterious, without brightness, — no greens or golds, silvers or pinks, blues or pearls, but just the dull, heavy red, like the ball the dragon tosses upon her own flag. The sun sinks behind the paddy-fields into the west, the twinkling lights, away down in the city and on the bay, admonish us, and when we enter the cable-car and are whirled down, and still down, the side of the hill, the romance is gone before we reach the city.

RESIDENCE OF THE TARTAR GENERAL, NEW CHWANG, CHINA.

CHAPTER XXIV

MACAO, CHINA

A TRIP from Hong-kong to Macao in one of the untidy little steamers which ply between the ports is very interesting and enjoyable. When the frantic yells of the officers, the blowing of steam, and the tooting of the whistle have ceased, the little craft heads for the Lymoon Pass, and all is quiet on board except the pulsating throbs of the exhausting steam. We run between scenes in brown and gray, leaden, wild, and weird, and the undulating motion of the ever-restless sea causes the little craft to dance upon the waters. Picturesque groups and crowds unwittingly pose about the decks, — Portuguese, Chinese, and half-breeds, who make up the list of passengers. The ever-changing groups are studies that leave pleasant memories; and long after the journey is done, we smile at the recollections of this or that incident of the trip.

Like all other harbors in this part of the world, Macao swarms with gay sampans, with their queer little shrines and mirrors and pictures, half-Christian, half-Buddhist. A strange mixture of beliefs have come through poor old China, and in coming have brought the soil with them, — religion musty and soiled. The town is situated on the southern extremity of the island of Hiang-shang, on a point of land formed by the intersection of the Chu-kiang with the Heung-kiang, in latitude 22° north, and longitude 132° east. The gayly colored, flat-roofed houses, red and blue and green, make a quaint little city, which nestles between bold, bleak, black rocky hills.

The old Portuguese forts, with their ancient guns frowning upon the river, are more picturesque than awe-inspiring in these days of rifle-guns and long ranges. The Praya Grande (here everything is "grande") is the promenade of the place, where the belles and the beaux of old Macao take their airings, passing before the palace, and among the little shops and gambling saloons which border its animated road. The old church of St. Paul has braved monsoons, typhoons, fiery flames, and earthquakes since 1594. St. Paul, with its deep-toned organ, and the old Hospital of the Misericordi, stand as living protests, — the cross against the lotus.

After climbing the rocks and bowlders beyond the city, we reach the grotto of poor Camoëns, the real object of our pilgrimage. Strewn with great granite bowlders, abraded and shorn by monsoon and typhoon, the spot is as wild as nature made it, — although trees and shrubs and vines have been transplanted, so that men of these latter times may not see the place in its native bareness. Sitting here, where Camoëns wrote his immortal "Lusiad," to recount the glories of his beloved Portugal, although an exile from her shores, we must admire the man, so filled with patriotism.

The history of Camoëns is interesting. He was born in Lisbon in 1524. Of noble parentage, well educated, with classical attainments, witty, courteous, and handsome, he was welcome at the Portuguese court, where he met the youth and beauty of the land. Here he soon became a favorite with the fair sex, while his sarcasm incurred the hatred of his own.

Camoëns formed a romantic passion for a lady of the court. The lady had a suitor whom her parents favored, and when Camoëns's passion became known to them, their influence procured his banishment from the court. Our poet joined the forces, went to Africa, and engaged in the war against the Moors, in which he lost his right eye. In 1550 he returned to Lisbon. In 1553 he had trouble with an officer of the royal household. The officer and two of the poet's friends were rollicking, when a dispute arose, and the poet came to the rescue. The officer received a sword-thrust in the neck, and the friends ran off. Camoëns was thrown into prison, but was soon released on promising to leave the country.

He started for the East Indies, and arrived at Goa in time to join a force against the Purientas, where he did some good service. He returned to Goa in the following year, but, giving loose rein to his caustic pen, he incensed the authorities and was banished. He found his way to Macao, and in the solitude of this grotto passed his days in writing the "Lusiad," recounting the virtues of his faithful Javanese slave Antonio, — the poor slave, who, in strange lands, among strange people, tended Camoëns so devotedly and with such solicitude, through exile, tempest, and wreck, who begged for him, and who tenderly closed his hungering, weary eyes in death.

Returning to Goa, Camoëns and his faithful slave were wrecked near the mouth of the river, and on their arrival were cast into prison. In Goa, Camoëns received news of the death of his beloved, news which crazed him; but the devoted Antonio guided him through his sorrow. Camoëns was at last released from prison, and after seventeen years of weary exile he returned to Lisbon, where he was quarantined for a year on account of the plague, which had carried off more than fifty thousand people. When he landed, he went to see his poor old mother, and then made arrangements for the publication of the "Lusiad." Its publication excited the malice of jealous poets, but Camoëns knew little of this, as he lived a retired life, and his friends were only a few fathers of the convent of Santa Ana. After the year 1578, he was reduced to extreme poverty, and on June 10, 1580, he died in a small, cheerless room, in a miserable house in the Rua de Santa Ana.

After the death of Camoëns, Fra José Indio, a Carmelite monk, wrote these lines on a fly-leaf of a first copy of the "Lusiad":—

"What thing more grievous than to see so great genius lacking success! I saw him die in a hospital in Lisbon, without a sheet to cover him, after having triumphed in the Indies, and having sailed five thousand five hundred leagues by sea. What warning so great for those who, by night and day, weary themselves in study without profit, like the spider weaving the thread to catch small flies."

In 1557, the Portuguese, in return for their services in combating piracy, were permitted to form a settlement on the peninsula. The Jesuit missionaries set up the cross, and in 1575 the Chinese built the wall across the island to separate this settlement from the rest of China. In 1583, a government was formed for the settlement, and in 1628, Jeronimo de Silveria became the first royal Governor. The Chinese claim that they have always retained control over the settlement through Mandarins, and have never surrendered their territorial sovereign rights. The royal Governor, De Amaral, in 1849, declared that the Mandarins had no more authority than the representatives of any other

WOMAN OF NORTHERN CHINA.

foreign nation. De Amaral was assassinated in the same year, but his successors have continued his policy, although the Chinese government refuses to recognize the claim.

The European powers consider Macao a *de facto* colony, and the King of Portugal appoints all the officers, including the Chinese magistrates. Macao has been occupied by British forces to prevent its seizure by the French.

There are 6,050 inhabitants of European extraction in Macao, 60,617 Chinese living on the land, and about 11,000 in boats. The people are engaged in commercial and agricultural pursuits, and nearly all the land is under cultivation. Macao has been a free port since 1846. The preparation and packing of tea is the most important industry of the port, and there is a good trade in Chinese manufactured goods from Canton. Gambling and opium dens are numerous, and are openly carried on.

The total value of the trade of the port is $15,000,000. The revenue is largely made up from taxes on gambling tables, and small dues and fines.

CHAPTER XXV

MANILA, PHILIPPINE ISLANDS

ON the afternoon of March 12, we ran out of Hong-kong roads, and anchored under the lee of a barren little rock. On the following morning, we had target practice with great and small guns, rifles, and revolvers; after which we picked up our targets, and headed out for Manila.

After leaving the fogs and gloom of Hong-kong, balmy air freshened into good topsail-breezes, drove off the chill, and gave us all new life. Even the old ship — as sail was made, and the engines put out of use — dashed ahead and bumped into the seas as though she enjoyed the delightful bath.

During the middle watch of the 16th, we lost the wind, but the heavy swell of the sea remained, and the vessel became a little too sportive for our comfort. Fellows were pitched out of their bunks in a very unceremonious fashion, and furniture and crockery were sent about the decks at a rate dangerous to our limbs and our pockets. We were not slow in getting the engines connected, and going ahead with them.

For the first two or three hours, after starting up, the vessel rolled deeper than before. Sleep was out of the question, and we wandered about the mess-room like white-robed spirits, securing the noisy articles, and declaring that we would gladly " sell our farms " and come to sea, where we could always have such pleasant surroundings and so much comfort.

On the morning of the 17th, we sighted Luzon, and ran along Manila Bay, in full view of the land. For miles we ran almost beside the beautiful white surf-washed beach, which met the low, rolling land, and lost itself on the sides of great mountains, that rear their black heads full five thousand feet into the clouds. We reached the outer harbor at about noon, and anchored there.

Manila, the capital of Luzon, as well as of the Philippine Islands, is situated on the eastern side of the Bay of Manila, at the mouth of the Pasig River, in latitude 14° 36′ north, and longitude 120° 52′ east. The immediate surrounding country is low, rolling land, almost flat, and being bare of vegetation in the dry season has a barren appearance. The Mafonso and Mateo Mountains form the background for Manila, and give color and variety to the otherwise monotonous scenery.

Old Boreas and Neptune paid their respects to us on our first night in the port, in the form of a little blow. The sea dashed into our ports, drowning out some of the rooms; and after the ports were closed it became so intolerably hot that it was impossible to sleep in the ship.

The next morning we made a trip to the shore. After crossing the bay in the steam-cutter, we entered the Pasig River, between the grim old Spanish fort and the massive granite lighthouse which guard the entrance. Keeping on up the river for about a mile, passing between and dodging lines of busy shipping, where unloading and loading was being done, we heard all the noise and witnessed the confusion made by Spanish sailors and longshoremen, — poor fellows! — who cannot lift a weight without an accompanying yell or song, in which the song is seven-eighths yell and one-eighth music.

We landed on a flight of granite steps at the customhouse, and were assailed — but in a friendly way — by a crowd of natives, anxious to serve us in almost any capacity :

Manila, Philippine Islands.

to act as guides over the city, to sell the lucky number in the lottery, cakes, fruits, or cigars, or to furnish teams to see the sights. After some parley, we entered a trap driven by a native and drawn by a pair of lively little ponies, and started off for the Club. Our driver more than earned his fare by the vigorous manner in which he conducted his part of the expedition. He would strike at the flank of one pony and then at the other, all the while yelling as if the city were on fire, and he driving the only fire-engine in the place. We soon discovered this to be a ruse, a cheap way of showing his importance and zeal. The dash-board and not the ponies received the blows, and the yelling is simply a Manila fashion. It became evident that the Jehu did not know where the club-house was; neither did we, and as the day was hot, the trap comfortable, and we were seeing interesting, novel sights, we let him drive on at will.

After wandering about in this fashion, we dashed up a street where the "Stars and Stripes" were floating over our Consulate; and through an open window we saw our representative decked in all the glory of full dress, ready for a dinner at eight. He was slowly pacing the floor, trying to keep cool, with the mercury bobbing 100° in the shade. The Consulate gave us the bearing of the Club, and we headed directly for it, soon arrived, and laid ourselves out in long easy-chairs under the "punkhas," which the coolies kept moving at a vigorous rate, wafting gentle breezes over us, as we enjoyed the perfection of laziness, while awaiting the preparation of luncheon.

After having given the ponies a breathing spell and the Jehu time to rest his lungs, we re-entered the trap and started off to see the sights.

The Pasig River divides Manila into two parts, which are connected by a fine old stone bridge and a handsome suspension bridge.

The old city, the Plaza de Manila, is enclosed by the walls of the old fort, and is entered by low, arched gateways. Its streets are broad and very çlean, and run at right angles to each other; but as there are neither shops nor traffic, they are dull and gloomy, only brightened by the many little parks of refreshing green, and by the tinkling bells of the poor car-horses who are beaten through them.

AN INDIAN WARRIOR OF THE PHILIPPINE ISLANDS.

The Governor's palace, the administration building, and the cathedral face a large garden of beautiful tropical flowers, which shed their fragrance about a colossal bronze statue of Don Carlos IV. of Spain. The University and Academy of Arts, the arsenal, mint, museum, hospitals, many churches, and religious houses are also within the gloomy walls of the city. Outside the city walls, handsome villas, situated in beautiful grounds, extend along the roads for miles. La Luna is a promenade facing the bay, where all Manila resorts in the evening, to hear the bands play.

"New Manila," on the opposite side of the river, contains extensive warehouses filled with the products of these islands and with wares from all parts of the world,— the Escalto, lined with gay Chinese shops, the native suburb, which struggles for miles up the river, the busy Beriondo, and the fashionable San Miguel.

Manila, Philippine Islands 423

Dashing over the moss-covered stone bridge which spans the Pasig, thence along the river's bank, by the old, cracked city wall and the monument to Magellan, and under the low archway in the wall, we found our spirited little ponies trotting through the consecrated streets of old Manila. We

NATIVES OF MANILA, PHILIPPINE ISLANDS.

kept on through the sleepy streets to the cathedral, a massive old pile of granite, in the composite style of architecture, Romanesque, with Corinthian cornice. Founded in 1575, one hundred and fourteen years after Columbus discovered America; several times shattered, wrecked, and rebuilt, — it now stands (surrounded by the noblest specimens of architecture in Manila), bearing the scars and rents of the earthquakes of 1863 and 1880.

Venerable, historic, and altogether grand, the old battered walls still enclose and guard beautiful chapels and altars, the grand choir and organ, the golden throne, the cunningly wrought statues, and wonderful paintings, — all magnificent fittings for this old Christian church in this far-eastern isle.

Inanimate witness of masses, glorias, and triumphs in the fair days, when the people had cause for thanksgivings and rejoicings for bounteous harvests, the stay of the pestilence, or some triumph of the Spanish arms, or the witness of misery and heart-rending distress, when terror-stricken women and half-dazed men flocked here and prayed to Heaven to stay the rumbling and quaking earth, that rent and shattered massive piles of man's handiwork, tore great rents in the earth, and swallowed up hundreds and thousands of people, burying them from the sight of their fellows forever.

With its scars and rents, its chime of sonorous bells, and with clusters of old trees growing from its top and sides, the cathedral bell tower (now a ruin) stands like a solitary sentinel on the opposite side of the street. The native ringer, stationed within its walls, rings out the half-hours upon the musical chimes, by time measured with a Yankee clock which has superseded the ancient hour-glass.

The only modern thing in the vicinity, besides the clock, is the colossal bronze statue of Don Carlos IV. of Spain, in robes of state, which stands in a handsome garden of flowers, facing the cathedral. The inscription on the pedestal reads, —

"IN GRATITUDE FOR THE INTRODUCTION OF VACCINATION IN THE PHILIPPINE ISLANDS."

The noble pile of moss and creeper-covered granite yonder is the ruin of the palace, another result of the earthquake. The top and front of the building were thrown down, leaving the grand stone stairway exposed, like an ascent to some old tomb. These ruins are in the centre of a noble park of luxuriant growth. It is said that on moonlight nights, in the monsoon season, shadows from the trees thrown across stairway and park appear like a procession of black-robed monks wandering about the ruins. The superstitious natives stare with frightened eyes, and run in wonder and awe from the mysterious apparition. All about the city there are ruins of fine houses that were thrown down by the earthquake, and have remained untouched since that time.

The Church of the Sacred Heart is a magnificent pile, long and broad and high. Its exterior is plain and unpretentious, like the ecclesiastic architecture of old Spain and Mexico, and the missions of California; but its interior is encased with exquisitely carved sandal-wood, the work of native Christians of India, from designs furnished by native priests here. There are no gorgeous greens, golds, and scarlets, or bold, grotesque carvings, such as we see in the Buddhist temples, but beautiful reliefs and bas-reliefs that tell the stories of the Saviour, the Apostles, and Fathers of the Church. A great cabinet of sweet-scented woods is so finely executed as to bear the glass. Each section and panel is a wonderful work of art, and the whole a collection of masterpieces.

There are a few fine old historical paintings in the Church of Santo Domingo. One represents the murder of the priests in 1260 by the Arabians, on the Pescadores. On the opposite side of the doorway a painting represents a number of priests assembled, in the sanctuary, around the mutilated body of a white man, while the heavens are open, and the priests hold consultation with the Holy

Family. The light was poor, and we could not decipher the inscription upon this very old and dim picture.

On one side of a chapel, there is a fine painting of the "Jesuits preaching to the Japanese," and a picture opposite represents the "Persecution of the Jesuits by the Japanese." These pictures are carefully guarded and shown with much pride by the brethren of Santo Domingo.

About two hundred and fifty years ago, Japan was almost converted to Christianity by the Jesuits. The Dutch were jealous, and intrigued with the Japanese government, persuading it that the Christians designed its overthrow. The Japanese became alarmed, and waged a relentless war of extermination against the Jesuits and native Christians. Thousands who would not renounce their religion were thrown over the causeway of Papinberg, and drowned in the sea.

Cigar manufacture is a monopoly of the government, and the manufactory covers several acres of ground. It is a very interesting place to visit; twelve thousand women and girls are at work, some handsome, some plain, some neat, and others untidy; but all chatter gayly, and many a hearty Spanish laugh rings out while their little heaps of tobacco are manipulated. Here one sees all the processes of stripping, assorting, filling, rolling, pasting, counting, and packing in boxes the rolls of fragrant weed. At the noon-hour and in the evening, when the women leave the premises, they are all searched, to make sure that no scraps of tobacco are taken away. They are even required to take down their hair. The examinations are made under the superintendence of a Spanish beauty.

The cemetery, like those at New Orleans, is surrounded by an outer and an inner wall, with level compartments between them, shelved in rows one above another. On the arrival of a body, it is taken from its casket and placed in one of these compartments. Quicklime is placed around it to hasten the process of decomposition; the opening is then sealed with a memorial stone, and the casket is taken back to the undertaker's shop to await the next body that will fit into it.

A NATIVE OF MANILA, PHILIPPINE ISLANDS.

The old church near the cathedral contains some art treasures worth seeing. The painting representing the "Baptism of the Saviour by Saint John" is a fine composition, rich in coloring. The stained glass window behind the altar has "angels hovering about in the heavens." The altar-piece is a marble statue of the Virgin; and when the sun shines through the window, the effect is of "angels hovering about the Virgin." A heavy white veil hangs before the altar and heightens the effect of the picture, so that it appears like a beautiful dream.

Every afternoon San Miguel, the fashionable drive, is gay with hundreds of Spanish dowagers, black-eyed señoritas, and interesting children, who recline in elegant carriages, which are drawn by handsome ponies. The ladies are gowned in black or pink or yellow silks, with black mantillas arranged in the hair and falling gracefully about the shoulders, as they drive back and forth over the length of the noble street. As night approaches, the street is filled with people, the sidewalks are crowded, and all Manila seems to be out on parade.

Driving through a beautiful suburb that is lined with handsome villas and well-kept grounds of luxuriant green, we keep on with the throng, and reach "La Luna," an oblong plot of ground near the bay shore. La Luna, "the night," is about a quarter of a mile long, several hundred yards wide, and is illuminated by reddish-black flames from hundreds of kerosene lamps. A band from one of the regiments discourses music from dark until ten o'clock, while hundreds of carriages containing fair women and brave men drive slowly round and round. Their occupants enjoy the cool breezes from the wide bay, the beautiful, moving panorama, and the sweet music, or perhaps alight to promenade upon the greensward, and to exchange greetings with friends. The men, in white linen clothes, with black derby hats, lounge about with their cigars, or drop into the little wine-shops at the turn of the promenade to discuss the news over a glass of claret.

Wherever one goes in the evening, whether to church, theatre, on the streets, the beautiful promenade, or to call upon friends, he is always met by the sickly, reddish-black,

Manila, Philippine Islands 429

smoky flame of kerosene. The dread of earthquakes and fires should teach these people to throw the treacherous oil away, and to adopt gas or electricity.

A NATIVE OF MANILA, PHILIPPINE ISLANDS.

The Spaniards live in fine stone houses, which have an air of wealth and elegance; while the natives live in huts of straw or in poorly built houses of wood, often situated on low ground, where they are built on piles of wood, and can only be reached by rude ladders from the outside. The living part of all houses is on the upper floors, the lower floors being used as shops and store-rooms. Many of the citizens are very rich, and we did not see evidences of the extreme poverty that is met with in other places.

The native women dress in skirts of red or pink and white material, — usually large plaids, — a loosely fitting bodice of "penia cloth," with flowing sleeves of white lace. Their bare feet are encased in blue, red, or green plush slippers that have no backs, and their hair is always neatly dressed, as they never wear bonnets or hats. The native men wear white trousers and shirts (the latter always worn outside of the trousers), and slippers like those of the women. If it can be afforded, a black derby hat completes the male costume.

The street cars are dirty, and the service is indifferent. The cars are only used by the poorer natives, — even the Chinese coolies refuse to patronize them. The city had no adequate supply of water until very recently, when a wealthy citizen gave to it water-works and a reservoir. A contract has been made to supply the city with electric lights, but such matters move very slowly in old Manila. The only steam railway on the islands is one from Dagupan, twenty miles from Manila, which was opened for traffic in 1892.

After our return from La Luna, we went to the "French Restaurant," where we thoroughly enjoyed dining in public with Spaniards and some natives of the better class. There was an air of cheerfulness about the place. Everybody seemed to be in good humor, and tobacco-smoke curled about the room in an atmosphere already rich with garlic. As our appetites had been well sharpened by the day's work, we fully appreciated the *menu* and our surroundings. The dinner was excellent, consisting of fine soup, fish, and boiled potatoes, mystery, shrimp salad, Spanish meat-balls, more mystery, capon and fried potatoes, claret *ad libitum*, assorted fruits, small cakes, ice cream, black coffee, and good cigars,—all for sixty-six cents a plate. After dinner we rode out to the English Club, about two miles up the river, where, in a little summer-house, we enjoyed fragrant Manilas, while some of our friends were trying to keep cool by bowling in the alley. The night was quite warm and clear, with a half-moon to light the way and make the dingy kerosene lamps ashamed of themselves. Many residences were thrown open and rooms brilliantly illuminated gave a bright, showy effect from the street.

The amusements in Manila are the opera, theatre, evening receptions with cards and music, cock-fights, and the lottery.

A COCK-PIT AT MANILA, PHILIPPINE ISLANDS.

CHAPTER XXVI

THE PHILIPPINES

THE Philippines are a group of more than five hundred rich islands, which lie well off the coast of Asia, between the Tropic of Cancer and the Equator. For administrative purposes they are divided into twenty-seven provinces, and contain about eight millions of people. In the early days of the Spanish settlement, Jesuit missionaries came to the islands in great numbers, and met with success in the conversion of the natives. There are now about two thousand priests on the islands, who exercise almost unlimited authority over the natives. There are about six millions of natives who acknowledge the Spanish authority, and pay taxes in some form; but there are more than a million, in the inaccessible mountains, who live a guerilla life, and resist all efforts to bring them under subjection.

Ever since the Spaniards planted their standard upon the soil, in 1565, there have been strife, rebellions, and wars in the islands. In early days, the Portuguese and the Dutch were jealous of these rich possessions, and annoyed the Spaniards at every opportunity. Bold pirates sailed out from Chinese ports and raided the islands, and differences between the civil and ecclesiastical authorities have frequently led to internal dissensions and conflicts. In 1762 the British captured Manila, but restored it to Spain after two years' occupation.

There are about twelve thousand troops on the islands, of whom one half are natives with Spanish officers, and

The Untamed Indians of the Philippine Islands.

The Philippines

there is always a fleet of small Spanish war-vessels cruising about the islands to maintain order. There are a large number of "mestizos," or half-breeds, children of native mothers and foreign fathers.

In the wet season, from March to July, the rivers become swollen and flooded, and travel is difficult and dangerous. In the dry season, droughts often occur, when the ground is parched and vegetation burned by the sun. Locusts sometimes devour the crops, and terrific storms are frequent at the typhoon season.

The Philippines are a centre of volcanic action, and destructive earthquakes are of frequent occurrence. They have shaken down massive houses, desolated extensive tracts of land, filled up valleys, and opened passages from the sea into the interior. The history of the islands is full of accounts of these destructive visitations.

The Jesuits have an excellent observatory in Manila, for study of the weather, storms, and earthquakes. Instruments for determining the direction, force, and duration of earthquakes are fixed on a floor which is suspended from masonry. The whole arrangement is automatic and self-registering, so that if an earthquake should occur during the absence of the observer, it is supposed to record itself. How this arrangement will work in actual practice, under the given conditions, time only can determine.

The earthquake of 1796 was a calamity. In 1824, many churches, the principal bridge, the barracks, and a great number of private houses were destroyed in Manila. A chasm nearly four miles in length was opened, and six vessels were wrecked in the narrow river. The people all fled from the city, and a large number perished. During the earthquake of 1828, the great stones of the gates in the city walls were moved out of their places, and the bells in the church towers were set ringing. The walls of churches and other buildings were rent, and hanging lamps swung through an arc of about five degrees. The phenomena lasted for about three minutes, but there were no rumbling noises. A destructive earthquake occurred in 1836, and a terrible one made the year 1880 memorable in the history

NATIVES OF MANILA, PHILIPPINE ISLANDS.

of Manila, when a great portion of the city was wrecked. The people live in constant dread of these terrible visitations, and all possible precautions are taken for protection. The houses are located, planned, and built with reference to safety under such conditions. They are large and imposing, but have no architectural pretensions.

The Philippines 437

The city, with the suburbs, contains a population of three hundred thousand five hundred.

The people are good-natured and orderly. They have great respect for authority, and very few crimes are committed. The police force is strictly military, and its members are natives.

The lottery and several other forms of gambling flourish, and large revenues are derived from them. Race meetings are held every spring, when native and Chinese ponies are run. These entertainments are very popular, and attract large numbers of people from the islands and the Chinese coast.

The climate of these islands is healthy but hot. The maximum range of the thermometer is 103° Fah., but a sea breeze usually sets in about five in the evening, and lowers the temperature. The greatest annual rainfall recorded is 114 inches, and the least is 84 inches.

There are 323 Europeans and Americans, 4,506 Spaniards, 16,520 Chinese, 47,662 Chinese mestizos (half-breeds), 4,963 Spanish mestizos, and 200,966 pure natives in Manila. The population seems to be divided into the clergy, the officials, the half-breeds, and native Indians.

The business hours are from five to nine in the morning and from five to midnight. The middle of the day is devoted to quiet lounging and sleep.

There are four daily newspapers published in Manila, "El Diario de Manila," "La Oceania Española," and "La Voz de España" in the morning, and "El Comercio" in the evening.

Manila Bay is about one hundred and thirty miles in circumference and almost circular in shape. Its great size and the absence of shelter make it an unsafe anchorage for vessels during the typhoon season. The anchorage is about three miles from the landing, but small vessels go up the river and make fast to walls. Since 1880, a tax of two per cent has been laid on all imports, and one per cent on all exports, the income thus obtained to be used in building a breakwater within which vessels can lie in safety at all seasons of the year. Hurricanes, earthquakes, and fearful thunder-storms are frequent in the rainy season.

The Spanish naval station at Cavite, opposite the mouth of the Pasig, has a small patent slip and shops for the repair of vessels.

NATIVE BULL SLED, MANILA, PHILIPPINE ISLANDS.

The public revenue amounts to about fifteen millions of dollars each year. The principal exports are two hundred thousand tons of sugar, seven hundred thousand bales of hemp, and five thousand tons of coffee. The United States and Great Britain are the chief markets, and one hundred million cigars go to China and the East Indies annually.

The bay is full of harmless little water-snakes. Sometimes sharks make excursions up the bay, but they are *not* believed to be harmless.

Beef and other meats are poor, but the vegetables and

fruits, which are in great variety, are excellent and abundant.

Manila hemp is a product of the leaf-stalks of *Musa textilis*, indigenous to these islands, which the natives call "abaca." It is one of the most valuable products, and requires the least care and attention of them all. A false stem, or cluster of enclosing leaf-stalks, grows up from its rhizome to a height of about twenty feet, then spreads into unbroken leaves similar to those of the banana. It is rudely cultivated for its fibre. When about three years old it blooms, and this is the most favorable time for gathering the fibre. The stock is then cut, and the enclosing stalks are torn into narrow strips and cleaned while fresh. The cleaning is done by drawing the strips between a sharp knife-edged instrument and a block of hard wood, and repeating the operation until the soft cellular matter which surrounds the fibre is removed, when the fibre is hung in the open air to dry.

NATIVE WOMAN OF MANILA, PHILIPPINE ISLANDS.

Two natives will cut stocks and separate about twenty-five pounds of fibre per day. The fibre from the outer layer of leaves is tough, fully developed, and strong, while the product of the inner leaves is increasingly thin, fine, and weak.

The fine fibre is used by the natives, without spinning or twisting (the ends of the single fibres being knotted together), and from it a beautiful, fine, thin, translucent, and comparatively strong texture known as "penia-cloth" is made, which is used for articles of dress and ornament.

Having nearly completed our three years' tour of duty, we left Yokohama on August 15, and after buffeting the storms, calms, and fogs of the broad Pacific for about thirty-eight days, we sighted the highlands of California on a beautiful morning, and entered the Golden Gate. We gathered on the poop-deck and sang " Home Again " and " Praise God," while every fellow of us was filled with the sentiments of the hymns, for even the brown hills on each side of us were home; and if we could have done so, I have no doubt that some would have been quite willing to hug the old hair seals on Cliff Rock because they were Americans. Soon we dropped our anchors off the Custom House wharf, and later proceeded to the Navy Yard, where the flag was hauled down just three years after it had been raised.

APPENDIX

Appendix

THE JAPAN—CHINA WAR

EVER since the settlement of foreigners in Korea, there have been periodical outbreaks of more or less violence against the new-comers, — the Japanese. These outbreaks have been instigated by secret societies, known as "Tan Haks," or anti-foreigners, whose hatred was hereditary, and whose jealousy was excited and intensified by the beautiful civilization of the Japanese, and by the evidences of progress and advancement among the new settlers.

A Japanese would be found murdered in one part of the kingdom, a serious outbreak would occur in another part, the authorities would be resisted somewhere else, and law-abiding people lived in a state of alarm and unrest.

After the snows had disappeared, the ice had melted, and the roads became passable in 1894, a rebellion broke out in Korea, and soon became so formidable that the government forces were unable to suppress it. Korea called on China for assistance, and China, as by treaty bound, notified Japan that she would send a force to suppress the outbreak. On June 7, Japan gave China notice that she would also send a force to protect her own subjects resident in the troubled districts. On June 9, the town of Asan, about forty miles south of Seoul, was the scene of great excitement caused by the landing of about two thousand Chinese troops; at about the same time the Japanese landed five hundred men from their fleet at Chemulpo, and pushed them on to the capital.

The Japanese government appreciated the gravity of the situation, and by the end of the month had about five thousand men of the fifth division of its army divided between Chemulpo and the capital. There were one thousand on the southeast coast, one thousand at Fu-san, and one thousand at Gen-san. All the available vessels of the navy were being made ready for war service, notice was sent to the reserves to join the colors, war material was assembled for speedy transportation, and transports were secured and made ready for service. The people were patriotic and enthusiastic, and Japan commenced to send her forces to Korea, well supplied and well guarded while on the way.

With the view of protecting her own subjects resident in Korea, and to protect her commerce with that country, Japan demanded that certain methods of the Korean government be changed, under the joint protection of Japan and China. China declined the proposition, and demanded the withdrawal of the Japanese forces, claiming that the rebellion was suppressed. After grave consideration, the Japanese government, on the 14th of July, informed the Chinese government that "in this juncture the Imperial Japanese government find themselves relieved of all responsibility for any eventuality that may in future arise out of the situation."

On June 30, 1894, the Japanese navy consisted of the following vessels which were available for active war service: —

Name.	Class.	Displacements.	Speed.	Where Built.
Matsushima	Coast Defence	4,277	16	France, 1891
Itsukushima	Coast Defence	4,277	16.75	France, 1891
Hochidate	Coast Defence	4,277	16	Japan, 1894
Fuso	Armored Cruiser	3,700	13	England, 1878
Chiyoda	Armored Cruiser	2,450	19	England, 1890
Hiyei	Protected Cruiser	2,250	14	England, 1878
Kongo	Protected Cruiser	2,250	14	England, 1878
Naniwa	Protected Cruiser	3,650	19	England, 1886
Takachiho	Protected Cruiser	3,650	18	England, 1886
Yoshino	Protected Cruiser	4,150	23	England, 1893
Akitsushima	Protected Cruiser	3,150	19	Japan, 1894
Tsukushi	Gun Vessel	1,350	16.8	England, 1883
Takao	Cruiser	1,774	....	Japan, 1889
Musashi	Cruiser	1,476	....	Japan, 1888
Yamato	Cruiser	1,476	....	Japan, 1887
Katsuragi	Cruiser	1,476	....	Japan, 1887
Teurin	Cruiser	1,547	....	Japan, 1885
Kaimo	Cruiser	1,358	....	Japan, 1884
Amagi	Cruiser	1,030	....	Japan, 1878
Banjo	Cruiser	656	....	Japan, 1880
Yaeyama	Partially Protected Cruiser	1,600	....	Japan, 1890
Oshima	Partially Protected Cruiser	639	....	Japan, 1892
Maya	Gun Vessel	614	13	Japan, 1890
Atago	Gun Vessel	614	13	Japan, 1890
Akagi	Gun Vessel	614	13	Japan, 1890
Chokai	Gun Vessel	614	13	Japan, 1890

The fleet was organized into five squadrons, — the first squadron being composed of the "Matsushima," the "Itsukushima," the "Hochidate," and the "Chiyoda;" the second squadron, of the "Yoshino," the "Takachiho," the

JAPANESE MOUNTED INFANTRY. BY A JAPANESE ARTIST.

"Akitsushima," and the "Naniwa;" the third squadron of the "Fuso," the "Hiyei," the "Kongo," and the "Takao;" the fourth squadron of the "Katsuragi," the "Yaeyama," the "Musashi," and the "Teurin;" the fifth squadron, of the "Oshima," the "Banjo," the "Maya," the "Atago," the "Akagi," and the "Chokai." The fleet of torpedo boats was divided into three divisions, consisting of six boats each in the first and second divisions, and of four boats in the third division.

The Japanese army, with the colors, consisted of six divisions of about nine thousand men each, and the three divisions of the Imperial Guard of about six thousand men each, — a total of about seventy-two thousand men. To reinforce these were the first and second reserves, each containing about sixteen thousand men, making a grand total of about one hundred and four thousand men available for active service. During the hostilities which ensued, the forces serving with the colors were increased by recruits from the reserves, bringing the active divisions up to an average of fifteen thousand men each.

The Chinese army consisted of about one million men, less than two hundred thousand of whom had modern arms, and these were of many styles and patterns, while their equipments, organization, and training were far from being up to the standard of Western nations.

The Chinese navy consisted of the following-named vessels which were available for active war service: —

Name.	Class	Displacements.	Speed.	Where Built.
Chen Yuen	Battleship	7,430	15.5	Germany, 1883
Ting Yuen .	Battleship	7,430	15.4	Germany, 1883
King Yuen .	Coast Defence Vessel	2,900	15	Germany, 1887
Lai Yuen .	Coast Defence Vessel	2,900	15	Germany, 1887
Chi Yuen .	Coast Defence Vessel	2,355	17.5	Germany, 1884
Ping Yuen .	Coast Defence Vessel	2,600	10.5	China, 1890
Ching Yuen	Protected Cruiser . .	2,300	18.5	England, 1887
Chih Yuen .	Protected Cruiser . .	2,300	18.5	England, 1887
Ying Wei .	Gun Vessel	1,350	16.2	England, 1881
Chao Yung	Gun Vessel	1,350	16.2	England, 1881
Kuang Yi .	Third-Class Cruiser .	1,030	16.5	China, 1891
Kuang Ping	Third-Class Cruiser .	1,030	16.5	China, 1891
Kuang Kia .	Third-Class Cruiser .	1,030	16.5	China, 1891
Wei Yuen .	Old Corvette . . .	1,300	. . . .	. . . .
Kong Chi .	Old Corvette . . .	1,300	. . . .	
Chao Kiang	Despatch Vessel . .	500	. . . .	
Chen Pai .	Gun Vessel	440	. . . .	. . . .
Chen Pieu .	Gun Vessel	440	. . . .	
Chen Li . .	Gun Vessel	440	. . . .	. . . .
Chen Chung	Gun Vessel	440	. . . .	. . . .
Chen Nau .	Gun Vessel	440	. . . .	. . . .
Chen Tung	Gun Vessel	440	. . . .	. . . .

China called out her troops for the purpose of driving the Japanese out of Korea, and Japan determined on her own action. On July 22, China sent eight transports laden with troops from Taku to Asan, and on the next day the Japanese, believing that an attempt had been made to abduct the King of Korea and take him to the Chinese camp, sent troops to the palace, drove off the guards, and posted their own guards at the entrances for the protection of the King.

Transports arrived off Asan in the afternoon of the 24th, and landed twenty-five hundred troops (reinforcements for General Yeh) under cover of the Chinese war vessels " Chi Yuen " and " Kuang Yi," and, on the next afternoon, the " Wei Yuen " arrived from Chemulpo, with news of the troubles at the king's palace.

Early in the morning of the 25th, the " Wei Yuen," " Kuang Yi," and " Tsi Yuen " started for China, and at about seven o'clock, when off the island of Poung Do, they were met by the Japanese war vessels " Yoshino," " Akitsushima," and " Naniwa," under command of Rear-Admiral Tsuboi. Turrets and guns were cleared for action. The " Yoshino" and " Akitsushima" engaged the " Wei Yuen," while the " Naniwa " went in hot pursuit of the " Kuang Yi," damaging her so badly and pressing her so hard that her commander was forced to run her aground on a shoal place off the entrance to the bay. The " Naniwa " next joined in the pursuit of the " Tsi Yuen," which was fleeing towards the island of Shopajul, with badly damaged turret, steering gear, and other works.

The transport " Kowshing," under the British flag, was now discovered coming in from the direction of China, and, to the southward, the Chinese steamer " Tsao Kiang " was seen on her way from Chefoo to Asan. The " Naniwa " made signal for the " Kowshing " to anchor about a mile from the island, and sent an officer to examine her. Later in the morning, the "Yoshino" continued to chase the "Tsi Yuen," and the "Akitsushima" started for the "Tsao Kiang," which vessel attempted to escape to China. The "Kowshing" was now directed to follow the "Naniwa," but the Chinese officials on board would not permit her English officers to obey the order. After several repetitions and non-compliance with the order, the "Naniwa" discharged a torpedo at the "Kowshing" and opened fire upon her, sinking her in about a half-hour, after which the "Naniwa" steamed about the wreckage, and saved some of the people. The "Tsi Yuen" finally eluded the "Yoshino," when the latter vessel dropped her anchor, and in the early afternoon the "Akitsushima" returned with the "Tsao Kiang" as her prize. The next morning the little fleet steamed south, and, falling in with the "Yaeyama," transferred their prisoners to her for transportation to Japan.

On the 25th, General Oshima, at the head of thirty-five hundred troops, left Seoul for Asan, where the Chinese were in force. The Chinese checked the advance guard of one of the attacking columns, but later the Chinese were met in considerable force at Seikwan, near Asan, and defeated. The main position at Asan was abandoned during the night, and an immense quantity of stores fell into the hands of the Japanese. The Chinese retreated, by a circuitous route around Seoul, to Ping-yang, and the Japanese returned to the capital.

PING-YANG AND THE YALU

On July 31, the government of China made a formal declaration of a state of war, and the government of Japan did the same thing on August 1.

The most important duty assigned to the Japanese navy was to keep the sea communications between Japan and

Korea safe, and to support the landing of their armies, and the work was admirably done. The fleet's base of operations was in the neighborhood of the Kokun Islands, and its guard vessels were kept hovering about the Gulf of Pichili, watching Ping-yang Inlet and the Shantung Promontory, while the fifth division of the Japanese army and war material of all kinds were rapidly pushed into Korea under this protection.

The Chinese fleet remained in the Gulf of Pichili, apparently indifferent to the movements of the Japanese, and Chinese vessels accompanied their transports from Port Arthur to the Yalu without interference from the Japanese.

On August 10, a Japanese fleet of twelve vessels and some torpedo boats exchanged shots with the forts at Wei-Hai-Wei, but, finding no large Chinese vessels in harbor, they returned to Korea.

The Chinese were in considerable force at Ping-yang, some having been sent from Taku, and great numbers having crossed over from Manchuria. The Japanese prepared to dislodge them, and on August 15 their main body left Seoul and took up the march for Ping-yang, while a column of infantry and artillery left Gen-san, the marches being so directed that a junction was successfully effected before Ping-yang was reached. On August 21, the first reserves of the fifth division under General Nodzu arrived at Chemulpo, in transports, and on the 25th they made a forced march to Ping-yang, where they assisted in the assault and capture. In August, a brigade of eight thousand men of the third division landed at Gen-san, when Colonel Sato marched across the mountains to Ping-yang, with five thousand men.

On September 10, thirty-five transports arrived on the west coast of Korea, when six war vessels assisted them in landing the second brigade of the third division (about ten thousand men), the pontoon bridges for crossing the

Yalu River, a large number of coolies, and vast quantities of stores and provisions; while the main body of the fleet remained outside on the lookout.

Ping-yang, naturally a strong position, had been greatly strengthened by the Chinese, who had about fifteen thousand men for its defence. The Japanese attacking forces amounted to about seventeen thousand. On September 15, the Japanese assaulted the outer works, advancing in three columns, the fighting lasting until night. The Chinese retreated towards the Yalu under cover of the darkness. The next morning, the Japanese took possession of the works and the city, and sent a force in pursuit of the fleeing Chinese; but they were badly demoralized, and made no further stand on Korean soil. The Japanese moved up to the Yalu River, where they halted to await reinforcements. Their forces now in Korea consisted of the third and fifth divisions, with strong garrisons at Ping-yang, Seoul, Fu-san, and Gen-san.

The Japanese fleet arrived at Ping-yang Inlet on the morning of September 15, when the Admiral sent four men-of-war and some torpedo boats up the river to assist the army in its operations against the Chinese. The remainder of the fleet was formed into two squadrons, and steamed up the coast, leaving the inlet the next morning. The first squadron, under command of Admiral Ito, was made up of the " Matsushima," " Chiyoda," " Itsukushima," " Hochidate," " Hiyei," " Fuso," and the " Akagi." The second squadron, under command of Rear-Admiral Tsuboi, was composed of the " Yoshino," the " Takachiho," the " Akitsushima," the " Naniwa," and the armed steamer " Sakyo."

The Chinese squadron cruised about Taku, Port Arthur, Wei-Hai-Wei, and the Gulf of Pichili, until the evening of September 14, when it headed for Talienwan Bay, where it was joined by the smaller vessels, and some torpedo boats. The entire squadron, under the command of Admiral Ting, and convoying five transports, with about five thousand troops and stores, sailed for the Yalu River, where it arrived on the 16th and landed the troops and stores under the guns of the "Ping Yuen," "Kuang Ping," and the torpedo boats, the "Ting Yuen," the "Chen Yuen," the "Lai Yuen," the "King Yuen," the "Chi Yuen," the "Ching Yuen," the "Chih Yuen," the "Chao Yuen," the "Yung Wei," the "Kuang Kia," and four small gunboats guarding the approaches.

On the morning of the 17th, smoke was reported, whereupon Admiral Ting got his fleet under way, and formed his line of battle, — the two battleships being in the centre, the smaller vessels on the flanks, and the gun and torpedo boats under cover of the fleet. The Chinese steamed slowly up to meet the approaching Japanese squadrons, which were advancing in column.

The first squadron, Admiral Ito, was in the lead, and headed for the centre of the Chinese column, then slowly changed its course and passed its right wing. When the advance vessels of the Japanese squadron had approached to within about six thousand yards, the Chinese vessels opened fire upon them. The Japanese continued to advance upon their enemy's right flank, and when within about three thousand yards opened a deadly fire.

After passing the flank, the "Ping Yuen," the "Kuang Ping," and the torpedo boats were attacked, but they avoided the assault. The squadron now hastened to the support of the "Hiyei" and the "Akagi." The Chinese vessels kept their bows toward their enemy, and slowly swung to starboard, as the Japanese vessels approached their right flank. The "Fuso" steamed close in front of the Chinese line, and the "Hiyei," having lost her position in line, was compelled to cross the Chinese line, between the "Chen Yuen" and the "King Yuen," and in so doing was so badly damaged as to compel her commander to seek protection under cover of the vessels which had turned the Chinese flank, and were now in the rear of that fleet.

The "Akagi," not being able to keep up with the first squadron, was exposed to the assault of all the vessels of the Chinese left wing. She was closely pressed by the "Lai Yuen," which vessel was set on fire, when the "Akagi" was enabled to withdraw. The second squadron was called to the assistance of the "Akagi," and fiercely assaulted the front of the Chinese line, while the first squadron was attacking it in the rear. The combined attack was maintained with great vigor, the Japanese vessels slowly withdrawing to long range, where they re-formed their columns.

Early in the action, the Chinese fleet was thrown into disorder, and was not able to re-form. The "Chao Yuen" and the "Yuen Wei," disabled and on fire, headed for Talu Tao, where the "Yung Wei" sank soon after reaching shoal water, when her crew were taken off by one of the torpedo boats. The "Chao Yung" and the "Kuang Kia" were cut off from the fleet by the Japanese first squadron, and started to run from the battle. In the panic, the "Chao Yung" was rammed by the "Chi Yuen," and sank in deep water, and the "Chi Yuen" soon sank as a result of her injuries. All the other vessels were more or less damaged, and were dropping away from the "Chung Yuen" and the "Ting Yuen," which bravely kept up the fight.

The Japanese slowly drew their vessels out of range, but were followed up by the Chinese battleships, when the battle was soon renewed. The Japanese second squadron was sent after the retreating Chinese vessels, and sank the "King Yuen," while the first squadron of five vessels circled round and round the two Chinese battleships at long range. The "Matsushima" was seriously injured, and had a large number of her people killed by being struck by a twelve-inch shell from the "Ting Yuen."

At half-past five in the afternoon, after a hot engagement of seven hours and a half, the Japanese vessels steamed out of range, and closed the action. The remaining Chinese vessels steamed to Port Arthur, where they were repaired. The "Kuang Kia" being lost in the vicinity of Talienwan Bay, Admiral Ito transferred his flag to the "Hochidate," and during the night the fleet stood out to sea, returning in the morning, when the "Matsushima," the "Hiyei," and the "Akagi," being badly injured, were sent to Japan for repairs. The rest of the fleet returned to Ping-yang Inlet on the 19th, where all the other vessels were repaired. As soon as the vessels were ready for service, they were sent to cruise in the Gulf of Pichili, taking in Port Arthur and Shantung.

Thirty-seven transports, containing eighteen thousand men of the first division, arrived in Ping-yang Inlet from Heisoshima, on October 22. They were convoyed from here by the Japanese fleet and sixteen torpedo boats to Kwayeus, about eighty miles northeast of Port Arthur, where they landed on the 24th. The entire division was landed without opposition by the 29th, and the troops of the twelfth brigade of the sixth division, about nine thousand men, which had been encamped at Chemulpo, were brought over and landed by November 4. These movements were guarded by the vessels of the fleet, which were kept cruising in the vicinity.

The Japanese moved on to the town of Pitsewo, and occupied it. The advance guard was then pushed on to Kinchau, which was defended by fifteen thousand Chinese troops. After an artillery duel of several hours' duration and an assault, Kinchau was captured on the 6th, the Chinese fleeing in the direction of Talienwan and Port Arthur.

On November 6, the Japanese fleet, in company with

some tenders, sailed to the entrance of Talienwan Bay, leaving the vessels of their third squadron and a few others to protect the enemy's base. The tenders searched for mines, while the war vessels steamed back and forth across the entrance to the bay to draw upon themselves the fire of the forts.

On the morning of the 7th, three of the vessels entered Talienwan Bay, and two entered Keu Bay, where they found that the forts had been abandoned by the Chinese, and were occupied by their own troops. The mines were soon removed, and Talienwan Bay was made the base of operations for the Japanese forces.

The vessels of the Chinese squadron that had been injured at the battle at Ping-yang Inlet were now repaired and ready for service; and having received their stores at Taku, they sailed for Wei-Hai-Wei on the 12th. The Japanese Admiral Ito, with the first, second, and third squadrons, and six torpedo boats, steamed about the entrance to Wei-Hai-Wei on the 16th and 17th, in the hope of drawing the Chinese vessels out. On the 18th, he returned to Talienwan Bay, leaving the second squadron to watch the Chinese fleet. On the same day, the " Chen Yuen " struck upon a rock off Hwang Island, at the entrance of Wei-Hai-Wei Bay, and received serious injuries.

On the 13th the twelfth brigade reached Kinchau, and on the 17th the march was taken up for Port Arthur.

The works at Port Arthur were very strong on the sea side, and on the land side were formed of redoubts of stone and earth, which commanded the hills for about three miles from the arsenal. These were connected by a wall that was of some value as a means of defence, and mounted guns of various calibres, from Krupps down to machine guns and Gatlings. Ten of these works were located on the left hand and two on the right hand of the main road, and lines of rifle-pits covered their rear from the top of a steep ridge, being garrisoned by about thirteen thousand troops, while the Japanese force was twenty thousand, of whom about fifteen thousand were in the action.

On the 18th, when about eight miles from Port Arthur, the Japanese advance was met by a large body of Chinese, who wounded a number of the Japanese, and drove them back to their main body. The Japanese steadily advanced in three columns, having fifty field and mountain and twenty-four siege guns. On the 20th, the Chinese made a sortie in force in two columns, threatening the Japanese right. A single shell put one column to flight, and the other was driven back after some little fighting. A Chinese force of about one thousand advanced to meet the Japanese right column, and was soon repulsed. The Japanese commander of the right column then paid his respects to the forts on the west of the main road, which he soon captured. The centre and left then pushed forward under cover of the artillery fire, and captured the works in front of them, meeting with little resistance. The Chinese fled in the direction of Port Arthur, leaving guns, stores, and ammunition in good condition. They were pursued, the rifle-pits on the ridge were soon captured, and at two in the afternoon the Japanese troops occupied the camp.

Several of the forts on the sea side were captured on the same day, and the remaining works were found abandoned on the 22d. The Chinese garrison was badly demoralized, and no attempts have been made to destroy any of the works, as forts and navy-yards were found to be in good condition.

On the 21st of November, the Japanese fleet, except the third squadron, which was on guard at Talienwan, steamed about the entrance to Port Arthur, some of the vessels of the fourth squadron exchanging shots with the forts. Late in the day, two torpedo boats came out of the harbor, when some of the Japanese torpedo boats destroyed them under the guns of the western forts. The fleet remained off the harbor all night, and on the next day found their army in possession of the place. The entrance was soon cleared of mines and torpedoes, when Port Arthur became the base of Japanese operations.

THE INVASION OF MANCHURIA

While the Japanese were awaiting reinforcements on the left bank of the Yalu River, the Chinese had selected a naturally strong position on the right bank, and erected earthworks. On October 24, the Japanese began the passage of the Yalu in columns. One column forded the river about twenty-five miles above its mouth, while the main body crossed on a pontoon bridge near the city of Wiju. On the next day, the Japanese charged the Chinese and defeated them, part fleeing towards Kiuliencheng, and the others towards Antong. The Japanese followed the Chinese and captured Kiuliencheng on the next day without opposition. The Chinese forces in these encounters amounted to about twenty-five thousand.

The Chinese retreated in the direction of Fenhugangen, on the main road to Monkden, and through Antong on the road to Takushan, about thirty miles west of the entrance to the Yalu River. They were hotly pursued in both directions, and were so badly demoralized that they abandoned fieldpieces, small arms, and great quantities of stores and ammunition.

General Tatsumi entered Fenghuanchung at the head of his brigade on the 31st, and found the Chinese fleeing in two directions, some on the road to Monkden, while others went in the direction of Haichang. General Oseka pursued the enemy to Siyuen, when they fell back to Semencheng, which is situated on the Siyuen and Inku cross-roads.

The third division, under General Katsura, attacked the

Chinese near Sumuchang, and drove them towards Haichang, which was captured and occupied by the Japanese on the 13th. Here they intrenched themselves and rested. About the same time, General Tatsumi, with the fifth division, was doing some hard work in forced marches, fighting his way towards Liaoyang, where the Chinese offered considerable resistance, and made numerous attempts to cut off their communications. The Japanese advance met a force

IMPERIAL CHINESE TROOPS.

which checked them at Matien Pass, on the Monkden road, but they made no effort to capture the pass, and General Ito harassed them by making several attempts, all of which were unsuccessful, to cut off the Japanese communications with the Yalu River.

The Japanese found the Chinese in considerable numbers a few miles west of Haichang, and only succeeded in driving them off after several hours of hard fighting, during which the loss on both sides was very heavy. The Chinese retreated towards Nieuchwang.

About the end of December, General Nogi left Kinchau for Kaiping with a brigade of the first division of the second army, which had been engaged at Port Arthur. He reached Kaiping on January 10, and drove the Chinese out with great loss, and as he was now within supporting distance of the third division at Haichang, he opened communication with it. The first division soon came up, under the command of Lieutenant-General Yamigi, when their forces were united.

The Japanese now held Kaiping, Haichang, and Fenghuanchung, and kept their communications open with Takushan, Kiuliencheng, and Antong, which position remained practically unchanged until the end of February. The Chinese confronted them in superior numbers, there being a corps at Liaoyang, another at Nieuchwang, and one at Tienchwangtai, which also held the Inku. In January and February they made several attempts to recapture Haichang, but they were driven off with small loss to the Japanese.

After the capture of Port Arthur, the Japanese fleet steamed about the Gulf of Pichili, and the entrance to Wei-Hai-Wei, using coal that had been captured at Port Arthur. On January 18, the "Yoshino," the "Akitsushima," and the "Takachiho" made a demonstration before Tenchan, about seventy miles west of Wei-Hai-Wei, which was repeated on the next day. These vessels then rejoined the fleet in Talienwan Bay, where they found the whole of the second division, and the eleventh brigade of the sixth division, — about twenty thousand men in all, — assembled on fifty transports which had arrived from Uijina.

In the evening, the fleet convoyed twenty of the transports, with troops, to Yungching Bay, on the Shantung Promontory, after which they took a threatening position at the entrance to Wei-Hai-Wei. By the 23d, all the transports had arrived and landed their troops, not, however, until one of the vessels had opened fire and dispersed the Chinese who opposed the landing.

Wei-Hai-Wei was defended against attack from the sea by strong earthworks on both the mainland and the islands, and heavy guns commanded both entrances. The land side was protected by earthworks that were mounted with field-guns, and the eastern islands had a clay wall about five feet thick. On the western side, a parapet of sand-bags had been built, and mounted with a number of 10.5 centimetres, and a machine gun. The approaches were all mined. The island of Lingking had in barbette a number of guns, ranging from field-guns up to 9.4 inches calibre, and there was a well-built fort on Channel Island which mounted two 8-inch and a number of smaller guns.

The Japanese advance guard occupied Yungching on the 20th, and on the 25th the Japanese moved forward in two columns. The eleventh brigade moved along the northern road, while the second division took the southern road, having daily encounters with a large body of Chinese who were retreating before it. These roads were very difficult,— mere bridle-paths, and almost impassable.

Notwithstanding the fieldpieces had not come up, the eastern works were assaulted at about nine o'clock on the morning of the 30th, and by a quarter of one o'clock were in the possession of the Japanese. The larger vessels remained in position to assist in the attack if necessary, but the active work was done by the smaller ones. A party of officers and men from the fleet manned one of the captured forts at the eastern entrance, and opened a hot fire on the Channel Island fort. The fort on Channel Island, the eastern forts, and the imprisoned Chinese fleet replied with spirit. A battalion of Japanese troops was deployed across the beach to intercept the Chinese, who were fleeing from the eastern forts. While engaged with the Chinese, their line was enfiladed by the fire from several of their own vessels, and the battalion was nearly annihilated. On the next day, the Japanese southern column took position across the western promontory. The left of this line encountered the frenzied Chinese, who were fleeing from the western forts, and sustained great loss. After receiving reinforcements, they drove the Chinese off in the direction of Chefoo. The western forts were abandoned, and Wei-Hai-Wei was occupied without further resistance.

The smaller vessels of the Japanese fleet were compelled to leave their station at the entrance to the harbor, and find shelter from a severe gale and snowstorm which raged for three days. On the 3d, the vessels returned and exchanged shots with the forts to divert attention from the parties who were examining the entrances to the harbor. A channel was found on the east side, and at two o'clock on the morning of the 5th, ten torpedo boats left the lee of Three-Peaked Point, and raced for the entrance. Eight of them succeeded in entering the harbor, and immediately attacked the Chinese fleet, firing eleven torpedoes. One torpedo from boat No. 9 struck the "Ting Yuen," when she was run into shoal water and sank; later the Chinese blew her up. No. 9 received a shot in her boiler, and, being helpless, was abandoned. No. 22 grounded in trying to leave the harbor, and was lost. On the morning of the 6th, under cover of the darkness, five torpedo boats started for the harbor. Four succeeded in entering, and discharged several torpedoes, sinking the "Lai Yuen," the "Wei Yuen," and the tender "Panfah." After the exploit, all the torpedo boats returned safely, when some of the Japanese vessels and the eastern forts manned by Japanese opened fire on the Chinese fleet and island forts. On the 7th, the magazine on Channel Island exploded, and the fort was soon abandoned. The Chinese torpedo fleet tried to escape by the western entrance, but they were chased, and were all captured or destroyed by the first squadron. On the 9th, the Japanese placed mortar batteries in position near the western forts, and opened fire on the Lingking batteries at the same time the eastern forts opened on the island and the Chinese fleets. The firing lasted all day, and the " Ching Yuen" was sunk. On the 11th, the Japanese fleet opened fire on the island forts, but a strong wind and heavy sea compelled the ships to stop firing, and draw out of range. During the winter months, the operations of the Japanese fleet were frequently interrupted by foul weather.

On the 12th, Admiral Ting proposed to capitulate to Admiral Ito, and on the 17th the Japanese fleet steamed into the harbor, and took possession of the remaining vessels of the Chinese fleet, and of the forts. Admiral Ting committed suicide. The officers who had been captured were sent, with the dead Admiral, to Chefoo in the prize vessel " Kang Chi," which the Japanese furnished for the purpose. The " Chen Yuen," the " Tei Yuen," the " Ping Yuen," the " Kuang Ping," and six of the small gunboats were among the prizes, all of which were sent to Japan, except the " Chen Yuen," which was sent to Port Arthur for repairs. The forts and guns on the mainland were destroyed, the army was gradually withdrawn to Talienwan, and by the end of February there only remained 320 men, and a naval force to look after Lingking.

The Spring Campaign in Manchuria

The first division of the second army, under command of Lieutenant-General Yamagi, was at Kaiping, and part of the fifth division, under General Nodzu, was at Haichang, when an advance was ordered. On February 24, troops were sent out from Kaiping, and, after some hard fighting, Tapingsham was captured. A few days later, General Katsuma left Haichang with a force, and pushed the Chinese

464   An American Cruiser in the East

back some fifteen miles on the Laiyang Road, and then went in the direction of Nieuchwang. At the same time, a part of the fifth division made a direct attack from Hai-chang, and captured the place on March 4, after a severe fight, which lasted from ten in the morning until eleven at night. The Chinese kept up a street fight, and defended themselves house by house. Lieutenant-General Yamagi

JAPANESE ARTILLERY.   BY A JAPANESE ARTIST.

pushed on to Inku, which he took possession of on the 7th, the Chinese fleeing in all directions across the frozen river.

On the 9th, the first army, assisted by a brigade of the second army, moved on the Chinese at Tienchwangtai, on the west side of the Liao River, and captured the place after several hours' fighting. The main body of the Chinese had retreated before the assault began, leaving a small rear-guard to repeat the story of Nieuchwang, a running street fight, and from house to house.

Appendix

THE PESCADORES AND FORMOSA

The first and second squadrons were refitted in Japan, and made ready for operations against Formosa. The remaining vessels of the fleet continued cruising about the Gulf of Pichili.

The seven war vessels under command of Admiral Ito convoyed five transports, with about three thousand troops and a battery of mountain artillery, and came to anchor off Pachan Island, Pescadores, on March 20. On the 23d, the troops were landed on Ponghan under cover of the fleet. Three of the vessels engaged a fort about four miles to the westward, and a fort nearer Makung. After the troops were established on shore, three more vessels were sent to assist against the forts, and at about two in the afternoon the Chinese abandoned the lower fort.

On the morning of the 24th, the Japanese advanced against Makung, on the west side of Ponghan, where the Chinese soon abandoned their works, fleeing to Fisher Island in junks. The Japanese soon found that the Chinese had carried off the movable parts of the guns. As soon as the Japanese flag was raised upon the fort, at half-past eleven in the morning, the Chinese forts opened fire upon it from Fisher Island. Lieutenant Inouye of the navy, with thirty men, had accompanied the army. He was able to get the disabled guns in working order, and turned their fire upon Fisher Island. Not getting a return fire, he crossed over in a sampan at night, and found that the Chinese had abandoned their forts and escaped to the mainland. After searching for mines, the fleet entered the harbor on the 26th, but moved outside again on account of cholera among the troops.

By the terms of the armistice, which became effective on March 30, active operations were suspended in the districts of Monkden, Chili, and Shantung. The Japanese were in force at Talienwan and Kinchan, and additional troops were being assembled in Japan. The Chinese were in force at Kuiu, at Monkden, at Sharhaiwan, at Taku, at Tientsin, and in great numbers in the vicinity of Peking, which city, it was feared, would be next assailed. The Japanese fleet had full control of the seas, and there was no important Chinese force south of the Japanese lines.

The Japanese Imperial Guard arrived at Kulung, Formosa, about the end of May, as an army of occupation.

The treaty of peace was signed by the representatives of the two Powers on April 17, 1895, and ratifications by the Emperors of Japan and China were exchanged on May 8. The treaty provided for the full and complete surrender of Korea; the cession by China to Japan of Formosa and the Pescadores; the payment of a war indemnity of 200,000,000 taels; the opening to trade of several Chinese cities hitherto closed; the extension of Japanese steam navigation to several rivers in China; and the security of certain rights to Japanese subjects in China. Japan agreed to evacuate Chinese territory within three months, but to occupy Wei-Hai-Wei temporarily, at the partial expense of China, as a guarantee of the faithful performance of the stipulations of the treaty; prisoners of war were to be exchanged, and Chinese subjects who had been compromised in their relations with the Japanese army were not to be punished.

Japan was also to have possession of the southern part of the Feng-tien, including Port Arthur, but by an Imperial rescript, dated June 10, 1895, the Japanese Government expressed the intention of leaving this territory under Chinese jurisdiction. The document reads thus: —

"Since, then, the Government of their Majesties, the Emperors of Russia and Germany and of the Republic of France, have united in a recommendation to our Government not to permanently possess the peninsula of Feng-tien, our newly acquired territory, on the ground that such permanent possession would be detrimental to the lasting peace of the Orient.

"Devoted as we unalterably are, and ever have been, to the principles of peace, we were constrained to take up arms against China for no other reason than our desire to secure for the Orient an enduring peace.

"Now the friendly recommendation of the three Powers was equally prompted by the same desire. Consulting, therefore, the best interests of peace, and animated by a desire not to bring upon our people added hardship, or to impede the progress of national destiny by creating new complications, and thereby making the situation difficult and retarding the restoration of peace, we do not hesitate to accept such recommendation."

Formosa and the Pescadores were formally transferred from China to Japan at Kulung, Formosa, on the 2d day of June, by the Chinese High Commissioner to Admiral Kalayama, the Japanese Governor-General. He found that the Chinese officials and troops had been withdrawn, but the aboriginal natives, whose fears and prejudices had been played upon, were in a state of rebellion and war. His troops, therefore, had to fight their way and restore order out of the chaos which reigned in those beautiful islands.

During the entire war, 623 Japanese were killed in battle; 2,489 died of cholera; 2,981 died of other diseases; and of the 3,155 wounded, 172 died of their wounds. It is not known how many Chinese were killed and wounded, as their organization was too imperfect to justify even an approximate estimate of the numbers.

There were some splendid duels on field and deck, but the discipline, steadiness, and equipment of the Japanese were too much for the ill-armed and worse-disciplined troops and sailors under the "dragon flag."

Through innumerable hardships, in the face of the typhoons and during the terrible winter of Manchuria, the Japanese sailors and soldiers bore themselves as men conscious of their strength, and were humane and generous to their vanquished foes. Scanty rations and medicines were shared with enemies. The wounded, the women, and the children were cared for and succored. Safeguards and protection were thrown about the captured towns and villages, and justice was shown toward the humblest.

www.ingramcontent.com/pod-product-compliance
Lightning Source LLC
Chambersburg PA
CBHW051237300426
44114CB00011B/778